A Nation of Realtors®

A Nation of Realtors®

A CULTURAL HISTORY

OF THE TWENTIETH-CENTURY

AMERICAN MIDDLE CLASS

Jeffrey M. Hornstein

© 2005 Duke University Press

All rights reserved

Printed in the United States of America on

acid-free paper ∞ *Designed by Amy Ruth Buchanan*

Typeset in Dante by Keystone Typesetting, Inc.

Library of Congress Cataloging-in-Publication Data

appear on the last printed page of this book.

The symbol "®" following the word "Realtor" on the cover and title page of this book is a symbol of the National Association of REALTORS®. It tells you that the person using the title is a member of the local, state, and national association of REALTORS®, and voluntarily subscribes to the Code of Ethics of the organization. Except when cited as part of a quotation, throughout this book the term "Realtor" will be used in its strict legal and trademarked sense, to designate a broker who held membership in the National Association of Real Estate Boards (NAREB), which changed its name in 1973 to the National Association of Realtors.

A Nation of Realtors®

A book in the series RADICAL PERSPECTIVES:

A RADICAL HISTORY REVIEW BOOK SERIES

Series editors: Daniel J. Walkowitz, New York University

Barbara Weinstein, University of Maryland, College Park

History, as radical historians have long observed, cannot be severed from authorial subjectivity, indeed from politics. Political concerns animate the questions we ask, the subjects on which we write. For over thirty years the Radical History Review has led in nurturing and advancing politically engaged historical research. Radical Perspectives seeks to further the journal's mission: any author wishing to be in the series makes a self-conscious decision to associate her or his work with a radical perspective. To be sure, many of us are currently struggling with what it means to be a radical historian in the early twenty-first century, and this series is intended to provide some signposts for what we would judge to be radical history. It will offer innovative ways of telling stories from multiple perspectives; comparative, transnational, and global histories that transcend conventional boundaries of region and nation; works that elaborate on the implications of the postcolonial move to "provincialize Europe"; studies of the public in and of the past, including those that consider the commodification of the past; histories that explore the intersection of identities such as gender, race, class, and sexuality with an eye to their political implications and complications. Above all, this book series seeks to create an important intellectual space and discursive community to explore the very issue of what constitutes radical history. Within this context, some of the books published in the series may privilege alternative and oppositional political cultures, but all will be concerned with the way power is constituted, contested, used, and abused.

Hornstein's book is a landmark contribution to the study of middle-class formation. It subtly negotiates materialist notions of class and the cultural terrain in which subjectivities are forged. In this way, the book provides innovative and significant methodological and conceptual strategies for understanding how class was used and negotiated by women and men imbedded in a dominant culture that celebrated classlessness. Hornstein's choice of a case study is brilliant: the members of his labor force—realtors—inhabit a liminal class location as "business professionals" engaged in the marketing of the quintessential bourgeois product, the home. Moreover, gender is central to divisions within the real estate labor force, much as it shapes middle-class identity. As Hornstein demonstrates, the real estate industry in the last half of the twentieth century developed a gendered labor force divided between the male realtors' commercial market and the women realtors' domestic market. This book therefore not only provides a sustained gender analysis: it is one of the first texts to place the professional identities of men and women, as they inform class subjectivities, in a dynamic historical relationship.

CONTENTS

ACKNOWLEDGMENTS

This book is the culmination of a long intellectual and political journey that began during my junior year at MIT, when I first became interested in housing and identity through an internship with the Boston Coalition for the Homeless. My senior thesis, written under the strict supervision of Michael Lipsky with assistance from Richard Vallely and Ellen Immergut, explored the relationship between homelessness and the marginal social status that necessarily came with it in twentieth-century America. As a political science graduate student at the University of Pennsylvania, I began to shift emphasis from the urban Other to the suburban Self, in order to understand the middle-class subject position which has so shaped my existence. At Penn, I learned social theory from Ian Lustick and political economy from Peter Swenson and Tom Callaghy. I was very fortunate that Gary Gerstle decided to spend a year at Penn just as I was deciding to take my first graduate-level history course. Under Gary's tutelage, I stumbled upon the question that would ultimately drive this study: How did virtually all Americans come to think of themselves as "middle class" in the twentieth century?

I decided to pursue the cultural history of the American middle class and enrolled in the history department at the University of Maryland to study with James B. Gilbert, to whom I owe enormous debts both intellectual and stylistic. Without Jim's fanatic dedication to elegance and clarity in historical writing, I'd still be writing obscurantist prose for the "four initiates of the logos," as he was fond of saying. Jim also made the offhand suggestion one day that I consider exploring the real estate business. At Maryland, David Sicilia taught me everything I know about business and economic history, Robyn Muncy and Gay Gullickson introduced me to gender analysis, Mary Corbin Sies grounded me in suburban history, and Marshall Grossman made me rethink everything I thought I knew about subjectivity. Dorothy Ross's seminar at Johns Hopkins sparked my interest in the history of social science, David Harvey's course on Marx's *Capital* ensured that I wouldn't lose sight of the political in economic and business history, and a chance encounter with Burton Bledstein at the OAH led me to think about Realtors and professionalism. Danny Walkowitz has been an unflagging supporter of my work and the most meticulous and generous reader a young historian could hope for.

Many organizations and institutions made my research possible. First and foremost I owe a huge debt of gratitude to the National Association of Realtors. Its executive vice president Terry McDermott was gracious enough to allow a non-Realtor to use the organization's well-organized library and archives, without which this project would have been impossible. The capable and kind folks at NAR's Information Central, particularly John Krukoff, Mary Martinez, and Nancy Pavkovic, as well as the staff at the Women's Council of Realtors, made my lengthy research jaunts to Chicago productive and enjoyable. The Maryland history department's William Randolph Hearst Fund paid for my stays at the quaint Motel 6 in the heart of Chicago's Magnificent Mile. The staffs at the Realtors Association of Metropolitan Pittsburgh and the Columbus Board of Realtors courteously made archival materials available to me. The archivists at the Wisconsin Historical Society, the Historical Society of Pennsylvania, and the Urban Archives at Temple University were enormously helpful. The staffs at both the Herbert Hoover and the Franklin D. Roosevelt Presidential Libraries were uniformly obliging; I am grateful to the HHPL Association and the Lubin-Winant Fund at the FDRPL for research support. The Mary Savage Snouffer Dissertation Fellowship at the University of Maryland granted me a peaceful yearlong respite from teaching to finish writing. The conscientious public employees in the Manuscript Room at the Library of Congress as well as those at the National Archives were a great help.

One professional organization, the Business History Conference, figures centrally in my intellectual and professional development. The annual meetings were unfailingly provocative and stimulating—as well as much more fun than one would imagine a bunch of business historians having. David Sicilia encouraged me to become active, and Phil Scranton, Roger Horowitz, and Angel Kwolek-Folland were very supportive of my work. The BHC kindly awarded me the Herman E. Krooss Prize for Best Dissertation in 2002, which encouraged me to think about publication.

I was fortunate to have been part of two graduate student communities in Baltimore and College Park. Fellow Maryland graduate students, especially Linda Sargent, Dusan Korac, Ed Wehrle, and Adriane Kinnane (who rewrote my dissertation prospectus at a crucial moment), made for a stimulating intellectual atmosphere. My co-editor of *Maryland Historian*, Mark Tacyn, made sure I read something other than dissertation-related material. My Baltimore friends Dirk Bonker, Frances Clark, Carolyn Eastman, Chris Gardner, Maiju Lehmijoki-Gardner, Jeff Mullins, and Rebecca Plant provided excellent distractions from the grind of graduate school. Friends on the research and conference circuit such as Steph Dyer, Jennifer Kerns-Robison, Tina Manko, Jennifer Pettit, and Kevin Reilly made it fun and cool to be a historian. I'll never forget the pleasurable hours that Luca Burgazzoli and I spent drinking coffee during breaks from writing in the year we both spent in exile in South Carolina working on our dissertations.

My lifelong friends Steve Carver, Eric Hornstein, and Darren Dorkin, as well as my parents Allan and Elaine Hornstein, brother Neil, and sorely missed grandmother Ruth Moran, fulfilled the requisite "when-the-hell-are-you-going-to-finish?" function. I would be remiss if I did not express gratitude to the AFL-CIO's Organizing Institute and the American Federation of Teachers, particularly my mentor, Rich Klimmer, who made it possible for me to embark on a new career as a union organizer. The intellectual community and political camaraderie I've found working with Graduate Employees Together–University of Pennsylvania / AFT have been most welcome. The energizing experience of working on an organizing campaign enabled me to make time to turn an unwieldy dissertation into this book.

In the end, I do not think I would ever have finished the dissertation or the book if it were not for the emotional sustenance and joie de vivre that Pamela Barnett brought into my life at the most crucial of moments. Her love enriches my life and her careful eye and intellectual precision made this a much better book.

INTRODUCTION

Anomalous, mutable, with tenuous fringes, the middle classes never have been and are not now a fixed entity, to be encompassed by a simple, rigid definition . . . The meaning of the middle classes is likely to remain with good cause in a state, so to speak, of suspended definition.

—Charles F. Palm, 1936[1]

In this country all men are realtors. As the prime symbol of our civilization, neither the pilgrim father, nor the pioneer, nor the captain of industry, suffices so well as the real estate man to explain certain habits of mind, certain ideals and certain inconsistencies of the behavior of the American people.

—Robert C. Binkeley, 1929[2]

A Nation of Realtors?

Around the beginning of the twentieth century, a group of prominent American urban real estate brokers, dealers in commercial property and developers of residential subdivisions, made a concerted effort to organize their occupation into a "profession" on the national level. They were motivated both by their desire to rehabilitate real estate as a commodity in the wake of the depression of the 1890s and by their desire for "unification of thought and purpose among the country's real estate interests," in the words of a prominent broker from New York.[3] The men who led this group were primarily from rapidly growing cities in the Midwest and the West. Men like William Washington Hannan of the Detroit Real Estate Board, Alexander S. Taylor of the Cleveland Real Estate Board, and Edward S. Judd of the Chicago Real Estate Board aimed to refashion real estate brokerage into a vital, ethical, and progressive calling. These real estate men were also trying to spur the development of their own regions. It was no coincidence that the impetus for organization came from the newest and fastest-growing regions of the continent, places where organized real estate men had had, and would continue to have, tremendous influence over both the structure of local real estate markets and the shape of metropolitan landscapes.

The men at the vanguard of the professional project in real estate participated in an organizational revolution on the municipal level, establishing dozens of local real estate boards in the 1870s and 1880s, creating the rules and practices that governed local real estate markets.[4] They then acquired national aspirations, culminating in the formation in 1908 of the National Association of Real Estate Exchanges, later renamed the National Association of Real Estate Boards (NAREB). Through national-level organization, they sought to join what the historian Robert Wiebe called the "national class"—the new middle class of educated, cosmopolitan men and women, bound loosely by a consciousness of their "unique skills and functions," who would achieve a "revolution in values" in the early twentieth century.[5]

This moral transformation, particularly the valorization of organization and expertise over politics and popular participation, was part and parcel of the phenomenon called "progressivism"—the loosely connected and often internally contradictory social and political reform movements of the period from roughly 1890 to 1920. The Progressive era was marked by the ideological incoherence characteristic of "middle-class" values. Such themes as anti-monopolism, the interdependence of humanity in complex society, and social efficiency combined to form a social language deployed by various groups to agitate for a wide range of social reforms. This language provided a semblance of consistency across widely disparate movements.[6]

Historians most often characterize the Progressive era as a period in which "middle-class" values triumphed over those of the working classes and immigrants, though little critical scrutiny is given to those alleged middle-class values, or the means by which they are constructed and disseminated. The social meaning of the term "middle-class" was in great flux from about 1890 to 1940, reflecting and reflected in the real estate brokers' ideological inconsistencies at the same time, as the signifier "middle class" became increasingly dominant as a category of identity.

The "Inner Secrets" of Middle-Class Manhood

In the early years of the twentieth century, George Horace Lorimer's *Saturday Evening Post* extolled the virtues of entrepreneurship, ostensibly to persuade more young men to embark on careers that entailed risk taking, a cornerstone of true manhood in the Victorian view of the world. Promoting small business values as truly American values, Lorimer saw real estate brokers as potential exemplars of the ideal American. In fact, there were natural affinities between the professionalizing real estate men and Lorimer himself. Like Lorimer, the real estate men combined "the pious weight of traditional values" with the "heady promise of the present and future."[7] Natural optimists and champions of individualism and private property, real estate men were also proponents of "modern" business methods. From 1910 to 1930, Lorimer published numerous articles by and about real estate brokers, providing an alternative to the unflattering image of real estate brokerage in the public mind as a refuge for the "down and out" and the disreputable.

The real estate man made his public début as a literary hero in 1912, when the *Post* published Edward Mott Woollcy's story "The Inner Secrets of a Real Estate Broker's Rise." An example of commercial realism and a business morality tale, "Inner Secrets" was structured as an interview with an anonymous, prosperous broker reflecting on his gradual adoption of the values and practices that led almost inexorably to his success.[8] The title of the story evoked an ancient notion of a profession as a master craft—defined by a body of "inner," secret knowledge imparted to an apprentice by a master practitioner. Yet the narrative itself was an archetypical American success story—a tale of the hero's ascent from a lowly, dependent clerical position and his achievement of self-mastery through entrepreneurship—clearly meant to convey the sacred and "secret" knowledge to a mass audience. The story defined success in terms of not simply achieving pecuniary reward but more importantly finding a meaningful career as a self-directed and autonomous businessman, predicated on accepting and internalizing the value of "honest service" over that of pure profit maximization. The narrative argued for the self-transformative and self-mastering potential in applying "ethics" to business practice. Real estate brokerage and kindred occupations, practiced ethically, represented salvation from corporate servility, in both the moral and the remunerative senses.

The protagonist of "Inner Secrets" confides to the interviewer that when he was a twenty-four-year-old "young chap in love," he was not satisfied with his lowly job in the corporate hierarchy as a cashier because it neither paid well nor provided satisfaction. He seemed to despair of his ability to earn a suitably large salary to establish a secure and comfortable household. Currently a "man who has passed the forty mark," with a smattering of gray hairs marking a "right royal battle" to be his "own master," he hopes to impress on young men, "whether they sell real estate or not," that they need not be stuck in the subservience of menial work. Real estate brokerage offered a young man long on ambition but short on material means an opportunity to be his own man and succeed through hard work and risk taking. Woolley's hero was a clear rejoinder to the popular image of real estate as a means to reap a "very large fortune for a very minute outlay."[9] The path to meaningful success in brokerage was arduous, but worthwhile.

However, the salutary effects would flow only to those who practiced real estate brokerage properly. After a year of attempting to make money in the standard, not-quite-honest ways of the "overcrowded" and "ordinary real estate ranks," Woolley's hero had an epiphany. Presented with an easy opportunity to cheat an old woman thinking of investing what little was left of her late husband's estate in the purchase of a business property, he was struck by the "innocence" of her "old soul." Because she knew so little about real estate "and the factors that influence it," the "sharks" had already made off with a large part of the bequest. Rising to the occasion, he provided her with an appraisal report that "fairly sizzled with honesty," pointing out that the "land was badly situated from the standpoint of business development," that "merchants of the better class were migrating from the neighborhood," and that "undesirable elements" were "invading the district." Having saved her from "a sham," he perceived the "dawning of a real opportunity" to "educate" and "guide" customers toward "goods that had real value."[10] He was reborn with an ethical consciousness, leading directly to his business success.

The moral lesson of Woolley's story was straightforward: the "inner secret" of achieving full satisfaction from one's work inhered in protecting the vulnerable and the weak, of putting honesty and integrity before all other considerations. Ethical practice was not only honorable and proper—it also ensured the modern businessman's prosperity. Professionalism paid *and* provided moral satisfaction. Protecting the "widow" from the "shark" and similar acts of chivalry were important themes in the early narrative of the professional real estate broker. The emerging occupational identity melded an older theme in the history of masculinity—chivalry, protection of the weak—with an emergent version of manhood built on efficient expertise, a "technocratic" masculinity. But this was not all.

For Woolley's hero, the rewards for making the transition from "shark" to "professional" went beyond feelings of moral superiority, beyond the achievement of public confidence that led to stable business and profits. There was a *personal*, subjective benefit of achieving honest professionalism, which the transformed broker articulated in terms of *stability*. "I was happy when I got down to this point," he avowed, "for I was doing something definite . . . I was through with aimless wandering. There is a magic country that hangs over the heads of most men; they see it, though it is above and beyond them; but usually there is a road that leads to it."[11] The territorial metaphor was no accident: with the frontier only recently declared officially closed, with no *actual* real estate left to "conquer," the ambitious young man was supposed to "find his place" in the "magic country" of a stable, honorable, and perhaps remunerative white-collar career. In terms of traditional middle-class masculinity this was discomforting, because the typical white-collar job entailed subordination within a corporate hierarchy. Real estate brokerage offered a man an opportunity both to exercise his ethical faculties and to engage in autonomous, risk-taking, entrepreneurial activity, to attain the character-building benefits of both small business and the independent professions. At the same time, the real estate man performed an invaluable service: dealing in land, in space, in providing places for those on the move, the broker's essential function brought together the migrant and the hearthstone. Two sets of ostensibly antagonistic tendencies at the heart of American culture—mobility and stability, business and the professions—met in the figure of the real estate man.

Thus the young man seeking "something definite" now had a heroic narrative with which to identify: a story of transformation from unethical to ethical broker, from mediocre mendacity to successful honesty. A young man could be both entrepreneurial and ethical. The story itself mirrored and materialized a transitional moment: the protagonist transferred his "secret" knowledge to prospective brokers in the process of describing his self-transformation. This new identity, that of the ethical or professional real estate man, offered a solution to the problem that the narrative of the story posed, by creating a career that was relatively easy to enter and that satisfied the desire to do "something definite," to *be* something in a world defined by rapid change. The ethical real estate broker presented a vocational model that a young man would find satisfying because it would both test him and allow him to express the full range of his talents. He could find in real estate brokerage the excitement, occupational autonomy, and potential pecuniary rewards of entrepreneurship, as well as the prestige and ethical standards of white-collar "head work." Real estate brokerage held itself out as an ideal pursuit in a world in which occupational categories and the realities they attempted to represent were in flux.[12] Ethical brokerage promised to solve the problem of instilling manhood, though the nature of that manhood was not completely unambiguous. On the one hand, Woolley's protagonist conformed to the model of the "self-made man," the dominant nineteenth-century conception of "marketplace manhood" that valorized entrepreneurship and autonomy.[13] At the same time, however, the real estate hero figured in relation to an emergent technocratic discourse of white-collar professionalism that would coexist uneasily with marketplace manhood throughout most of the twentieth century.

The rise of professional real estate brokerage provides an ideal window into the internal dynamics of the cultural transformation of the American middle class. Emerging as a full-time occupation in the early twentieth century, real estate brokerage embodied a variety of early twentieth-century cultural, social, and economic trends, including the drive to professionalize business, the rapid expansion of white-collar labor and its feminization, the rise of independent contracting as a prominent form of labor relations, and the enormous growth of the home-building and home-selling industries. The home became a crucial site of both consumption and middle-class identification in the early twentieth century. Yet few scholars have focused on the interrelationship between the "demand" and the "supply" sides of housing in America.[14] Real estate brokers were intermediaries between "house" and "home," and analysis of their attempts to elevate their occupation to the status of a profession reveals something new about both the operation of the housing industry and the complex processes of middle-class formation. In many ways the real estate brokers' professional project exemplifies the cultural history of the twentieth-century American middle class.

Dreaming the American Home

While ideal notions of "Home Sweet Home" may be traced to the 1820s, it was with the emergence of "domestic science" in the postbellum years that the American home truly became an object of expert knowledge and professional intervention. By the first decades of the twentieth century social workers, home economists, architects, urban planners, housing reformers, housing officials, and real estate brokers planned, regulated, inspected, designed, and sold houses, and wrote and spoke prolifically on the subject of the American home. Never before had "home" become such a sustained focus of scientific, technical, reformist, political, and business discourse, shaping the identity of several emergent occupations. A specific notion of home became symbolic of ideal family relationships and notions of citizenship.[15] The conception of a real estate brokerage as an occupation-*cum*-profession depended upon the existence of "home" as an intellectual and cultural object, and the discourse of professionalism surrounding it. As putative home experts, real estate brokers would reserve central roles for themselves in the promotion of homeownership and the creation of housing policy from the early 1920s onward. But the home was also indelibly marked as a feminine space, and this fact complicated the models available for real estate men to draw upon in their drive to professionalize. A small number of women were involved in real estate brokerage in the early twentieth century—in rough proportion to their participation in other white-collar fields of endeavor—and the early professionalizers would attempt to ignore their existence. But because the home was feminine terrain, successful women brokers discovered clever ways of insinuating themselves into the professional project, ultimately creating a field that was far more open to women than any other business profession.

Thanks in large measure to organized real estate brokers' cultural and political work, the single-family home on a quarter-acre lot in a low-density suburban development became the "American Dream," and the vast majority of Americans bought into it, literally and figuratively.[16] Proponents of so-called modern housing who stubbornly demurred and called for high-density, publicly funded, ecologically sound land development after the European model, or who noted the irony of having housing produced by the "private" housing market massively subsidized by the public at rates four to five times that expended on public housing, were tarred as "socialists" when they were not ignored.[17] Americans, particularly white Americans, came to think of themselves as inhabiting a classless society, composed of one big "middle class," its membership defined to a large degree by actual or expectant home-ownership.[18] Choices other than a detached, single-family home in the sub-urbs came to be stigmatized as transitional at best, the "ladder of life" presup-posed to extend naturally from renting to owning a home of one's own. A social stigma came to be attached to those who chose to rent rather than own their homes.[19] Those who "fell through the cracks" and became "homeless" were, by definition, exiled to a residual category later called the "underclass," an ideological term that functioned to deny social relationships between those in the "middle class" and those in the group "below."[20]

Aside from going a long way toward making homeownership both a dominant cultural trend and a material reality, real estate brokerage exempli-fied the "professionalization of everyone," in the words of the sociologist Harold Wilensky. Real estate brokerage as a career and a self-styled profession conformed to the profile of neither the female-dominated "semi-professions" like nursing and social work nor the traditional, male-dominated "learned" professions like medicine and law.[21] Neither a professional in the accepted sense nor a white-collar cog in the corporate machine or a strictly autono-mous entrepreneur, the "professional" real estate broker hinted at a potential new paradigm for staking a claim to middle-class identity. If in the eighteenth and nineteenth centuries a man established himself as a member of the middle class by achieving economic autonomy through success in business, amassing property, or completing a masculine rite of passage that included years of rigorous education and apprenticeship, in the American Century middle-class status became, like much else, a commodity available for sale to an ever-wider consumption community. Additionally, if the only path to middle-class status for a woman in the nineteenth century was marriage to a man of standing, the opening of real estate brokerage to women in the twentieth century made possible the establishment of an independent female, middle-class subject position. By the late twentieth century, in large part because of the efforts of pioneering women brokers, it became possible for a divorced or single woman to stake her own claim as "middle class."

Theorizing the Realtor

The men who launched the real estate brokers' professional project in 1908 were at the vanguard of a movement to reinvent the businessman by transforming business into a profession. It was a thoroughly progressive movement, albeit conservative in its progressivism. Organized real estate brokers structured the rules of the real estate market to create a demand for their services, positioning themselves as the principal purveyors of what came to be the quintessential symbol of middle-class status, the detached, owner-occupied, single-family home. At the same time, they attempted to appropriate middle-class standing by participating in—and reinventing—the discourse of professionalism, staking claim to expertise as city builders with a profound role to play in American society. Real estate brokers helped to "democratize" professionalism by partially delinking it from higher education and by infusing it with entrepreneurialism. Real estate brokers attempted to retain a sense of creativity in white-collar work in the face of the increasingly standardized world of the corporation, at the same time as they attempted to figure themselves as "professionals" in the modern, technocratic mold. The real estate man understood himself as an artisanal creator (*homo faber*), a man of technical skill and scientific objectivity, a socially conscientious reformist businessman and a profit-oriented entrepreneur, often at the same time.[22] These ostensibly antagonistic ideas formed a tense and productive synthesis— a new model of profession, part of the core of a new middle-class identity.

The aspiring professional real estate brokers aimed to follow the course of many occupations before them. The national association's founders sought an occupational monopoly through a combination of voluntaristic and legal means; they promulgated ethical precepts and used their accumulating social capital to intervene in the public policy arena. The membership of the National Association of Real Estate Boards encompassed a wide range of brokers, from principal owners of small brokerages to large, integrated development companies, and this occasionally made it difficult to establish a unified policy agenda; at different times various factions within the organization prevailed. Nevertheless, in a consummate work of *bricolage*, the organized real estate brokers combined prevailing notions about proper gender roles and relations and long-standing ideals about property ownership, republican virtue, and American entrepreneurship with a modicum of economic science and a distinctive professional label, "Realtor," in an attempt to forge an

identity as creators of domestic spaces and builders of cities even as they
created demand for their services. This identity, like the "middle class" of
which it was a part, cobbled together a diverse range of interests.[23]

Though the creators of official categories in the U.S. Census Bureau and
the ivory towers of academic sociology failed to bestow the title "profession"
upon them, the Realtors succeeded brilliantly as a cultural, political, and
business movement, in sum, as a *hegemonic project*. As a leading element in the
rising twentieth-century American middle class, the Realtors helped to organize social, cultural, political, and economic relations in such as a way as to
make their particular interests appear to be the universal and natural interests
of *"the* middle class"—which was itself reconstituted in this organizational
and definitional process. By the 1950s, the white suburban homeowner was
embedded in mainstream American culture as paradigmatically "middle
class," and the struggles of the 1930s over housing policy were foggy memo-
ries at best.

This is not in any way meant to suggest a conspiracy, or even to imply a
new version of consensus history. Most Americans in the mid-twentieth century thought of themselves as "middle class" and of their society as composed
mostly of "middle-class" people. Americans had long thought of their society
as open and largely free from the rigid class structures associated with the old
order of Europe, devoid of extremes of wealth, privilege, and power, a society
in which a man could get ahead by dint of pluck and luck.

The Realtors appealed to prevailing institutional arrangements and cultural sensibilities to forge an organic political movement rooted in existing
structures and ideologies. Their major achievement came in creatively combining the ideology of homeownership, the languages of professionalism and
entrepreneurship, and shifting gender notions into a potent political force, in
the process welding together what social theorists call a "historical bloc."[24]
The Realtors drew together various elements into a relational whole, manifest in a wide range of institutions (local real estate boards, the National
Association of Real Estate Boards, the National Association of Home Builders, state real estate commissions), laws (zoning ordinances, real estate brokerage licensing laws, federal mortgage insurance), business practices (commission schedules, the multiple-listing system, standardized subdividing
procedures), social relationships (racial exclusionism and redlining, lucrative
career opportunities for women), and cultural common sense (the inalienable
right to private property, unfettered individualism, and the right to privacy).

The Realtors played a leading role in spinning the webs of relationships and meanings that constituted the fabric of the twentieth-century middle class.

But like all hegemonic formations, the new social identity, "middle class," contained tensions that persistently threatened its stability and required constant reinforcement. My analysis of the transformation of real estate brokerage from a part-time endeavor to a highly organized "business profession," an often lucrative career engaging millions of men and women, focuses on the tensions within the professional project, the ongoing internal effort to negotiate the relationship between gender and work in the real estate field, as well as on the external project to advance a positive public face for their field and to maintain demand for their primary product, the home.

CHAPTER ONE

"Doing Something Definite":

The Emergence of Real Estate Brokerage

as a Career, 1883–1908

[Bilfinger the real estate man] was the most enterprising and forgetful gentleman I ever met. He was, too, a genius in his way. I fear, if the angel Gabriel had passed that way, Bilfinger would have called him into our office and skinned him out of his trumpet.

—"Bilfinger," *Harper's*, August 1889[1]

The circumstances were right for a reconfiguration of American culture in the early twentieth century. Men who might once have gone into business for themselves were drawn into the work force as white-collar employees, destined to spend the rest of their adult lives climbing a corporate ladder, rung by rung. At the same time, middle-class women were "discovering" that their solemn duty to "the race" and "the nation" was to (scientifically) manage the home, though some, albeit unfortunate ones such as widows, were also drawn into the world of remunerative labor. American culture had historically connected work and character formation, but this relationship became problematic, for men in particular, because of the rapid spread of the corporation. Numerous commentators called for new sources of social validation, particularly for men. Ordinary occupations like mid-level management, bookkeeping, teaching, social work, insurance sales, and real estate brokerage attempted to refashion themselves into "professions," vital to the functioning of American society. In real estate, like many other fields, the professionalizing impulse was embodied in an organizational impulse, beginning on the local level with the proliferation of real estate boards and exchanges in the 1880s and 1890s and culminating in 1908 with the formation of the National

Association of Real Estate Exchanges, later renamed the National Association of Real Estate Boards.

Herod M. Bilfinger, Real Estate Broker

The term "real estate broker" entered the American lexicon in the mid-nineteenth century, but it was not then associated with a respectable occupation.[2] In nineteenth-century popular culture, the figure of the real estate man—always a man—was unflattering. His detractors, particularly the lawyer intent on establishing himself as the ultimate defender of civic virtue, portrayed him as a devious swindler. In a story in *Harper's* in 1854, for example, the lawyer-narrator describes how a real estate broker, Stephen Halliday, bilked Durand, a wealthy yet naïve old gentleman, out of his fortune. Halliday, whom the kindly Durand trusted implicitly, skipped the country, leaving his victim in penury and indirectly causing the death of two of his children and the loss of his dignity—linked, of course, to his loss of creditworthiness. His ignominy was mitigated only posthumously with the recovery of his fortune by the upright attorney, who recounts the tale with evident great satisfaction at having saved the old man's beautiful granddaughter from a life of poverty and disgrace. This melodrama was clearly intended to bolster lawyers' claims to professional status and was not about real estate brokerage per se, but its narrative depended upon unvoiced assumptions associating real estate men with chicanery.[3]

Satirists beginning with Tom P. Morgan in the pages of *Harper's* in the 1890s and continuing with Ring Lardner, Sinclair Lewis, and H. L. Mencken in 1910–30 generated an alternative and almost equally unflattering representation of the real estate man. These writers depicted the real estate broker as a more or less likable hustler with at least some scruples about his occupation. Morgan's character Herod M. Bilfinger exemplified what the "high-class" real estate brokers who aspired to raise the status of the field called a "fly-by-nighter." Bilfinger made his fortune by attracting investments in new settlements that existed only on paper, getting away with the scheme in the end, or by selling the same homestead to five different families, escaping just as the victims caught on. Bilfinger "had a way of appearing, tarrying a little, and then departing, taking with him the financial pelts, as it were, of a goodly portion of the community." As "perpetrated" by Bilfinger, the real estate business "resembled somewhat a jug with a remarkably large handle, the said

handle turned toward Bilfinger."[4] Toward the turn of the century, the figure
of the "curbstoner," the man with his office "in his hat," joined this menag-
erie of negative representations.

Despite the vocation's ill repute, tens of thousands of men made their
living as real estate brokers in the late nineteenth century and the early
twentieth. While many bankers, lawyers, and others in growing towns and
cities had dabbled in real estate since colonial times, in the final decades of the
nineteenth century significant numbers of men—and a few women—chose to
become full-time real estate brokers. The 1910 Census listed nearly 126,000
brokers, of whom 98 percent were men. Why did so many men choose this
occupation? Was it, as Morgan put it in a Bilfinger episode, because they were
"seeking something that would return a very large fortune for a very minute
outlay of labor"?[5] Or was there some other appeal? Real estate brokerage, as it
emerged in the first decades of the twentieth century, carved out a new and
promising career niche, that of the *business professional*.

Local Class Knowledge: The Urban Real Estate Board

As in many other spheres of American life, the organizational impulse began
to pervade urban real estate brokerage in the 1880s. Urban brokers formed
real estate boards for a variety of reasons, including the improvement of their
image, as well as the "establishment and maintenance of uniform rates for
handling real estate"—that is, the creation of more nearly perfect, less ruin-
ously competitive, and more oligopolistic real estate markets—and "the promotion of a spirit of good fellowship" among brokers.[6] Designed as a self-
selecting means to bring together only the "high-class" brokers who could
afford the generally expensive initiation and membership fees, real estate
exchanges and boards spread rapidly across the continent. Between 1875 and
1910, boards were formed in most major and minor North American cities,
from Buffalo to Jacksonville, Boston to San Francisco, Winnipeg to New
Orleans. The states and provinces of the Midwest and West led the movement
to organize real estate men; the overwhelming majority of the boards formed
in this early period were in these regions.[7] By the eve of American entry into
the First World War, nearly 150 boards representing more than 7,500 members
had joined the National Association of Real Estate Boards. While many
boards and brokers remained outside the national association—in 1920, only
about 9 percent of all brokers were members of boards affiliated with it[8]—its

membership certainly comprised the largest and most prominent boards, and by extension, the most prominent brokers, by about 1915. As various local editions of *Who's Who* attested, by 1917 the major figures in virtually every metropolitan real estate market were members of an affiliated board.[9]

Local real estate boards wrought profound changes on local real estate markets; in many ways, it can be said that they created the modern real estate markets. Boards standardized the rules for participation in real estate transactions by creating standard lease forms and uniform commission schedules, collected and organized data about available properties, and helped buyers and sellers come together much more efficiently than they could have done on their own. Boards, particularly those affiliated with the national association, established the internal standards of the occupation as well as the local customs and state laws governing real estate practice. And the national association collected, standardized, and disseminated this local knowledge across the nation. By the 1920s, for example, the national association promulgated model real estate broker licensing and zoning laws drawn up by member boards, and municipal and state governments often adopted them verbatim.

Boards facilitated real estate transactions, standardized commission schedules and leases, and more generally attempted to "stabilize values," as real estate men often put it. They coordinated and centralized information about real estate to solve both their own and consumers' problems of uncertainty and information asymmetry. Real estate boards generally emerged in periods of rapid community growth, and frequently they stimulated further growth by coordinating the efforts of the most active brokers and developers in an area.[10] Modeled after stock exchanges, early real estate boards initially provided a specified place and time where brokers representing owners and purchasers of real property could meet to negotiate. Boards soon developed into stable institutions, with constitutions, boards of directors, bylaws, paid staffs, regular meetings, and often their own lodge-style meeting houses or boardrooms. It became a point of pride for boards to own their own "homes," as it were, consistent with the emerging ideology of the occupation.

Boards developed rules and practices for the conduct of real estate transactions, and attempted to influence legislation pertaining to real estate, often successfully. When the Detroit Real Estate Board was formed in 1906, members immediately agreed to raise commission rates from 2 to 3 percent on improved property, and because the city's most prominent brokers were members, the board's standard soon became the city's standard. The Detroit

board also instigated litigation to test the validity of a mortgage tax law. The
Baltimore Real Estate Exchange introduced a bill repealing the mortgage tax,
which became state law.[11]

Prospective buyers, clients, and brokers themselves had legitimate concerns about the validity of information received from other brokers, and more
generally about the trustworthiness of the purveyors of such information.
Stories abounded, sometimes apocryphal but often authentic, about corrupt,
fly-by-night swindlers who gypped innocent people, typically portrayed as
widows or naïve young couples, out of their life savings. In rural areas,
unscrupulous real estate "pirates" "infest[ed] the trains and depots," luring
unsuspecting new settlers into their lair, refusing to let the prospective buyer
"get in touch with anyone else until after he has been sold a piece of land."[12]
Popular culture reflected this concern in stories like Morgan's "Bilfinger," Ring
Lardner's "Own Your Home," and Sinclair Lewis's *Babbitt*.[13] Typical early-
twentieth-century real estate frauds included selling land to which the vendor
had no title; purchasing worthless land, mortgaging it to a confederate, and
selling the mortgage to unsuspecting persons; and selling land owned only on
contract-for-sale.[14] Thus, boards emerged in large part for "high-class" real
estate men to distinguish themselves from the less scrupulous, or at least from
the perception that most brokers were not to be trusted. Boards attempted to
establish and enforce rules of real estate practice and publicize their good
efforts, to gain the confidence of consumers and boost the image of the
occupation. To the latter end, local boards courted editors of real estate
sections of local newspapers and engaged in major publicity efforts.

Perhaps the greatest business innovation wrought by local boards in the
formative stages of organized real estate was the development and spread of
the multiple-listing system. The architects of MLS intended to address both the
issue of trust and the related problem of incomplete information in a highly
fragmented market. Boards established elaborate, cross-indexed card systems
for compiling all the properties listed by each member, and devised systems of
commission sharing. Typically, a board established a multiple-listing bureau
that members could join for a fee beyond their annual membership dues.
Bureau members were obligated to post all listings with the board's multiple-
listing card file, to which any bureau member was entitled to have access.
Thus, a broker-member had at his disposal the listings of every other member,
assuring owners of widespread exposure of their property and buyers of comprehensive information on market prices and available properties. Through

MLS, organized real estate men aimed to achieve a perfect market, in which every piece of real estate would be for sale by every real estate broker—or at least by every member of the board, and thus on offer to many more potential buyers. As the Toledo board's slogan put it, "Property Listed with One Is Listed with All."[15]

To forestall the potential for deleterious competition facilitated by the MLS, boards introduced the practice of exclusive agency. Under this arrangement, the original, "listing" broker bound his client through a sixty- or ninety-day exclusive contract to sell a listed property. "Owners sulked at first," according to the secretary of the Toledo board, "but when they saw it was the exclusive contract or nothing, and that signing an exclusive contract gave them the services of every office in the Board, they gradually came around to our method of doing business."[16] Any broker who found a buyer for an exclusively listed property would be obligated to share any commission with the listing broker. The idea spread slowly in the second decade of the century, but by 1925 some form of MLS was in operation in more than two hundred cities. As the long-time executive secretary of the national association, Herbert U. Nelson, noted in 1925 in his book on administering real estate boards, the development of multiple listing and exclusive contracts permanently transformed the practice of real estate brokerage.[17] The spread of MLS in turn expedited the process of organization, as access to the MLS was generally contingent upon membership in a local real estate board.[18] MLS helped to transform the local board from an élite club into a true service organization, and a growing number of medium-sized and small operators began to join.

Real estate boards aimed to tame the anarchic conditions of the turn-of-the-century urban real estate market, and in so doing to create a more stable, oligopolistic market in real property managed by a relatively small group of "high-class" real estate men. And in some respects they succeeded, as real estate experienced periods of great growth in the period 1905–25, during the zenith of the real estate men's initial professionalization efforts.[19] However, the boom and bust cycles characteristic of the American urban real estate market were partly a function of the failure of real estate brokers to fully professionalize the field. Organized real estate brokerage never managed to accrue enough disciplinary power to enforce adherence to consistent doctrine or practices, or to achieve true occupational closure and completely drive from its ranks the unscrupulous operator and the speculator driven purely by short-term profit.

Real estate brokers began to impose self-control through local collective action in part to reestablish the confidence in real estate as an investment lost by the ruinous competition and land speculation in the 1880s and the resultant deep and prolonged realty bust in the 1890s. The public's opinion of the real estate broker in the nineteenth century was low to begin with, and the crash of the 1890s exacerbated this poor image. The real estate men who established local boards from 1880 to 1920 aimed to instill in the public mind a sense of their competence, of the value and integrity of their information—after all, this was their primary commodity—and of their desire and ability to transcend base profit motives and provide a "public service." Through organization, real estate brokers hoped to reform themselves and rehabilitate their industry. In the process, they inadvertently created a new sort of hybrid identity, that of a "business professional."

The Chicago Board

By the second decade of the century, local real estate boards had become social institutions through which brokers developed a particular sense of their common interest and identity as members of a significant vocation. Local boards made the first efforts to develop standards of quality for men who dealt in real property. The Chicago Real Estate Board was in many ways the paradigmatic local board, formed as the city rebuilt itself and its population exploded in the aftermath of the Great Chicago Fire. Unlike older eastern cities, Chicago and other rapidly developing metropolises in the Midwest and West were virtual blank slates for ambitious real estate men.[20] The men who founded the Chicago board in 1883 directed their energies not only toward tangible concerns such as commission rates, legal forms and leases, and the relationship between agent and office but also to "questions . . . of a broad character, relating to the future of the city and improvement of its physical and governmental conditions." From the beginning its members imagined the board not as a narrow business association but as a civic one that would promote the common good of property dealers and owners, and also as a men's social club.

The Chicago board was involved in questions of public improvements and their relation to land values, championing tax reductions for property owners and supporting zoning laws in the early twentieth century. The board aimed, as the sociologist Everett C. Hughes put it in 1931, to "separate the community into tax-paying sheep, and tax-devouring wolves," fashioning itself as the "protecting watch-dog of the innocent, productive flock" of property owners, large and small.[21] Thus, very early in the history of local board organizing, the rhetoric of the real estate man as protector of civic virtue, as advocate of the property owner, was central.

The Chicago board played a significant role in civic affairs and city politics. Members of the board subscribed more than $100,000 to promote the city's successful bid to be the host in 1893 of the World's Columbian Exposition,[22] and the former board president William Kerfoot served as its director. The board was also well represented on the Chicago Civic Federation, a harbinger of the close relationship that would develop in the period 1910–20 between organized real estate and the American Civic Association. The Chicago board was among the prime movers behind the "City Beautiful" movement for wider streets and an expanded public park system in the early years of the century, along with the Chicago Civic Federation. It championed comprehensive zoning ordinances and city planning, and was the chief promoter of homeownership during the "Own Your Own Home" campaign after the First World War. The Chicago board demonstrated its political muscle in its formative years, forcing the city council to overturn a revenue ordinance in 1893 that established an annual license fee of $50 for brokers. It wasn't that the board was opposed to fees in principle; in 1893, its annual dues were the exorbitant sum of $200. Rather, the board sought to control its own membership, and chafed at what it perceived as government mandates. The matter of occupational licensing and its relationship to "self-control" was a point of intense controversy for many members of local real estate boards, and this concern would later reappear at the state and national levels.

Because of the predominance of renters in the Chicago real estate market, the Chicago board's original charter of incorporation stated as an explicit purpose the protection of landlords from "dishonest and immoral tenants"[23] (the pejorative language was later expunged). One of the board's first collective actions was to devise a system for rating tenants according to their paying habits and care of premises, a policy adopted by many landlords. The public understood that the new organization stood on the side of the property owners. The Chicago board devised uniform leases, the *Chicago Tribune* noted, in which "the tenant promises to do everything, and . . . all the landlord agrees to do is to receive the rent in advance."[24] In some respects the board's position was understandable in the context of growing anti-labor sentiment in the 1890s, in Chicago in particular, as many formerly socialist-leaning reformers became champions of private property and homeownership. The Chicago board, like most other well-organized urban boards, was successful in imposing the standard lease upon the entire market, translating vocational practice into public policy.

The development of the standard lease represented the very earliest attempt by real estate brokers to create a technical language of their own, an esoteric vocabulary that might endow their occupation with a veneer of expertise. The brokers appropriated arcane terminology from the law to create an imposing document that became familiarly incomprehensible to virtually every adult American. The standard lease transformed a simple agreement between owner and tenant into an eight-part document replete with obscure legalese and Latinate terms. "Witnesseth," began the "recital" and "demise" section of the Chicago Real Estate Board's standard apartment lease, "That Lessor, for and in consideration of the covenants and agreements hereinafter contained and made on the part of the Lessee, does hereby demise and lease to Lessee for use only by Lessee, and for a private residence or dwelling only, the premises known and described as follows." There followed the "habendum," defining the start and length of the lease, the "reddendum," or reservation of land, and a twenty-item list of covenants and restrictions. These last included proscription of "unlawful or immoral practice, with or without" the tenant's knowledge or consent and the use of the premises as a lodging or boarding facility or for giving instruction in music or singing. "Immoral practice" was defined as an injury to "the reputation of the premises or the building." Responding to the widespread perception that the standard lease was heavily biased in favor of the landlord, a prominent real estate text admitted as much, noting that the lease was "for the sole purpose of protecting the owner of the property against depredations committed by irresponsible tenants; the desirable tenant secures all the protection he needs, but the trouble maker will find his way made hard for him."[25] The standard lease was one of the first elements in the developing body of practices that helped to define the profession. However, the creation of a body of special real estate practice and knowledge proceeded spasmodically, and neither local boards nor the national association was ever able to establish anything like complete authority over the production and dissemination of real estate knowledge.

In the first five years of its existence, the Chicago Real Estate Board enrolled upwards of two hundred members, hired a secretary, and established a headquarters on State Street with meeting rooms.[26] It developed the rudiments of corporate solidarity, organizational spirit, and the sort of future-orientation that comes with an expectation of permanency. Its official organ, the *Chicago Call Board Bulletin*, distributed both information about properties for sale and transactions under way, as well as news and gossip about the board's members. Members began to conceive of the board as a meaningful institution from which at least part of their social identity derived.[27]

Though the Chicago board never managed to draw every Chicago real estate man into its ranks, its membership and influence grew tremendously. By 1917 the board boasted several hundred broker-members, making it among the largest boards in the national association, and its members owned, managed, and disposed freely of huge swaths of property. Though comprising only about 10 percent of the real estate agents listed in the Chicago City Directory, the Chicago board exercised a great deal of control over the rules of the local real estate market, particularly with respect to standardized leases, eviction procedures, and commission schedules. Hughes estimated that the brokers who composed the Chicago board conducted three-fourths of the city's real estate business. In the process of building an organization, the men who founded the Chicago board also built a city.

Further, the board was an organized and visible force in the corridors of power, a presence in city hall and the state legislature to a degree greatly disproportionate to the size of the membership roster. The board claimed credit for defeating legislation that would have increased the city's bonding limits by assessing higher taxes on property. It also claimed to have been instrumental in putting an end to the common speculative practice of buying land in a well-to-do neighborhood and then announcing the construction of a livery stable or some other nuisance, in essence blackmailing residents into buying out the speculators to prevent the construction.[28] The board successfully pressured the city government to pass ordinances requiring frontage consents for nuisance properties.[29] These regulations foreshadowed the sorts of comprehensive zoning laws for which the Chicago board and most other urban boards would lobby in the years following the First World War.

The sort of real estate broker licensing laws favored by the Chicago board never came to complete fruition, though in 1921 Illinois created a real estate commission under the control of "experienced real estate brokers"—meaning, in practice, members of the Chicago board and other organized real estate men from other parts of the state. This pattern was replicated across the nation. The norms of proper conduct were beginning to congeal in response to particular problems. Of special concern was the question of how to remunerate the broker for his services, especially in the frequent case in which more than one broker was involved in a transaction. Who gets the commission: the broker who made the initial listing of the property, or the one who actually found a buyer for it? By the turn of the century, the board had developed a solution in the form of the exclusive agency contract, a short-term binding agreement between agent and client, along with a standard commission schedule.

Through the Chicago Real Estate Board, Chicago's élite brokers set the terms for participation in the city's real estate market, and these were eventually codified into law. The Chicago board's energetic approach to self-regulation, political lobbying, and civic participation was copied across the country, thus altering not only real estate practice but the very shape of the American metropolis.[30]

The Philadelphia Board

The Philadelphia Real Estate Board was established as a nonprofit corporation on 21 April 1908. Given its age and high levels of homeownership and real estate activity in general, Philadelphia was a surprisingly late entrant into the organized real estate world, the last of the major colonial cities to organize a board. The Philadelphia board would come to embody the Progressive era's oft-contradictory urbanization agendas. The city's traditionally high rates of homeownership provided a natural constituency for the formation of a real estate board, yet its major concentrations of both urban industry and poverty meant that struggles over the roles of government versus private enterprise in urban development would be particularly acute.

With more deeply entrenched interests and far higher population densities than the cities of the West—and consequently, less land to develop—eastern cities needed to discover their slums before "new frontiers" emerged for real estate men. It was no coincidence that one of the most influential housing reform movements of the Progressive era, the National Housing Conference, emerged in Philadelphia, out of the Philadelphia Housing Association. From the beginning, the Philadelphia Real Estate Board was composed of two distinct groups: those who subscribed to emerging "progressive" notions about zoning and planning, and those who fiercely opposed such ideas. Interestingly, these divisions often fell along ethnic and religious lines.

The Philadelphia board's stated purpose was to "encourage trade and commerce in Real Estate, to inculcate just and equitable principles in trade, to [protect] against imposition and fraud, to bring about greater uniformity and certainty in business practices, and to establish closer ties of business association among the members." Aside from emulating its predecessors by organizing the rules of the real estate business in Philadelphia through self-regulation among members and wielding political influence, the Philadelphia board established itself rather quickly as both an educational institution and a social organization. It conducted intensive courses in real estate practice as well as weekly seminars for salesmen and continuing education for brokers. Its weekly luncheons, monthly dinners, and semiannual stag parties and golf outings were generally well attended and featured prominent local, state, and national politicians and business leaders as keynote speakers. The board quickly attracted a large membership, which by the end of 1910 numbered four hundred.[31]

The Philadelphia board screened applicants largely on the basis of demonstrated character and experience. A three-stage process of nomination, reference, and election winnowed out the undesirable and the untrustworthy. A typical letter of reference mentioned an applicant's "honesty," "reliability," and "integrity," and often that an applicant was "young, energetic and conscientious, and qualified to conduct a real estate business." Referees also generally mentioned the quality of the applicant's office. For example, a referee noted that one fifty-one-year-old veteran broker "conduct[ed] a well-equipped office in a business like manner."[32] The office became an important marker of a businessman's competence and character.

Applications for membership on the Philadelphia board provide insights into the characteristics that "high-class" real estate men valued in their colleagues, as well as their conception of the organization. The board asked each referee to state the nature of his relationship to the applicant. Typically, a referee was a long-standing familial or business acquaintance.[33] The board left it to the referee to ascertain whether the applicant was "qualified to conduct a real estate business" and whether he was financially sound. Three of the nine questions on the application pertained to social qualities. Was the applicant "gentlemanly in deportment"? Did he enjoy a good reputation? Was he regarded as "a man of integrity and honor"?[34] The Philadelphia board sought not simply "successful" brokers in purely financial terms—though of course fiscal soundness was an important consideration, and one not entirely divorced from moral concerns. Its aim was to attract men of character and standing, "gentlemen" at least in deportment, who had been in the business long enough to acquire solid reputations, and who were likely to enhance the board as both a business organization and a social institution. The idea, in sum, was to keep the unscrupulous, fly-by-night broker out.

The Philadelphia board was very much a social institution, and its calendar was filled with events. An annual banquet typically drew several hundred brokers and their wives, along with members of the local, regional, and national power élite. The social functions created a sense of belonging to an occupation that transcended day-to-day concerns of financial success. Minutes of meetings reveal a sense of confident camaraderie, most evident when the organization experienced a transition in elected officers or suffered the loss of a member. Most boards leased boardrooms, which functioned as social centers for the organization's members. Beginning in about 1910, boards began to construct their own headquarters buildings, often designed to accommodate not only business but pleasure as well, often replete with a barbershop, a smoking room, and a Turkish bath, among other amenities. The Philadelphia board built its "home" in 1922, and it soon became the envy of real estate men across the nation. The *National Real Estate Journal (NREJ)* noted the "elegance and taste displayed in the architectural construction, as well as the furnishings of the general executive offices, the private secretary's office, the lounge room, [and] the general meeting room," which exuded "the warmth of fellowship." A board "home" was the key to bringing real estate men into "closer friendly relationship." But, the *Journal* concluded, "it must be a real home, with all the charming and cozy conveniences that go to make up a home."[35] Of course it was a purely homosocial "home," since women were excluded from membership in the Philadelphia board from its founding in 1908 until late in the Depression. The board occupied its lodgings on the corner of Thirteenth and Locust Streets in Center City Philadelphia for more than five decades.

Business Republicanism

The local real estate board was a republican microcosm of sorts, where men participated in their own governance by enacting and observing rules, writing and amending constitutions, nominating and electing officers, forming committees, debating topics of concern to their business lives, and disciplining wayward members. This last, self-disciplinary function was essential in the period 1910–30 to the real estate men's professional self-image, which demanded that all disputes between brokers be handled by internal mechanisms of adjudication. Each board had its own arbitration and ethics committee that handled cases of fraud, disputes over commissions, and various other ethical infractions. Self-governing men had no need for meddling lawyers. However, since real estate boards never acquired control over the credentialing process, this system was only partly effective; a board could expel a man from membership, but not from the business entirely.

Finally, the local real estate board engendered camaraderie among members and loyalty to the organization and to the occupation through a multitude of social functions. Newsletters, weekly luncheons, banquets, and entreaties to simply drop by the board's headquarters to read the business pages and enjoy a pipe or cigar reinforced a sense of brotherhood and gave members a chance to perform manliness in ways that were impossible in the course of everyday business or home life. Meetings and banquets abounded with oratory, both scripted and impromptu, demarcating the boundaries of white masculine belonging, with racist and sexist jokes about "Chinamen," "darkies," and "hens." Many boards emulated fraternal organizations, inducting new members in formal initiation rituals laden with metaphors from chivalric legends and the ministry. A new member swore never to be "recreant to his vow" or "an apostate to the noble principles of the real estate profession." In return for inclusion in the order of worthy real estate men, the individual broker pledged himself before his brethren to "foster public improvements and worthy enterprises," "promote patriotism and public spirit," and "put forth every effort to establish the profession . . . in a position of dignity and responsibility." The ceremony concluded when the president of the board grasped the hand of the initiate while a chorus of real estate brethren loudly welcomed him into their ranks.[36]

"Initiation" into "manhood" was an important notion for many American men in the nineteenth century and the early twentieth. Success in the competitive marketplace had long been a prominent rite of passage from boyhood to manhood in America. But the increasing incorporation of the American economy at the turn of the century threatened this notion of "marketplace manhood."[37] In response, men of the working and middling classes—especially those in the tertiary, distributive sector of the economy such as salesmen and brokers—began to articulate a vision of themselves as successors to the heroic artisans, the rugged pioneers, and the captains of industry of American masculine lore. "A good salesman is without doubt one of our finest types of manhood, and a desirable citizen for any community. He stands on his own feet. He is independent—quite self-sufficient," stated a real estate man from Pittsburgh. In the new corporate economy, the young man who wanted "to make good in business" ought to be tossed out on the road alone as a salesman, with a sample case, a train ticket, and compensation only on commission. This would test his mettle and "instill in him an appreciation of the word produce, of what a struggle the average business man has to make to gain headway against a field always strong." It would make him realize like nothing else why "the greatest rewards in business so frequently go to the man who has gone through the hard school of selling, who has earned his keep and comfort by the stern standard of dollars and cents and sales."[38]

The real estate man imagined himself as the greatest of all salesmen. He "must work hard, act quickly, and think fast, and above all, be fair to both buyer and seller . . . He has made glad the hearts of millions of wives and mothers when he induced the husbands and fathers to purchase the little spot she called home, where her work was made easier, and her life made happier."[39] Thus, real estate brokerage fashioned itself as a manly calling both because it required a quick mind, strength of spirit, integrity, and perseverance, and because it was by definition an exercise of power over other men, a triumph of will aided by aggressive sales techniques. The desired results of this hard work were to expand homeownership, broaden civic virtue, and make women's work easier and their lives happier. These attitudes reached their fullest expression in the years following the First World War, during the "Own Your Own Home" and "Better Homes for America" campaigns, both instigated primarily by organized real estate men.

By the early twentieth century real estate boards had become ubiquitous institutions that performed crucial functions in terms of both regulating real estate markets and creating among brokers a sense of their own occupational self-worth. They seldom made front-page news, except when a convention came to town, but a glance at the real estate section of any urban newspaper provided ample evidence of the vital activities of board members in shaping towns and cities. By the time of the First World War few urban or suburban Americans had been untouched by the handiwork of a real estate board, whether directly in the form of a lease or a commission on property purchased, or indirectly in the form of legislation that a board had helped to write or implement. The designs of local boards were embodied in regulations concerning building materials for houses and offices, the width of streets, and the distance between streets and front doorsteps. Local boards wrote or helped to write land-use ordinances and other restrictions on building, and they promoted ideas about the "City Beautiful" and comprehensive zoning. One commentator quipped that "only the hoboes" escaped the influence of the board.[40] Paradoxically, while the individual real estate man was overrepresented in the news, mostly as a villain in stories about fraud and abuse, the real estate board was very much an underacknowledged institution. The movement toward national-level professionalization that took root in the first decade of the twentieth century would raise the profile and increase the power of local boards tremendously.

CHAPTER TWO

Real Estate Brokerage and the Formation of a (National) Middle-Class Consciousness, 1907–1915

We are the men who handle the earth,

Wet with dew from the great hand of God;

Ornate with buildings of infinite worth,

Covered with tints of the emerald sod,

Sliced into parcels of one certain size,

Groaning 'neath weight of brick, stone and steel,

Spreading, a plane, or a grim mountain's rise,

Binding within it a man's woe or weal.

—The Song of the Real Estate Dealer[1]

It was through his local board that the broker established himself as a fraternal member of the "high-class" real estate order, but he began to think of himself as part of a national movement of "professional" brokers through the National Association of Real Estate Exchanges. The most active local boards came together in Chicago in 1908 to formulate and spread the gospel of ethics, establish durable and reproducible institutions, influence public policy, and try in earnest to define, operationalize, and promote real estate brokerage as a respectable career and ultimately a "profession." The leading men in this movement promoted an image of an ideal real estate broker possessed of integrity, prescience, and a strong sense of responsibility for "man's woe or weal," as the poet proclaimed in "The Song of the Real Estate Dealer," written in honor of the national association's annual convention in 1915. They endeavored to foregather men fitting this description into an organization in order to institutionalize high standards for occupational entry and standardize real estate practice across the country. They faced considerable obstacles, as real estate brokerage was almost by definition a local or at best regional occupation. While they readily formed local organizations, and plainly saw the wisdom in doing so, real estate men tended to have a weak sense of connectedness to the world beyond their hometowns. However, the depression of the 1890s had impressed upon some of them that increasingly national and even global forces affected the local real estate market in ways they did not fully comprehend.

In the first half-decade or so of their professional project, the men who founded the National Association of Real Estate Exchanges constructed an image of a "high-class" broker around an implicit two-part masculine ideal. On the one hand the real estate man was a visionary artist, exercising his creative will on cities like the sculptor on a block of marble. On the other, he was a risk-taking entrepreneur, boldly utilizing his innate tact to draw investors to his far-reaching, profitable development schemes.

In the first phase of the effort to nationalize and regularize the vocation, which lasted from 1907 until about 1915, the local fraternal cultures were woven together into a tenuous national brotherhood that served to unite men with disparate interests and experiences. This national masculine vocational ethos was developed, enacted, and continually revised at the annual convention of the National Association of Real Estate Exchanges and in its official organ, the *National Real Estate Journal*. While women were beginning to engage in real estate brokerage in this period, their voices were completely absent from the discourse of professionalism emerging in the local real estate boards and the national association until the 1920s. The national professional consciousness that emerged among real estate men was deeply inflected by gender in this period, an especially unstable and transitional moment in the history of both American manhood and the American work ethic.

The Conventions of Middle-Class Masculinity

"What is our annual convention?" asked William W. Hannan, outgoing president of the national association, in 1910. "To my mind this is one of the most important features of our national organization. Meetings of representative real estate men, the live men of the leading communities, each endowed with the practical experience and practical problems which confront us, serve to disseminate thoughts and ideas that are of inestimable value to all." The annual convention of the national association drew together hundreds of real estate men from across the country, facilitating the development of new acquaintances, bonds of "brotherhood" that would enable members to do business outside their own communities and transcend the limits of localism. The meetings took place in a different city each year, and local boards competed fiercely for the honor of hosting a convention. The annual convention, along with the official organ, the *National Real Estate Journal*, formed what Hannan called the "backbone" of the emerging profession.[2] A fragile web of masculine ligaments, to continue Hannan's anatomical metaphor, loosely linked the vertebrae of the organization.

The various masculinities enacted on the stage of the convention both reinforced and undermined the real estate brokers' claims to respectable, professional status. As Hannan's words suggested, the convention served two equally important functions in the early years. The real estate men produced and distributed technical knowledge, in the process defining their profession. They also constituted a "brotherhood," performing and revising business republicanism at these annual gatherings. In and through such rituals as the journey to and from the convention on a specially chartered Pullman car crammed full of their peers, the business meetings and speeches, and especially the social events of the convention, the real estate men became aware of themselves as part of a national, masculine business world. Through the experience of the convention and the post-convention reporting in the *NREJ*, the national association's members began to develop a sense of themselves as part of a broad, national class of professionals. They participated in the making of a national language and a national style of middle-class manhood, emerging from concrete discussions about the nature of their enterprise and the role of real estate men in local and national affairs.

The formative meeting of the National Association of Real Estate Exchanges in Chicago in May 1908 brought together a group of men who believed that real estate brokerage, properly organized, could among other things save American civilization from the ills of unfettered urban and rural development. For three days 120 men representing nineteen boards from thirteen states met in the YMCA Hall in Chicago. These men and their boards, which represented merely 1 or 2 percent of the more than 120,000 brokers enumerated by the 1910 census, founded the national association explicitly to represent the national interests of real estate as an occupation. They also aimed to establish as ground rules for the real estate field as a whole the practices and norms of their relatively élite coterie. In fact, they attempted to construct real estate brokerage as a "national" enterprise and to instill a "national" consciousness into a decidedly parochial group of men who bought, sold, and developed real estate primarily in one particular place. More precisely, a small group of real estate brokers with national ambitions set out to create a generic image of a "professional" broker that would elide local differences. For this, they stipulated a set of attributes that defined the generic, professional real estate man, and a set of principles and practices that defined the profession itself.

Fiercely loyal to their local boards, yet desirous of creating an effective national body, the delegates to the founding convention decided upon a loose, federal style of organization, with local boards as the constitutive units. The first version of the constitution and bylaws gave the national organization few powers and minimal financial resources in the early years. Local boards would set membership standards and collect dues, which were passed upward to the national organization, albeit not always expeditiously. The convention decided to establish the national headquarters in Minneapolis, in the offices of the prominent Detroit broker Samuel S. Thorpe, and hired Edward Halsey as executive secretary. Halsey, the only truly "national" official because he belonged to no local board, presented his goals for the organization at the first convention. These included a rating system for real estate men along Dun and Bradstreet lines, based on "moral qualifications" rather than financial ones; some sort of signification of membership; uniform state laws governing deeds, mortgages, and real estate contracts; and the establishment of exclusive agency, a short-term agreement by which the local board would enforce the right of any one member to be the sole representative of a client. All these measures were intended to curb reckless, speculative, fly-by-night practices and ruinous competition by attracting a better breed of broker. From the beginning, "character" was central to the brokers' nascent professional self-image, and the state was conceived as a relevant participant in the development of the profession, through licensing law and the law of contract. Aided by the power of organization, the founders imagined that oligopolistic practices like exclusive agency would keep the field narrow.

The founding convention drafted a constitution and bylaws. The preamble of the constitution stated that the organization aimed to "unite the real estate men of America for the purpose of exerting effectively a combined influence upon matters affecting real estate interests." The members aimed to standardize transaction procedures and lobby for laws that would improve access to financing for homebuyers and builders, thus facilitating investment in real estate and restoring confidence in real property in the wake of the debacle of the 1890s. But real estate was (and to a large degree still is) a very decentralized "industry," and the new organization faced from its inception the daunting task of identifying and cultivating issues that cut across local concerns. These included coming to consensus on standards of ethical practice, enhancing the public image of the occupation, and deciding whether to endorse zoning, city planning, and state licensing laws. Because these issues all turned out to be contentious, the bonds of fraternity formed at the annual meetings among participants were crucial to the endurance of the profession.

The founding convention debated the role of organized real estate men in the political process. R. Bruce Douglas, president of the Milwaukee Real Estate Exchange, argued that organized real estate should keep out of politics, with the exception of attempting to secure "liberal immigration laws." Douglas and others argued that immigration was crucial to the expansion of the real estate business, and that colonization by foreigners made good business sense. Interestingly, there was no recorded objection to Douglas's advocacy of liberalized immigration, but several delegates were adamantly opposed to his plea for political detachment. W. T. Graham of Omaha insisted that real estate men were obliged to show a keen interest in politics, because politics was constantly impinging upon the real estate business. "We wield a potent influence," he asserted. Organized real estate men could and should "subdue" their officials to achieve "reasonable legislation."[3] This position was implicit in the constitution's preamble, and was the de facto stance of the organization for the entire twentieth century. From the outset, however, there was an articulated philosophical position that the profession, and implicitly any profession, should not take anything other than a disinterested position in relation to politics. A sizable minority of men believed it beneath the dignity of a true professional to sully his reputation by participating in the inherently corrupt and compromised political process. A true professional could only serve the public good in a position insulated from the compromises inherent to politics.

Despite its reservations some twenty-five years earlier about the one-sided intentions of its hometown real estate board, the press in Chicago viewed the establishment of the national association as a positive development. In describing the organizational meeting, the *Chicago Tribune* asserted that real estate "sharks" were now in "danger of extermination": the real estate dealer was "no longer a mere speculator in land or buildings," but an influential and positive force in the community. "High-class" brokers did not succeed through chicanery and fraud but through "knowledge of many matters." Ostensibly, these were not the same men so squarely on the side of the "grinding landlord" in 1883.[4] If they charged high rents, the *Tribune* implied, it would be for reasons having only to do with public health and welfare and based on a dispassionate analysis of the realities of land values.

Publicly, the real estate men declared a role for themselves as protectors of society—implicitly marked feminine, childlike, or working class—against the unscrupulous, nefarious swindler who populated the ranks of the commonplace real estate agent. Participants in the founding convention called for "extermination" of the "curbstone brokers" who bring naïve "lambs" "into their fold," the rough and tumble world of the realty market, "to skin them."[5] The curbstoner and other devious characters were the fount of misery, and professional brokers had a solemn duty to expose and banish them from the vocation. How to do this, and how to decide where to draw the line between ethical broker and miscreant? Would membership in a real estate board in itself serve as sufficient guarantee of integrity?

Utterances about responsibility for protecting the public referred implicitly to a conundrum inherent in the founding of the organization and the development of the profession. The founders of the national association believed that they were, as "high-class" brokers, in the minority. There were at least three types of brokers—good, indifferent, and bad. The middle, and largest, group was more or less ethically agnostic, susceptible to education and persuasion: it might join the bandwagon of professionalization. How were the reformers to "eliminate" those in the third group who refused to play by their rules? Would doing so require bringing the police powers of the state to bear? There were dangers in such a strategy, among them a perceived loss of autonomy. But this was not all. Could the national association's leaders persuade even all the prominent brokers who made up their ranks that they ought to see themselves as "professionals" rather than mere businessmen? Why would or should a proud American businessman identify himself as a "professional"? What was to be gained? Was anything to be lost? The debate over the professionalization of business was fraught with multiple and often antagonistic meanings, and went right to the heart of what it meant to be a middle-class American man in the twentieth century.

From the beginning of their organized efforts, the real estate men developed an occupational culture that linked the sale and development of real estate with particular notions of middle-class manhood. As brokers, real estate men were mediators, structurally speaking, between production and consumption. While many brokers were also developers—"community builders" who planned, platted, and sold entire neighborhoods and subdivisions—most were only intermediaries, who assumed the task of adjusting the supply of real property to demand, and used their local knowledge to bring together appropriately matched buyers and sellers of real estate. As organized high-class brokers, though, they had unavoidable civic responsibilities that went well beyond the simple harmonization of supply and demand. It was incumbent upon them to make sure that their clients used land responsibly. "All the progress of the whole people depends upon the real manhood," asserted the Buffalo real estate man Fenton M. Parke before the New York Real Estate Association in 1910. Hence, he continued, the "need of men of vision, men who will co-operate, men who will give their time, energies, ability, and money not only to philanthropic matters, but to business, labor, social, and other organizations." This "touching of elbows" in cooperative work would teach every man "regard for the common good which is the hope for our citizenship," and would level "class distinctions."[6] The real estate men developed a vision of themselves as part of a larger cohort of men and women whose cooperative work in balancing various interests would redeem American civilization and mitigate the harsh impact of rapid industrialization and haphazard urban development. Real estate men of the better sort envisioned themselves as part of an emerging stratum of public-spirited men and women to whom was delegated, by virtue of their innate ability and learned skill, the role of uplifting society. Many reformers urged that urban and rural land policy demanded moral guidance and intelligent action, and the more prescient among the real estate men saw an opportunity to appropriate and shape the emerging field as a jurisdiction of their own.

Real estate men were in the middle in other ways as well. As relatively small businessmen and entrepreneurs, they experienced the anxiety produced by the increasing incorporation of the American economy, especially after the depression of the 1890s. At the same time, as developers and as brokers of commercial and residential property, they were in a position to accrue income and status, as a rapidly growing number of white-collar workers sought new homes in new suburbs and as businesses sought property on which to expand and to build towering office buildings. As real estate men, they had a civic duty, so they thought, not only to intelligently create great cities but also to bring the benefits of homeownership to every American, especially the workingman. As Hannan put it in his farewell presidential address in Minneapolis in 1910, "there is no one element in our social life that tends to greater harmony, greater home life, and better citizenship than home ownership by the man who depends upon his daily wage for his livelihood."[7] Or as "B. A. Homeowner" poetically put it, "lives of all great men remind us we can make our lives sublime, by buying a home with golden dollars, ere they float away on the tides of time."[8] The real estate men claimed responsibility for increasing homeownership as the special moral burden of their occupation, along with the rational development of cities and suburbs. Such moral burdens required cooperation among strong, virile, live men, to borrow the language of the time. Part of their claim to professional status rested on their role as providers of homes, particularly for women, children, and wage earners.

The annual convention played a central role in the development of a national orientation and professional consciousness. The convention supplied a condensed time and space for defining peculiarly "middle-class" masculine styles and rhetoric. Virtually each part of the convention can be seen as a significant moment in a foundational ritual of middle-class manliness. The way the convention was promoted and the mode of invitation; the railway journey in Pullman cars; the appearance of hundreds of real estate men simultaneously at the host city's train depot; the trip from depot to conference venue; the mixing in the hotel lobby; the oratory and business on the floor of the convention; and especially the formal and informal socializing—all were charged with meaning worthy of an intensive anthropological study.

The spate of convention advertising that typically began to appear in the *National Real Estate Journal* three or four months before the event entreated the real estate men to join their brethren for a week of discussion, learning, and revelry. It encouraged them to invite their wives and at the same time to leave them at home, to be men among other men. The journey to and from the convention was an expressive rite of passage, a trip away from everyday domestic and business concerns for the large majority of men who left wife and children for the exclusive world of real estate men.

A convention delegate generally began his journey with other brokers from his own board, but each stop of the train added to the contingent of men headed to Detroit, Minneapolis, Denver, Louisville, Winnipeg, Pittsburgh, or

Los Angeles (the sites of the conventions in 1909–15). By the time they arrived at a major railway interchange like Cleveland or Chicago, there would likely be numerous real estate men from various places on board the train. For example, dozens of delegates to the convention of 1911 converged in Chicago to board a chartered Pullman car, the "Real Estate Special," to complete the trip to Denver. In the Pullmans the men smoked, talked, chanted, and sang, discussed the issues of the day, and swapped encomiums to their hometowns. This was the first step in the four-day ritual of male bonding.

After the lengthy trip, the men arrived in the host city, where invariably the convention committee had arranged to transport them in a caravan of honk-ing and bedecked automobiles from the train station to the conference hotel. Particularly in the early years of automobiling, the parade of cars symbolized adventure, wealth, and modern technical prowess, and this was surely not lost on the real estate men or spectators in the press and the public. Upon arrival at the hotel, members of the welcoming committee greeted the visitors heartily and gave them a distinctive badge. Thus marked as part of the in-group, the men began "mixing." "Let's go down and get acquainted," a local delegate implored a visiting broker as he grabbed him by the elbow and shepherded him into the commotion of the hotel lobby, where the two encountered hundreds of other real estate men. In this bustling crowd the individual real estate broker was likely to first feel himself part of a vital movement of men.

Interrupting the informal fraternizing, the local organizers marshaled the men into the massive convention hall for the opening ceremony, which fea-tured a benediction by a local religious figure, always Protestant, followed by a welcoming speech by the mayor or governor. The local notables regaled the visiting real estate men with tales of the host city—the most beautiful, hos-pitable, industrious, and forward-looking city in America, they inevitably claimed—and assured them that their opinion of the city was of extreme interest to every citizen, because theirs was a truly "progressive" and impor-tant calling. The real estate men responded to the compliment with thun-derous applause. The spectacle of the roll call followed, as various boards made dramatic entries in costume and performed ditties written especially for the occasion.

Next came the address by the local board president, a paean to real estate men that drew the delegates to their feet numerous times, stomping and whistling. The annual report of the president of the national association followed, recounting its great achievements that year, to which the men responded with a rousing chorus of "He's a Jolly Good Fellow" or some other sign of appreciation.[9] After the regional vice-presidents read their reports, an inspiring keynote speech ended the first day's activities, and the men adjourned to their rooms to prepare for the evening's social events. The convention reconvened in the morning at 9:30, and committee reports and various business meetings occupied the day until the next evening's social function. The third day typically consisted of a half-day of business followed by a mixed-sex outing, such as a picnic at Lake Minnetonka in 1910. On the fourth and final day, the delegates chose their new leaders and voted on various resolutions and policies to shape the workings of the organization for the ensuing year. This was the generic structure of the convention.

Massive publicity attended the openings of real estate conventions, beginning with Detroit in 1909, which garnered four complete columns of coverage in the *Detroit Free Press*, including a large front-page story on 26 June, the concluding day of the convention. The paper published much of the Detroit broker William W. Hannan's keynote address, "Organization," delivered at the male-only banquet. Hannan, president-elect of the national association, told the assembled men that "immeasurable good" would result from organization, that only organization could eliminate the "element which is the cause of criticism because of unprofessional conduct or breach of trust." Most importantly, Hannan asserted, organization "carries with it" cooperation and "brotherhood." Other speakers echoed Hannan's call for fraternal unity, and added other important themes. William E. Harmon of New York spoke on the need to develop a "science of real estate," noting that "the men who represent 50 per cent of the wealth of the country" operate "without any established principles or exact knowledge," and calling for university courses on the subject. Alas, Harmon's plea for putting brokerage on a scientific basis was premature, as we shall see. The convention concluded with a resolution that urged uniform legislation on real estate, and that instructed the officers to transmit the resolution to the leaders of the American Bar Association to be considered at their convention.[10]

The convention in Minneapolis in 1910 received even greater and richer coverage in the major newspapers. The *Minneapolis Journal* published anticipatory articles with headlines such as "All Ready for Real Estate Men," enumerating in detail the agenda of the convention, as well as the names of registered delegates. The mayor of Minneapolis and the governor of Minnesota both made an appearance to welcome the men. The convention itself was the subject of a front-page story and six to eight columns of coverage each day for three days. News stories recounted the discussions at the meetings in detail. Editorial pages were both laudatory of the real estate men and very deferential to their presumed expertise. One writer noted an important change in the nature of the occupation. While a convention of real estate dealers in 1900 would likely have consisted only of "recreation-seekers," by 1910 the real estate men were "capable of informing discussions of the most intimate municipal problems," and the real estate business as a whole was now almost deserving of inclusion in the ranks of the professions.[11] The journalist had posed as a self-evident proposition that the ability to have "informed discussions" was almost grounds for acceptance as a profession. This notion would serve as the benchmark for later discussions and debates over the nature of real estate professionalism.

From 1910 onward, it was customary for the editorial page of the host city's major daily newspaper to welcome the real estate men to the annual convention by recognizing their unique and expert perspective. "The Real Estate Convention brings together a collection of men whose actual opinion of this city is of value to us," declared a typical statement in the *Minneapolis Journal* in 1910. "It is the greatest compliment in the world if we are able to satisfy such men . . . The real estate dealers of the country are very welcome in Minneapolis. We have learned much from them. We hope they have learned something from us."[12] Editorial pages were effusive: "Real Estate!" trumpeted the *Rocky Mountain News* on the opening day of the convention in 1911. "The delegates are glad to be here; for they are men of intelligence. And Denver is glad to have them here. It is pleasant to play host to so wide-awake a crowd . . . Denver is one of the few cities . . . which can stand, unblinking, the scrutiny of a group of men trained as real estate dealers are trained."[13] Throughout the decade the national association garnered strong support and much praise in major daily newspapers, partly a result of shared ideals of moderate progressivism on the part of editors and the real estate men, and partly a result of the alliances with newspaper editors formed by local boards in their quest to improve the occupation's image.

The newspapers published a detailed convention program each day, and reportage from the convention was nearly always on the front page, despite the gravity of world events in 1914 and 1915. Stories recounted the events of the convention in unusual detail, quoting liberally from the various papers on subjects such as "Why the Chicago Real Estate Board Is a Success," "Our Local Exchange," "The Ethics of Our Business," and "Real Estate Booms." Images of camaraderie peppered stories about the high level of interchange in the meeting rooms. Numerous photos of men dining, shaking hands, and posing in large groups while wearing large hats adorned the pages of the major newspapers. Many newspapers also employed a cartoonist to sketch and caricature the delegates, helping to develop a gallery of vocational folk heroes. Among those in the pantheon were the early presidents of the organization, and the convention photographers never failed to snap a candid shot of early luminaries like Samuel Thorpe, W. W. Hannan, Thomas Shallcross, and others in amicable conversation. The cartoonist for the *Pittsburgh Courier-Post* in 1914 depicted the president of the hometown board, Henry P. Haas, as a dashing figure on a steed.[14] Each president became the subject of a myth, and the tales became the folklore of the vocation.

The annual rite of passing the gavel from one president to the next offered an opportunity for the real estate men to praise each other publicly, to emote in a manly manner. Eulogizing the outgoing president W. W. Hannan, Bruce Douglas (reelected to the secretary-treasurer's post for a second term at Minneapolis in 1910), noted that Hannan had kept his campaign promise to "do all the fighting" for the national association in its embryonic first year. While the president was "out looking for a fight," Douglas quipped, there was nothing left for the secretary to do but "the work." In the midst of "prolonged applause" and cries of "What's the matter with Hannan? He's all right," Hannan took the podium and reflected upon his presidency with "no small degree of satisfaction and pride," noting that it was not the "high honor" of the office or his specific accomplishments that were most satisfying but rather the "many friends" he made and the "many manifestations of loyalty, friendship and kindness" from the men with whom he came into contact. Often, when he was on the verge of discouragement at the immensity of his task, the "magnificent support" and "kindly treatment" he received provided moral sustenance.[15] Hannan helped to define the parameters for publicly acceptable masculine expressions of tenderness and warmth, and the audience responded with generous applause. Hannan's sentimental words drew the real estate men assembled at the annual convention deeper into the fraternity.

In the early years, the *National Real Estate Journal* published verbatim transcripts of the activities of the annual conventions. Remarkably detailed and formatted like scripts, the proceedings included notations about applause levels, laughter, and interruptions from the floor. The men engaged in lively debate about such issues as the bylaws of the national association's constitution, the fee structure for membership, ideas for running board meetings effectively, and how to increase the number of local boards affiliated with the organization. The convention reports conveyed a sense of the organization as a living, participatory body, a republic of businessmen conducting their affairs with both seriousness of purpose and levity of spirit. Committee chairs leavened their reports with humorous and off-color anecdotes, and the assembly often broke into spontaneous applause and cheers.

Even moments of disagreement—like a spat on the floor of the closing session of the 1910 convention between A. G. Bowes of Denver and Joseph P. Day of New York over the site of the 1911 convention—reinforced this business republicanism. Day made a rather long point in support of Denver's invitation to host the meeting, during which he praised the western cities in general for their leadership in the national association and for their superior organizational efforts. Day suggested that the organization develop a policy about convention sites, implying that they might be chosen to reward not only those regions or cities that were already well organized but those that needed help, like many in the East. When the time came for an eastern city to make a bid for the convention, Day implored, it ought to be allowed "to state its case fairly, squarely and manfully as to what should be done to make this organization successful in the East." Bowes thanked Day for supporting his city's bid for the convention. But in the next breath, he took exception to Day's policy suggestion and in the process expressed a nasty bit of provincial envy. "I feel it is no more than right that the West should have it a few years. [The national association] started in the West . . . Boston is called the 'hub of the universe,' and New York is pretty close to it. Denver is the geographical center of the United States, that is the axle, and the others revolve around the axle and that takes New York with it for a few years." Day leapt to his feet in protest. "Do you think that is a fitting return when we pledge harmony and our friendship? . . . The attempt of this Denver man to differentiate is against the policy I have outlined." President Hannan immediately intervened, to loud applause: "This is not of the East, West, North, or South—it is of the whole country." Denver won the nomination unanimously; the republic was preserved.[16]

The meeting in Denver in 1911, like that in Minneapolis before it, was marked by much masculine emoting. "Today we are forceful factors in the business world," declared the association president, Alexander Taylor, before the opening session, "identified with the most progressive and honorable business of the age—that of providing homes and proper surroundings for our people and the building up of cities." From the rostrum, Taylor admired the "faces of strong, true men, assembled here for action, banded together by ties of common interests."[17] The Denver convention was notable for the appointment of Thomas S. Ingersoll, the affable executive secretary who would serve the national association for nearly ten years. "Tom" quickly came to personify the national organization in the minds of rank-and-file members. Aside from the presidents, it was Tom who linked the members and whose image and words would define the public face of the organization. His friendliness and service orientation typified the organization's camaraderie and public-spiritedness. As one convention report put it, "Tom fits this important office [of the executive secretary] like the proverbial glove, and his boundless energy and enthusiasm seems to increase each succeeding year."[18] Through his image and his fieldwork as a traveling executive secretary, the members of the national association achieved fraternal connectedness.

A convention typically lasted three or four days, but real estate men were encouraged to prolong the trip to take advantage of the hospitality of their colleagues along the route, to get to know each other better. After the convention in 1911, the Colorado Springs Real Estate Board hosted a group of men and their wives.[19] Friendships among brokers from different cities and regions of the country that developed during the convention formed the webs of national vocational identity, helping real estate men from scattered jurisdictions to see themselves as part of one great national fraternity. Making acquaintances at the convention also had economic value, and the real estate men were admonished never to forget that "beyond the true friendships," the convention fostered "business transactions."[20]

Men who were unable to attend a convention often sent letters or telegrams to the national officers, with instructions to read them aloud to the assembly. Regretting deeply his inability to make the trip to Los Angeles in 1915, Hill Ferguson of Birmingham, Alabama, gushed: "[It] breaks my heart that I am not in California today and I am thinking of it constantly. Give my love to Shallcross, Kane, Ninde, Haas, Upham, Coates, and any others that remember me." A broker from Toledo, Irving B. Hiett, assured the men that his "heart is there," and passed on "greetings to all the boys. I know they will get lots of inspiration and have a jolly good time."[21] Masculine affection, camaraderie, and commerce mingled effortlessly on the convention floor, in the hotel suites, and in the Pullman cars.

The press also covered the social events in detail. The *Minneapolis Star* covered the baseball game and other outdoor events at the convention of 1910 in as much detail as if they had been professional sporting events. Three pages of photos embellished the accounts of the massive opening pageant at the convention in Denver in 1911—"the greatest pageant by any city," with "two miles of floats," attended by eighty thousand spectators and indelibly recorded on a "moving picture machine" brought in from New York. "Realty Men Romp in the Snow," read a headline about a post-convention jaunt into the Rockies for "snowballing in July," leaving readers with an image of a convivial group of men equally comfortable in the boardroom and playing in the great outdoors.[22] In 1912 the *Louisville Courier-Journal* reported with tacit approval that the "staid real estate brokers [broke] loose with noise" when they convened in the city, behaving more like "college boys" than the prominent businessmen and important civic leaders they really were.[23] The media coverage produced an image of a boy inside each businessman. This "inner boy" kept the real estate men honest and energetically optimistic.

With the exception of a few evening events, the "ladies of the convention" were entertained separately. The Ladies' Reception Committee for the meeting in Pittsburgh in 1914 organized an extensive program, including an automobile tour of the "country homes" of prominent local brokers and a visit to the "Home of the 57 Varieties." The group photo taken by the Heinz Company demonstrated that "several men were also interested in this trip," or at least felt compelled to join their wives.[24] The wives of prominent members of the national association created a sort of ladies' auxiliary to the convention. One female guest praised the real estate men for making the ladies feel welcome at their conventions, since so many other business and professional organizations excluded them. For the most part, however, the real estate men spent the convention in their own homosocial realm.

Oration played a large part in the social world of the convention. There were many spontaneous interchanges on the convention floor, and from 1913 onward each convention reserved a large block of time for "Five Minute Speeches." In these oratorical contests, delegates from various boards competed to outdo each other in praising their hometowns, and winner took home a silver cup. The speeches also served as bids for the subsequent convention. Except in 1913, when the lone female delegate to the convention, Eva Miller of Tampa, bravely participated to high accolades, this was a manly rhetorical brawl. Each speaker threw down the gauntlet, challenging any other city's representative to best his hometown's catalogue of unparalleled attributes. Omaha was the "third largest packing center" and "second largest sheep market." Denver possessed "the bluest skies, the sweetest air, the most glorious sunsets, the purest water, the grandest mountain scenery." Philadelphia was "a city that was, a city that is, and a city that will be, a city that renews her youth with each decade." Toledo was a city of "splendid men and women," a "progressive yet conservative city . . . where purity of life counts, and a square deal is given to its citizens, and where reverence for God and truth is prominent and predominant."[25] The grand old American ministerial and political tradition of muscular oration endured in the business republic.

The events at the convention in Los Angeles in 1915 garnered the most extensive newspaper coverage of all. Everything about that convention was big—the turnout of more than fifteen hundred real estate men, the immense displays of California flora and fauna in the Shrine Hall, the scale model of Los Angeles adorning the luncheon banquet table, and the two massive theme parties organized by the developer Harry Culver's entertainment committee. Despite the brokers' propensity for including ladies in the evening social functions, Culver's committee decided that the first event would be a male-only "smoker," with the gold rush of 1849 as the theme. Culver's committee fabricated a "Forty-Niner" mining camp in the Shrine Hall—obviously "no place for ladies." The invitation implored the real estate men to dress appropriately, which they did, as "halfbreeds, Chinamen, mule drivers, prospectors, Indians, cowpunchers, swashbucklers, and other heathen of the old, old days of Gold Hill." The real estate men, many of them "pillars of the church," who in daily life "would shrink from anything more wicked than a 10-cent dice game at a cigar counter," indulged in three-card monte and roulette, and recklessly galloped and whirled to the blaring music of the brass band. As the *Los Angeles Times* described the gala on the front page of its editorial section, "Bret Harte, with all his imaginative power, never could have pictured such a foregathering of the abandoned souls of the West" and "tenderfeet from the effete East." The *Times* published a quarter-page photo of a group of costumed brokers, asking, "Who are these dangerous men?" It was a perfect illusion, down to the "painted women brazenly leaning over the bars and gaming tables and breezily forcing their attentions upon the men." However, as the *Times* was quick to point out, the pancake makeup on the faces of these women could not completely conceal the features of the real estate men underneath—though, it continued, "most of them would not have been known and certainly not recognized by their own wives."[26]

In a similar vein, the *National Real Estate Journal* reprinted a cartoon (figure 1) from the coverage of the 1914 convention in the *Pittsburgh Gazette-Times*. At first glance, it appears to be an ordinary caricature of an elegantly dressed real estate man who, the editors of the *NREJ* inform the reader, is a former treasurer of the national association, Col. W. W. Price, shown dancing with a woman. On looking more closely, we notice the nails fastening the dress of his stylish partner to a dolly, while he literally dances circles around her. Would "the boys" be "jealous" of his "tango dancing at the reception"? Not likely, as a final glance makes clear—for "she" is in fact not a woman at all but a rag doll!

What is the historian to make of these gender-laden rituals and representations? Why would businessmen yearning for respectability and recognition by day engage in cross-dressing at night? Why would they publish a cartoon of a man dancing the tango with a rag doll? Why the apparent need to play like boys? Is there any relationship between these acts and images and the real estate men's professional project? The answer lies in the dual purpose served by the annual convention: it was a forum for defining the occupation, for working through conflicting interpretations about what it meant to be a professional broker, and for developing a consensus about the ethical, practical, and theoretical parameters of the field; but it was also a site for scripting, enacting, and reinforcing social identity.

The depictions of personages from the national association, the flow of events, the minor roles reserved for the "ladies" (of either sex), the endless speeches by delegates and adulation from local politicos, the frequent displays of manly emotion, and the serious discussions of policies and practices wove together into a delicate fabric of intimate masculine solidarity. The men-only social functions allowed the businessmen to form bonds of brotherhood with one another, to find solidarity in an otherwise competitive and increasingly impersonal commercial world. "Stag" functions helped to strengthen the private bonds of the world of the *homo faber*, the old middle-class realm defined by direct relationships among individual men, yet the impetus to organize such functions was symptomatic of the tenuousness of that world.

FIGURE 1. "Col. W. W. Price." *National Real Estate Journal* 10,
no. 3 (September 1914): 206.

The "boys" playing in the Rocky Mountain snow were both excited with the anticipation of the new world unfolding before them and fearful of losing the familiar one that was quickly receding.

The national convention helped brokers from distant regions of the continent to feel personally part of something much larger than their everyday business milieu, yet at the same time the convention by definition represented what seemed to be an inexorable trend away from the personal, local, and familiar and toward the remote, far-flung, and abstract. The bonds of manly camaraderie held together the middle-class republic of business, which the national association's leaders tried to push into the intangible, scientific, efficient domain of modern professionalism. This unsettled and unsettling liminal moment between old and new middle class, between the intimate and grounded social world of the local businessman and the abstract universe of the national commercial professional, inspired cross-dressing and boy-play, intimate homosocial experiences that drew its participants closer together as modernist impulses and the forces of modernity thrust them apart. The presence of women, however marginal (and even ersatz), reminded them of comfortable gender conventions in an otherwise uncertain world. Old and new gender and class roles vied for expression in the performative social space of the convention.

In sum, an anthropologist participant-observer at one of the national association's annual meetings in the 1910s would likely have concluded that the gender-laden ceremonies he witnessed were the condensed and incompletely disguised representations of certain aspects of real social life, serving a double and contradictory function. On the one hand they released and communicated "dangerous" thoughts and emotions about perceived changes in gender and class relations. On the other hand, they served to disguise and transform these anxious thoughts, containing the element of danger and making it an object of humor. Laughter, as Freud noted long ago, simultaneously conceals and reveals, serving both ameliorative and compensatory functions.[27]

Writing Profession

The national association's official organ, the *National Real Estate Journal*, founded in 1910, supplemented the annual convention as a regular forum for developing a technical vocabulary and rhetoric of middle-class masculinity, a middle-class prose and even poetry. Founded "on definite principles for the upbuilding of the real estate interests of the United States," the journal stood for "everything that will benefit the whole real estate fraternity, that will elevate the members of the profession and make real estate the best medium for the investment of capital for those who wish to control their own investments." Like most trade journals, the *NREJ* was decidedly sanguine if not hyperbolic about the occupation and its role in society. In their journal, the real estate men created a common culture, defined their field, and helped each other to learn about the real estate world beyond the scope of their local knowledge. As on the convention floor, prominent members of the national association became objects of folkloric interest, and local happenings became national news. In prose and poetry, photographs and cartoons, the journal constructed a special, exclusive world of and for real estate men. The symbolic world of the *NREJ* complemented the performative space of the convention, giving a semblance of black-and-white permanency to the real estate men's occupational world.

Changes in the structure and format of the journal roughly corresponded to transformations in the national association. In its earliest years, 1910–13, the *NREJ* was a loosely organized compendium of advice, local reports, and anecdotes. A typical issue included columns by both the executive secretary and the president on national issues, proceedings from national or state-level meetings, reports from local and state boards, a digest of legal decisions affecting real estate, and articles on topics ranging from the "psychology of sales" and city planning to running an efficient real estate office. Like the young organization itself, the journal spoke in a multitude of voices.

Aside from pieces by national officers or staff, few of the articles in the early years were written for the journal exclusively. The editors typically solicited a paper read at a regional or annual convention or republished a piece of interest from another journal. The journal aimed to incorporate the local into the national and to give the membership a sense of both the wide scope of their field and their commonalities, but in the early years the effect was less integrative than aggregative. The format of the journal became increasingly standardized as the association augmented its organizational capacities in the years surrounding the First World War, and the focus of the articles became more explicitly national.

The leaders of the national association used the journal both for exhortation and to conceptualize the field. In the first issue, they stated a syllogism that (they hoped) would shape the profession's self-image: "Any man who wants to know anything about law must go to a lawyer. Any man who wants to know anything about medicine must go to a physician. If he wants to know anything about real estate or land he must go to a real estate man." The editors of the *NREJ* and the leadership of the national association made a concerted effort to associate real estate with the established professions of law, medicine, and less frequently the ministry and engineering. They constantly employed figures of speech like "builders of cities" to rhetorically link brokerage with active construction.

Like the daily newspapers, the *NREJ* laced its post-convention coverage with photographs of personages eminent and lesser, as well as with numerous caricatures. The panoramic convention portrait was a staple, as was the banquet photo, and both conveyed the grandeur of the event and the earnestness of the men involved. The representations of real estate men from all over the country together at the convention, published largely for the benefit of those who could not attend, reinforced an image of a national class of men with important work to do and competent leaders to help them do it. Yet at the same time, these images conveyed and no doubt cultivated a sense of good-fellowship among both participants and spectators.

Among the few items of original content in the early numbers of the *NREJ* were feature articles on prominent brokers, rising stars, and members of the occupation engaged in civic work. These articles presented real estate men as important participants in civic life as well as successful businessmen. A story in 1911 featured Mayor George W. Dilling of Seattle, former president of the Seattle Real Estate Board. He was elected, the article noted, "without having made any promises," and thus was immune to "hindrance from political sources." Among Mayor Dilling's first acts was to dismiss a "corrupt" civil service commissioner and replace him with the current president of the Seattle Real Estate Board, R. C. Erskine. Dilling made the appointment, the reader is quickly reassured, "not as a recognition of the association in any way, but on account of Mr. Erskine's particular fitness for the position."[28] Real estate men were doers, but doers steeped in ethics, exemplars of conservative progressivism.

Finally, and perhaps most important, the *National Real Estate Journal* created for its readers—the men of the national association and its allies—a new genre: the real estate success story. The stories constructed models by which men could evaluate their own achievements—and implicitly, diagnose their failures. The first of these stories, in the issue of 15 October 1910, featured the youngest real estate broker in Kansas City, Albert Schoenberg, aged twenty-four. Schoenberg's success was explicitly framed as a corrective to the widely held belief that the real estate business was "a last resource [sic] of members of the 'down and out club,'" a field taken up primarily by older men who had failed at other ventures. Educated in the Kansas City public schools, Schoenberg began his business career in an insurance office at the age of fourteen and entered an "apprenticeship" in a real estate office five years later, in 1905. Just three years later, he started his own firm, specializing in leases and downtown business property.[29]

What was the key to Schoenberg's success? The young man was a firm believer in the most modern methods of advertising, particularly the relatively recent innovation of brand naming. He displayed large banners plastered with his firm's name on every property he represented, and soon his firm handled more than a million dollars in property a year. Schoenberg's strategy of creating name recognition had been so successful that in just its third year in business his firm was able to buy out and absorb an "old established real estate house." Endowed with the "necessary energy, pluck, and judgment," Schoenberg would have been a success at any endeavor, but it was his "determination to master every phase of the real estate brokerage business" that allowed him to accomplish in a few years "what many men have spent a lifetime doing."[30] The future in real estate was wide open for ambitious and bright young men like Albert Schoenberg. It was time for the public to acknowledge this fact and give real estate brokerage the respect it deserved. It was also time for real estate men themselves to recognize that the will to knowledge—the "determination to master every phase"—and the innovative application of new methods, such as Schoenberg's novel advertising techniques, were the hallmarks of professionalism and the keys to success.

Brokerage as a Career

William W. Hannan exemplified the profession in its transitional years. Practitioner, theorist, and promoter wrapped into one, he was a central character in the occupational narrative unfolding in the press and in the first few volumes of the *National Real Estate Journal*. Yet at the same time, the professional movement was developing in ways that would make him an anachronism. A tireless advocate, he traveled the country meeting with local boards and prominent brokers, trying to convince them of the benefits of joining the national organization. During his tenure as president in 1910–11, the membership of the organization grew nearly 50 percent, as the New York, Cincinnati, Toledo, Columbus, and Winnipeg real estate boards signed on. Hannan's passion for city planning led him to forge links with other civic organizations, most notably the American Civic Association, a wellspring of city-planning activity.

Hannan's great strength was face-to-face proselytizing of prospective brokers. Speaking before a class of would-be real estate men at the Detroit YMCA in 1912, he vividly depicted the qualities of the "high-class" real estate broker that his young association hoped to attract to the rapidly growing field. While the 1910 census counted more than 120,000 real estate brokers, less than 2 percent were members of the national association (though among those were the most successful brokers in the United States). A successful candidate for admission into this exclusive fraternity needed to possess above all else an extraordinary measure of "vision." Hannan virtually threatened the men assembled at the Y: "If all you can see in a plot of ground is so many square feet of dirt, for heaven's sake keep out of the real estate business and go and dig ditches." The successful real estate man, Hannan said, "never sees the ground at all." He "sees homes, schools, churches, skyscrapers, thoroughfares teeming with traffic, factories belching forth the smoke of a thousand furnaces, docks and harbors crowded to congestion with the argosies of nations."[31]

Hannan's was a thoroughly modern, planned, urban, and industrial imagination, though his idea of a true profession was rooted largely in an older, artisanal tradition. Real estate brokerage not only promised to test a man's heroism: it also compelled him to discover the artist within himself. Hannan's eloquence contributed new metaphors to the eclectic mélange then taking shape. "As the sculptor sees the imprisoned Venus in a block of marble, the artist a Madonna looking out from the bare canvas," he waxed poetically, so the real estate man, if he was "to earn his salt," must "see a vision of a city ten, twenty years hence and act accordingly." His charge was to intelligently plan cities with more in mind than simple pecuniary reward—though this would come, and was the real estate man's due for his "service."[32]

Real estate brokerage therefore would improve a man's character, at the same time as the broker would improve the character of his city and of the nation as a whole. But there are some things that cannot be taught or acquired, Hannan warned. Supreme among these—the "cementing force" bringing together the enumerated qualities into a unified whole, the "real estate man"—was "tact." And, unfortunately, tact was "unteachable—something hopelessly noncontagious." This mysterious quality was "a gift from heaven"—and like grace, the only way to attain it was to shut one's eyes and "devoutly pray for it." Without tact, a man would be ordinary, but the man so graced would "win out" and to him alone would "flow easily the rewards and perquisites" of the occupation.[33] It was the extraordinary man that Hannan sought for affiliation with the national association, and ultimately for membership in the future profession as he envisioned it. But there was clearly a contradiction in Hannan's position: if "tact" made the man, and if it was indeed "unteachable," why bother with real estate education at all? Or was there to be a permanent hierarchy in the field—the professional visionaries of the national association overseeing the run-of-the-mill broker? Would not that defeat the entire purpose of professionalization to begin with? As we shall see, these questions of character and competency would provoke much debate among the real estate men in the second decade of the century. For Hannan, the successful real estate man possessed irreducible, innate qualities; for his successors in the professional movement, systematic training and education trumped such notions.

Perhaps Hannan's most important contribution to the emerging discourse of real estate professionalism was his vivid portrait of real estate brokerage as a "career," something to which a man (it went without saying) ought to consider devoting his life. The challenges of brokerage were real, he declared, and the talents needed to meet them considerable. The real estate man would often be called upon to "sacrifice[] more in a moment for the general spirit of the community than he ever hope[d] to gain." But his rewards would be rich and enduring, in ways far more important than mere financial gain. The "high-class" real estate man would be "the real hero," he thundered, "in every epoch-making climax in the dangerous evolution of public progress."[34]

Hannan charged the real estate man with responsibility for such central tasks in American life as providing adequate housing for the population, building new communities, and creating vital commercial and industrial centers. As a calling, real estate brokerage promised a man the opportunity to use all of his finest and noblest qualities, like risk taking, tact, and vision, to face the "dangerous evolution of public progress" head on and make perhaps the ultimate contribution to the national good: "building cities" and helping families to acquire homes of their own, the foundation of civilization. In the process, he could "win out" and obtain the "rewards and perquisites" which were his due—as a risk-taking entrepreneur operating in the market *and* as a civic-minded "professional," one whose primary function was to put his expertise at the service of mankind.

For Hannan and his contemporaries, "entrepreneur" and "professional" were not necessarily contradictory positions. In fact, "professional" was an amorphous notion before 1915, neither fully divested of its roots in divinity nor fully invested with the notions of expertise. In Hannan's mind, the real estate man was a visionary and heroic artisan, fashioning whole communities out of his raw material, land. He was at the same time a progressive planner, scientifically prognosticating future urban growth to best serve the housing needs of humanity. As an entrepreneur, he was unapologetic about the pecuniary rewards that might flow his way. The promises of real estate brokerage for an ambitious young man were not illusory or abstract. It was a wide-open field, and it experienced tremendous growth in the first quarter of the twentieth century. While law and medicine were becoming "overcrowded," the opportunities were constantly broadening in real estate because of the increasing number of people seeking homes in the cities and suburbs every year. Perpetually in motion, American society needed regulation, required the "attention and guidance" of the real estate man, "a man of unquestioned integrity and upright dealing." The successful candidates for real estate brokerage included "any serious-minded, healthy young man with good walking power, imagination and determination to succeed, willing to work hard and wait for results." Though he should be forewarned that the "fruits of labor" were "often long delayed," the payoff for perseverance was that "the work [was] always absorbing and of infinite variety . . . never monotonous."[35]

For all of Hannan's charismatic preaching, however, claims to expertise rang hollow, as real estate brokerage lacked not only a set of standards by which to define itself but also the systematic knowledge that characterized a true profession. The real estate men of Hannan's generation had created a "jurisdiction," a realm of activity over which they could potentially rule. But the parameters and the contents of the jurisdiction were completely undefined. Competition for jurisdictional control, the hallmark of a professionalizing project, would derive almost entirely from within, from the real estate men's own uncertainties about the nature and scope of their field.[36]

CHAPTER THREE

Character, Competency, and
Real (Estate) Professionalism,

1915–1921

> [H]ere and now I wish to impress upon every man in this convention and all those
> who deal in real estate along ethical lines that ours is a profession, for if years of
> training, study, knowledge of values and principles and up-building of character
> does not warrant to us the title of profession, then medicine, law and other kindred
> professions are trading on but what is a title and OURS by right.
>
> —Alexander S. Taylor, June 1915[1]

From about 1915 to 1920 leading men within the nascent real estate profession attempted to articulate and codify its principles of practice. A professional identity was beginning to coalesce, but there were several fundamental issues at stake. What did it mean to speak of "business ethics"? Even if consensus on ethics could be achieved, the problem of enforcement remained, both within the national association and among the larger population of real estate brokers. Was self-regulation through an ethical code, or even state-enforced licensing, enough to create a positive and professional image of the real estate broker in the public mind? And finally, there was the problem of education for professional brokers, which raised a further question: What were professional real estate men supposed to *do*, and how were they to go about doing it? The answers to these questions were not simple, and spoke to many larger issues in contemporary American culture.

Real estate men tried to graft the new onto the old. In the second phase of their professionalization efforts they attempted to preserve their conception of themselves as craftsmen and entrepreneurs, as fabricators of the world and dealmakers, and also to fashion themselves as thoroughly modern, efficient,

and scientific businessmen—what we might call "commercial professionals."
During the period from roughly 1915 to 1920, the fraternal, inward-looking
clubbishness that marked the first years of the National Association of Real
Estate Exchanges, and its successor the National Association of Real Estate
Boards, began to give way to an emphasis on "service," an impulse toward
systematization and standardization, and the rise of technical competency as
a crucial element in the real estate men's vocational consciousness. New
leaders pushed the organization to codify its standards, attempted to accomplish some form of occupational closure, and tried to devise a plan for educating the next generation. Toward the end of the First World War the real estate
men invented a professional sobriquet, "Realtor." It was a brand name available only to members of the national association, and the newly minted
Realtors attempted to invest the name with social significance. Remarkably,
within four years of its fabrication, the name became generic. The term
proliferated across the nation, and local "Realtor Committees" sprang into
action to police its usage. In a series of landmark lawsuits, the national
association retained legal ownership of the term. Despite concerted effort,
"Realtor" was not destined to attain the social cachet or authority attached to
"physician" or "attorney." Nevertheless, there were significant benefits to
membership in Realtordom, including access to the growing multiple-listing
system, perhaps the Realtors' greatest business innovation.

The four developments analyzed in this chapter—the drafting of an ethical
code, a heated conflict over licensing laws, the invention and adoption of the
term "Realtor," and the first steps toward planning an educational program—
are part and parcel of the real estate men's efforts to deal with the problems
facing every profession. However, the tensions that surfaced in the process of
working toward solutions for real estate embodied larger cultural tensions
about what it meant to be professional and middle class in the twentieth century.
In the end, the inventive and tentative answers that the real estate men stumbled
upon helped to reshape the social meaning of middle-class membership.

The Meaning of Profession

From the organization's birth, leading members of the National Association
of Real Estate Exchanges desired to move the field beyond simple self-interested organization and toward what they understood as "professionalism."
By 1910 a large portion of the rank-and-file membership was more or less

behind this project. The leaders of the movement attempted to construct an image of a professional broker, different from and better than the disparaged mass of "curbstone brokers," "harpies," and "land sharks" who formed a rogues' gallery in the public mind. What did it mean to be a "professional" real estate man? What did a successful claim to professional status entail? What models could provide guidance for real estate men? Could the leaders of the national association construct an image of a professional broker that was inclusive enough to encompass the organization's membership, and at the same time exclusive enough to lend credibility in the eyes of the public to their claims to professionalism? More generally, could a businessman be a professional, and why would he care to be one? Was not the appellation "businessman" an honorable one? Of what was the drive toward professionalism in business symptomatic?

Many critics and reformers in the late nineteenth century and the early twentieth began to call into question the traditional linkages in American culture between work and ethical improvement. According to many commentators, industrialization had undermined the moral reward of work, had emptied it of ethical content, leaving the pursuit of profit as its sole justification. Work was reduced to mere labor, a means to an end rather than an expression of human creativity. Many men and women worried that newer occupations, specialized, routinized, and regimented, were not conducive to character formation. Some sought to reinvent social ethics, to stress efficiency and the material rewards and social benefits of work done at maximum efficiency. Others sought to construct compensatory arenas for achieving character development, such as the world of sport and other sorts of manly violence.[2] Still others sought to reinfuse their work with meaning by raising their occupations to what they invariably characterized as a "higher plane" through professionalization.

During the second decade of the century a consensus began to emerge in the social science literature on the nature of the professions. As Abraham Flexner put it in an influential and widely read tract in 1915, professions were primarily intellectual in character and assumed a wide range of individual responsibility on the part of practitioners. They possessed a scientific and learned basis that provided the "raw material" for their operation, which was employed to a practical end; professionals were not merely theoreticians. They transmitted their techniques and knowledge through education. Finally, professionals tended toward self-organization and public service, if not altruism. Members of the true professions expected compensation commensurate with their vital social role, but public service was the *ultima ratio* and the opportunity to promote social welfare its own reward. Professional work promised both financial and moral remuneration, but it almost went without saying that the latter was the primary goal. Yet Flexner himself demurred from establishing fixed, static criteria for designating professions: "What matters most is professional spirit. All activities may be prosecuted in the genuine professional spirit."[3]

The men who led the movement to professionalize real estate brokerage were not of one mind on the criteria for designating their occupation a profession. There was little consensus on the meaning of terms like "public service," "ethics," and even "education." While leading members of the national association readily imagined their work as developers and purveyors of homes and as builders of cities to be of vital importance to the public good, and while they had indeed made great strides in terms of self-organization locally and nationally, the field lacked definitive professional standards. Many among even the finest "high-class" real estate men were consummate entrepreneurs, believing that their year-end balance sheets were the only true measure of occupational self-worth.

Nevertheless, most of the prime movers in the national association believed that to be a profession, real estate brokerage needed a moral foundation, a system of values that would shape brokers' behavior and explain to the broker why he should not follow the path of least resistance and maximum returns. "Our own self-respect and highest success in our calling demands" a code of ethics, said the ethics committee chairman, E. Orris Hart. A code would be a "guide to him who wants to do the right thing and a warning to the other whose selfish instincts incline him to trespass on the rights of others." A code would be a "measuring stick" for judging conduct and adjudicating intraprofessional conflict. A body of ethical precepts would also justify to the public why it should trust the high-class real estate man as an expert and fiduciary. In any event, Hart noted, the national association was "simply following the precedents found desirable by other professions."[4] So it was not only the right thing to do; others were doing it too—even some, like the accountants, in the world of business.[5]

In the period between 1900 and 1920, dozens of occupational groups in the United States rushed to form trade associations, to organize for cooperative competition. All sought order in the frenetic proliferation of new organizations. Most of these formulated codes of ethics, systematic statements of principles linking the organization's and the occupation's purpose with some notion of a broader public good. For business groups, codifying ethics entailed defining what it meant to be scrupulous in business: that is, how morality and the market might be harmonized. It also entailed construing particular business aims as fulfillments of general public needs: that is, conflating self-interest and the public good.

The movement to reform business implicitly questioned some fundamental tenets of traditional middle-class manhood. The nineteenth century had left as one of its legacies a particular notion of the successful businessman as a fierce competitor in the jungle of the commercial world. Organization, particularly "ethics," meant discovering ways in which it could become manly *not* to compete, or at least to compete within a cooperative framework. The laws of the jungle would have to yield to the laws of business ethics. Yet totally suppressing animalistic competitiveness risked emasculating the businessman.

The real estate men were not alone in their quest to sort out profession from mere commerce—this issue spoke to the heart of progressivism. On the one hand businessmen, including real estate dealers and credit men, attempted to infuse their vocations with "ethics," while on the other, better-established professions such as law and medicine grappled with the impact of commercial values on their professional identities. The first two decades of the century witnessed an outpouring of literature on ethics, professionalism, and business. Books with titles like *Every-Day Ethics, Business: A Profession, The Ethics of Business, The New Competition*, and *The Law: Business or Profession?* reflected on the "ethical trend in business" as well as the commercial trend in the professions. Scholars, commentators, businessmen, and association executives sought "laws of ethics," part of a movement toward the "adjustment of our race to the particular kind of world in which we live." Most of the newly emerging trade and professional associations produced codes of ethics. In 1922 the American Academy of Political and Social Science devoted an entire volume to "the ethics of the professions and of business," and an author wrote of the "commercial professions," implying a near-equivalence of status.[6] In the words of the author of an early work on trade associations and their ethical impact, codes of ethics proliferated among businessmen because "the ideals of men best project themselves into reality when crystallized in written documents."[7] It was mostly a matter of squaring the proper ideals with actual practice.

When the national association's annual convention in 1911 formed the Committee on Ethics and charged it with devising a code to establish standards for membership in the organization and to articulate principles according to which members should deal with each other and with the public, its members went back to basics. "Ethics are as old as the world," said the committee chairman Frank S. Craven of Philadelphia, advocating the "Golden Rule" as a starting point. " 'Do unto others as ye would that others do unto you,' and not as we hear frequently quoted, 'Do the other fellow before he can do you.' "[8] Implied in Craven's rendition of the Golden Rule was a negative moment to the ethical movement, namely the suppression of the broker who would "do the other fellow first." Figuring out how to expel or at least marginalize the unethical broker occupied many leading Realtors.

Yet many real estate men did not understand why American businessmen needed a code of ethics at all. As articles in the *National Real Estate Journal* pointed out, George Washington and William Penn had been real estate men, and they had had no formal code of ethics to guide their behavior. But Washington and Penn notwithstanding, why shouldn't the real estate man look only after his own narrow self-interest? Why shouldn't he "do the other fellow first"? In the competitive, rough-and-tumble world of commerce, should not the businessman simply aim to maximize his profits, keeping the traditional onus on the buyer—*caveat emptor*? Was this not the manly approach? In any case, would not the magic of the market naturally weed out the dishonest man?

In short, what was wrong with business, as traditionally conceived and practiced? What might it mean to be a "professional" businessman? Louis D. Brandeis first defined this apparent oxymoron, the "professional businessman." Speaking at the commencement at Brown University in 1912, Brandeis challenged businessmen to rise to the spirit of the times and fully professionalize their endeavors. Putting business on a "scientific" basis and subjecting it to voluntary cooperation and regulation, he argued, would ensure stable prosperity for the greatest number of Americans. Brandeis associated professionalism with science, organization, cooperation, and self-regulation. The professionalization of business would help fulfill a core progressive aim, part of what the social critic and founder of the *New Republic* Herbert Croly had termed the "promise of American life," namely the development of a well-ordered, patriotic society guided by expertise.[9] Some businessmen had already fallen in line, and Brandeis implored the rest to join the ranks of the high-minded.

Brandeis's arguments resonated strongly for leading members of the National Association of Real Estate Boards. Business professionalism suited their purposes well. It was an attempt to square two tendencies in turn-of-the-century American culture and society, tensions embodied in the Progressive movement. There was an admiration for the "efficiency" and "progress" exemplified by large corporations, and at the same time an implicit fear of emasculation at the root of the movement toward trust busting, and the parallel defense of small business as a "school of manhood."[10] Business professionalism promised to preserve the sort of manliness associated with proprietorship and entrepreneurship, while also allowing for a variant of manhood consistent with the rise of the corporation and the proliferation of white-collar work, particularly managerial work. Two metaphors governed much of the discourse of the professionalizing real estate men in the period from 1912 to 1920—the self-reliant pioneer and the engineer—and rarely, if ever, did the underlying tension seem to attract their notice.

Hewing closely to the script of profession builders before them, especially lawyers, doctors, and engineers, the national association's ethicists drew on prevailing negative cultural imagery of brokers like Stephen Halliday and Herod Bilfinger to construct a generic villain. Most often called the "curbstone broker" or simply "curbstoner," he was the foil to the ethical, professional broker that the typical real estate man imagined himself to be, a "low-class" real estate dealer "with his office in his hat," conducting his business in the street. He had no office and no permanent place of business, and therefore his dealings were untraceable and he was unaccountable for his actions. The curbstoner was analogous to the "quack" in medicine, the "shyster" in law, and the "licentious libertine" in the ministry, according to one influential proponent of ethics. Unethical by definition, the curbstoner lurked in train depots waiting for unwitting victims newly arrived to the city. He—invariably the curbstoner was represented as male—employed nefarious tactics to undercut honest brokers. An unethical broker, for example, might split his commissions with "society ladies" whom he employed as clandestine informants to gain leads on potential clients and customers.[11]

The portrait of the depraved curbstoner reflected turn-of-the-century America's pervasive fear of vagrancy. In numerous speeches, real estate men qualified the term "curbstoner" with the phrase "tramp of the profession." The vagabond and the nomad were the masculine counterpart to the feminized neurasthenic and hysteric, symbols of maladjustment at the turn of the century. Articles with titles like "Causes of Vagrancy and Methods of Eradication" proliferated in middle-class journals, the ostensibly pervasive malaise of rootlessness reflecting the anxiety of the middle class about its own tenuous social status and its relationship to former nodes of stability like meaningful work. The middle class, disrupted by the uncertainties of industrialism, sought ballast.[12] In this context, Edward Judd's assertion that working with land would promote stability of character takes on a new meaning, as does the statement of Edward Woolley's hero in "Inner Secrets of a Real Estate Broker's Rise" about finding in real estate brokerage "something definite." Professional real estate brokerage posited itself as an opportune antidote to the problem of drift, famously identified in 1914 by Walter Lippmann.[13] The curbstoner was a compelling villain largely because he was an unaccountable "business vagrant."

Possession of an office of one's own was an index of professionalism, and by implication of stable, middle-class manhood. An ethical, professional man was responsible for his actions, and he proudly announced his firm's address on business cards and stationery. While an office of one's own did not automatically transform a real estate man into a professional, lack of an office was clearly tantamount to non-professionalism. The office stood for a wide range of sentiments about professional identity, and the real estate men expended much effort describing, planning, and flaunting their offices. Elaborate filing systems, telephones, the multiple-listing service, standard lease forms, trained stenographers and typewriters, accounting equipment, well-appointed conference rooms, plat maps, and blueprints all figured in the imagery of the efficient and modern office. Early conventions of the national association discussed the ideal real estate office in detail. In 1911 in Denver, President Alexander Taylor boasted that the model office in the center of the convention hall cost over $15,000 to equip.[14]

The "well-organized real estate office" embodied at least two aspects of middle-class masculinity at once. The office was an ethical statement itself, a visible manifestation of a broker's credibility in both financial and moral terms. ("Trust me, I can afford to hire a staff and buy good furniture.") The Model Real Estate Office displayed on the stage of the Denver Auditorium was equipped with roll-top desks made of "golden quarter-sawed oak of the very latest design" and costing $3,000. The office was also a symbol of the emerging technocratic conception of masculinity. Equipped with the latest in office technology, it advertised a broker's faith in modern, scientific business practices. The Model Office contained "flexo-type machines," "electrically operated sealing, stamping, and addressing machines," and of course a "complete telephone system in operation during all sessions of the convention with absolutely no dummy phones." Completing the Model Office were a dictaphone and dictograph systems, "expensive electrical fixtures," and a stereopticon machine and films.[15]

The office also made a statement about the state of the broker's mental apparatus. The "modern office standard," one commentator in the *National Real Estate Journal* asserted, is "a place for everything and everything in its place." Utilizing social hygiene rhetoric prevalent at the time, he suggested that using modern, scientific business practices was a form of "cleaning," keeping not only the work environment but also the mind orderly. The "operation must reach the mental processes of both broker and owner."[16] His office equipment and appearance were an outward manifestation of the broker's inner state.

The real estate men claimed a moral relationship to their clients rooted in inequality of knowledge. Theirs was a profession, their "mental labor" requiring "special preparation" and a "liberal education or its equivalent," and not a mere "livelihood," a means of subsistence.[17] Frank Craven had explained to the convention in 1912 that "the real estate broker is probably depended upon by his client more than any other profession or trade," since the "average individual buys possibly one or two properties in a lifetime." The buyer comes to his broker "for information and advice, believing that he will receive honorable treatment, and the broker who would take advantage of him or her deserves everlasting censure."[18] Professionalism in general hinged upon a representation of the "client" as relatively deficient in knowledge and experience and thus dependent upon the professional's expertise and honor. The broker needed to play his part in restraining himself, exercising self-control in order not to "take advantage" of those less powerful than himself. The increased specialization attendant upon the increasing complexity of modern society meant that those who possessed expertise in particular fields had a moral obligation to transcend pure pecuniary gain, to not "take advantage" of the vulnerable layperson, figured in the minds of the real estate men as a semi-helpless damsel, naïve widow, ailing patriarch, or semiliterate working-class man—like the memorable Fred Gross, the bumbling protagonist of Ring Lardner's serial "Own Your Home" in 1919 in *Redbook*.[19] In a crucial area of American life, namely the disposition of property, the member of an established local board had a tremendous information advantage over both non-members and non-brokers, and thus had a moral obligation to honorably provide his services.

The real estate men also grounded their ethics in a claim at once technical and moral: that national progress and prosperity depended on real estate brokerage in a fundamental way. Real estate men were "the connecting link," and only "through the medium of the broker" did the country and cities grow and prosper.[20] Brokers rationally allocated land, America's traditional chief asset. Some real estate men worked hand in hand with other professionals, notably planners and architects, to design useful and beautiful cities, eradicate tenements, and provide Americans with decent and affordable housing. Several high-profile members of the national association, such as William W. Hannan, Samuel S. Thorpe, and Jesse Clyde Nichols of Kansas City belonged to the American Civic Association. "High-class" developers often allied themselves with urban and regional planners and against small property owners whose imperatives were dictated by short-term profitability.

The notion of "development" itself linked the real estate men to the broader discourses of professionalism and progressivism. The professional real estate broker, like other like-minded progressives and professionals, had a duty "to think not altogether what the profit shall be to [himself] but what the profit may, at some day in the future, be to [his] brothers of the entire community."[21] The most lauded brokers in the national trade press were those who advocated planning and zoning and designed subdivisions with an eye toward permanency rather than quick profit. J. C. Nichols, the "community builder" of Kansas City, was perhaps the exemplar of the high-class developer, a pioneer in using deed restrictions to stabilize the character of communities and, consequently, property values. Most leaders of the national association, at least in the first two decades, were believers in some form of controlled development.[22]

In sum, the real estate men aimed by professionalizing to find a solution to the dilemmas that rapid, corporate industrialization created for their middle-class manhood. They fashioned their emerging professional identity, semiconsciously, around three distinct, interrelated, and mutually antagonistic conceptions of the relationship between work and self—the venerable "aristocratic" notion of the calling, the "democratic" entrepreneurial values of the mid-nineteenth century, and an emerging technocratic conception of work. They contended that real estate brokerage was not a mere business enterprise but had an ineluctable moral component. Real estate "deals with the most fundamental asset of the race," William W. Hannan had thundered, and rather than focus on mere profits, real estate men should be asking themselves "what have [we] contributed to the sum of human achievement?"[23]

Self-Regulation and Ethics

With the officeless curbstoner fixed in their minds as the personification of everything they were not, the professionalizing real estate men set about constructing a suitably stringent and enforceable code of ethics aimed at eliminating the "tramp of the profession." The curbstoner was a useful foil against which an ethical professional identity could take shape. The Code of Ethics was in a sense a containment strategy, an attempt to draw an unbreachable line between the curbstoner and the high-class broker. If the national association were able to effectively regulate its members' behavior and expel the unethical curbstoner, the public would perceive brokers like other ostensibly self-policing, autonomous professionals such as lawyers and physicians.

Any code of professional conduct contains not only an explicit statement of purpose but also an implicit argument about the nature of the vocation itself. Real estate brokerage continued to suffer in the years surrounding the First World War from the depression of the 1890s, which had deeply impressed the image of the broker-as-reckless-speculator on the public mind. The leaders of the national association intended to make it clear that brokers were no longer gamblers but fiduciary agents for their clients, operating on a fee-for-service basis underpinned by trust. The Code of Ethics was intended both for intraprofessional relations and for public relations—that is, it should be interpreted both as a prescriptive statement and as a wish fulfillment.

The Code of Ethics turned out to be more controversial than any of its initial proponents imagined, and it wended its way through the ratification process for two years. Presented and approved in skeletal form by the delegates to the Winnipeg convention in 1913, it was adopted in its complete version in Los Angeles in 1915. Many members initially expressed wariness that a national code might undermine local authority, fearing that the "national" was seeking control over membership policies, among other things.

The leadership effectively convinced members that enforcement of the code would be purely a local affair and that the national association did not intend to usurp local prerogatives. The Code of Ethics ratified in 1915 contained five sections, consisting of thirty-seven paragraphs altogether.

First and foremost, the Code of Ethics was voluntaristic. The national association provided local boards with copies of the code, and boards had new members pledge to uphold it in their daily practice. Member boards were charged with enforcing it through the establishment of local arbitration and ethics committees. The regulatory mechanism was designed to keep internal disputes among brokers out of the courts, to keep disputes intraprofessional rather than get the meddling lawyers involved. Professionalism depended on self-control, in all senses of the term.

All codes of ethics are morality plays, and a close reading of the national association's code reveals a number of moral dilemmas. The code admonished brokers not to criticize each other, noting that "a broker worthy of respect and confidence will never make unfair criticisms or untruthful statements regarding a fellow broker," but "will cultivate a friendly relationship and respect for all worthy competitors." Only members of the national association were "worthy" competitors, of course. The admonition implicitly recognized both the existence of "unworthy" competition—the curbstoner— but also incentives to deviate from the rule, to make "unfair criticisms" or "untruthful statements." The code exhorted real estate men to remain dispassionate and keep their anxieties in check rather than "knock" another broker's deal. Should a prospective buyer express interest in a property offered by a competitor, the broker should treat the proposition as well as the absent broker "with fairness, however anxious" he may be to sell the property that he represents. Disinterestedness and collegiality were juxtaposed with a recognition that real estate brokerage was a for-profit, competitive enterprise—a tension at the core of business professionalism.

Most important in the "public duties" section of the code, emphasized in capital letters as a "FACTOR of GREAT IMPORTANCE in . . . maintaining the vocation of the real estate agent upon a HIGH PROFESSIONAL PLANE," was the instruction to use "exclusive agency contracts," under which the vendor of a property signed a legally binding contract with an agent, giving him or her the sole right to sell the property for a stipulated time (usually 60–90 days). The code noted the "obvious mutual advantages" of an exclusive contract: the client, the owner of the property, will "secure services of an expert or specialist," while "the feeling of sole responsibility for getting results"—a hallmark of professionalism—"will stimulate the ingenuity and activity of the agent." Exclusive agency alone guaranteed the client the full "service" he or she deserved. The national association widely promoted the idea of exclusive agency, which was said to avoid misunderstandings, inhibit ruinous price competition, and minimize the possibility that an owner might be obligated for commissions to more than one broker. More generally, the profession-alizers justified exclusive agency and most of the other innovations to real estate practice introduced during this phase of institutionalization in terms of "service."[24]

Here again the tensions inherent in business professionalism were manifest. Exclusive agency, elevated to an ethical principle, essentially called for clients to contract away their right to freely dispose of property under free market conditions. Although exclusive agency may have been necessary to give a broker the "feeling of sole responsibility" and induce him to act like a professional, market imperatives pulled clients away from exclusive agency and toward free competition. The rule ran counter to the prevailing ideology of business, which took for granted that competition, not exclusivity, stimulated maximum performance in the client's behalf. It was up to the brokers, through the medium of the local board, to convince the public that the benefits of signing an exclusive agency agreement—having a broker represent a client's interests as if they were his own—outweighed the potential gains of having a number of agents working simultaneously to sell a property. In order to steer between the Scylla of ruinous competition and the Charybdis of price fixing, local real estate boards devised the mechanism of exclusive agency plus multiple listing. This circumscribed market competition without eliminating it; the code of ethics nationalized this compromise. The tension between regulation and the "free market" would manifest itself in other conflicts, for example in that between advocates of zoning and urban planning and their opponents. It was an antagonism at the heart of middle-class masculinity, which touted entrepreneurialism at the same time as it prescribed cooperation and technocratic efficiency.

The code of ethics enumerated a formidable list of proscribed behavior. An ethical broker did not "knock" another broker, use fictitious names on deeds, give advice outside his area of expertise, mislead clients, collect commissions from both buyer and seller, ruin a fellow broker's deal, sue a fellow broker, ignore fraudulent activities, rent flats for illegal purposes, or secure "undesirable" tenants. Many of these rules of conduct violated pure market rationality, and their codification insinuated that brokers were in fact prone to transgressing them. The rule about securing "undesirable" tenants was much discussed at the annual convention in 1911. Several boards, Chicago and Toledo among them, told the assembled delegates how to establish a system for blacklisting "bad" tenants. Upon evicting a tenant from a property under his management, a member of the Chicago Real Estate Board was obliged to report the nature of the eviction to the board's secretary, who kept a cross-indexed file of undesirables. When a member wanted to run a background check on a prospective tenant, the board provided a useful service for twenty-five cents per inquiry.[25] The definition of "undesirable" would become rather capacious in the 1920s, encompassing racial and national minorities as well as other classes of "nuisances" that adversely affected property values.

The code also scripted a role for the brokers' clients. The real estate men understood that their professionalism depended to a large degree upon their clientele's compliance with the rules of the game. Clients were entreated not to "promiscuously list" a property (to engage more than one broker to sell it), to recognize the broker's fiduciary obligation to maintain the confidentiality of prospective buyers, and to "secure competent advice and services" by putting "their proposition in one reliable broker's hands," because the complexity of real estate practice required expert knowledge, "the only master" of which was "the agent whose years of study and practical experience have given him the right to high professional standing." In short, one could hardly expect a broker to act like a professional if the client did not play his part, and there were significant temptations on both sides to breach the rules.

The code aimed to institutionalize norms designed to obscure core tensions in business professionalism, at once attempting to restrict the imperatives of a strictly entrepreneurial capitalism while instilling the public service–oriented, cooperative values of the ascendant organized capitalist political economy. In its invocation to the public, the code was attempting to call forth a clientele for professional brokers, and to establish in that clientele's mind the characteristics of such brokers.

A code that purports to regulate "intraprofessional" relations is relevant only in a historical moment and in a social context in which it can no longer be assumed that "professionals" operate according to aristocratic, "gentlemanly" rules.[26] By defining a particular type of real estate man as the norm, with a particular relationship to his colleagues, his work, his clients, and the public at large, the code may be seen as an attempt to inculcate gentlemanly, aristocratic modes of behavior in men presumed to be other than gentlemen. This project of attempting to impose behavioral norms on entrepreneurial activity, to limit competition, with the tacit understanding that such rules are somehow unnatural, is central to business professionalism. At the same time as it instructs the brokers in proper behavior, the code constructs an imaginary, ethical, well-informed public that demands professional real estate brokerage. Professionalism was, in the brokers' minds, a relational identity.

In its ambivalence about class and status and its overarching concern with integrity, the code anticipated a cultural theme that would emerge fully in the late 1920s and early 1930s in the form of a "crisis of character."[27] The code embraced at once a hope of instilling "aristocratic" norms of deference, recognition of the inherent competitiveness of the field, and a wish that if everyone played his part according to the script, real estate brokerage would become an accepted profession. The problem, of course, inhered in persuading or compelling each actor to perform his role properly.

Licensing (and) Manhood

While there was relative consensus regarding the need for a code of ethics, the debate over whether the organized real estate men should support laws to license real estate brokers sharply divided the National Association of Real Estate Boards. Some opposed licensing in any form, finding the notion antithetical to old middle-class notions of occupational autonomy and voluntarism. Advocates of licensing split into two camps: those who favored licensing criteria that emphasized character—essentially standardizing and generalizing prevailing board membership policies—and those who argued for licensing based on an objective test of competency. It was not until the 1950s that the "competency" argument won the day; the first wave of licensing laws passed in the 1920s established character as the primary basis for obtaining a license.

Those committed to changing brokers' behavior as well as the public perception of brokerage raised questions about enforcement. The discussions of ethics in the National Real Estate Journal almost inevitably spawned proposals promoting real estate brokerage licensing laws. As early as the 1890s, municipalities had experimented with occupational licensing for brokers, but such licenses had more in common with permits for peddlers and hucksters than with certificates of vocational competency or even trustworthiness. Most of the leading men in the national association supported state licensing laws, arguing that they would provide an effective means of weeding out disreputable brokers and establishing a distinction between high-class brokers and curbstoners. In the long run, the national association's task was clear: raise the standards of real estate men's behavior and change public perceptions of the real estate man through educational work. Proponents argued that licensing laws were in the occupation's immediate interest. The proposition quickly incited fierce opposition, as many brokers were appalled by the idea that prosperous, prominent, and upstanding businessmen such as themselves should be required to genuflect before the state for recognition of their legitimacy or qualifications. This was more than just a simple dispute about occupational gatekeeping. The licensing issue became a point of conflict over what it meant to be a *man* in business.

The discussion of ethics forced the young association to look closely at itself as the leading element in a profession in the making. By 1915 the real estate men had achieved relative consensus on professional standards of conduct. Two formidable problems remained. How could the national association ensure practical adherence to the vision of the "ethical broker"? An elaborate but poorly enforced code of ethics might breed contempt or ridicule rather than respect. Yet even if the national association could ensure that its own members were ethical, what about nonmembers? Winning the public's confidence in the profession required creating a readily discernible distinction between the ethical professional broker and the contemptible curbstoner. Until the national association could exercise disciplinary control over every broker, each public revelation of corrupt brokerage practices would bring ignominy on all brokers, members of the national association included.

Proponents of licensing saw it as a means to impose the national association's ethical code on the entire field of practice through government regulation. However, the idea that American businessmen somehow required the heavy hand of the state to guarantee their honesty caused a disagreement that nearly split the organization. John T. Kenney, chairman of the legislative committee of the Wisconsin Real Estate Brokers' Association, published an article in the *National Real Estate Journal* in 1912 advocating a nationwide campaign for brokerage licensing laws, sparking a contentious debate. On and off for more than five years, heated exchanges took place on the floor of the convention and in the *NREJ*. Kenney argued forcefully for "legal recognition" of brokerage, based explicitly on a generic definition of profession as "science practiced." He contended that only state licensing could assure the public of the integrity of real estate brokers by putting brokers on a par with other regulated occupations, like law, medicine, and engineering. Both of Kenney's positions provoked hostile reactions.

In making the strong pro-licensing case, Kenney appealed primarily to technocratic masculinity, asserting that a professional man distinguished himself from the nonprofessional by his understanding of "the underlying principles pertaining to his work, and the effort or lack of effort" he made to "apply those principles in that work." The professional man "makes an original study of the situation and the conditions surrounding him," and plans his enterprise accordingly. The nonprofessional man, by contrast, is "merely an imitator, artificer or artisan who copies the methods and plans of someone else in some other situation, wholly regardless of their applicability to his own case." The artificer has no right to be considered a professional even though his "may be a fine art or a legally recognized profession," yet the other man is a professional "just the same even though no one, not even he himself, is aware of the fact."[28] The application of esoteric knowledge in an original and creative way marked the professional man. Kenney's words echoed closely those of other technocratic professionalizers, such as Victor C. Alderson, president of the Colorado School of Mines, who had implored a graduating class of mining engineers in 1909 to stake out a position as "artist-engineers" rather than "artisans." The artist-engineer, he asserted, uses "the sum total of his past experience and all the constructive imagination with which he is endowed to solve the complex questions which come before him," while the artisan "works with his hands and lets his mind rest."[29]

Technocratic masculinity figured imaginative, mental labor as "constructive," real (man's) work, aimed at solving the complex problems of the day, while manual labor was by definition monotonous and unoriginal. Technocratic masculinity spoke tacitly to anxieties about the impact of industrialization on the nature of work, privileging the mental in a world in which much human labor amounted to little more than tending machines. The engineer was a creative mental laborer, and he also designed the machines and systems that made industrialization possible. While the mining engineers had a more or less uncontested claim to mastery of scientific knowledge and technical skill as a basis for their professional identity, it would be well into the 1920s before real estate brokerage developed anything like a scientific or technical foundation.

The advocates of the strong pro-licensing position such as Kenney offered an alternative to W. W. Hannan's model of the real estate broker as Renaissance man. Professional training was not, Kenney argued, analogous to an apprenticeship program. To the technocrats, professionalism entailed a rigorous course of training, during which a man systematically accumulated the requisite scientific knowledge and learned how to apply it in unique situations. The paradigmatic professionals were the physician and the engineer, diagnosticians who used extensive and arcane scientific knowledge creatively, case by case, to solve particular problems. Unfortunately, from Kenney's point of view not only were state law and popular culture confused about what constituted a profession, so were many practitioners themselves. Those who did not apply scientific knowledge case by case did not merit consideration as professional men, regardless of legal recognition, and those who did, did. It was incumbent upon the state and national organizations to make real estate men "aware of the fact" that they were professionals, and legal recognition through licensing was a definite means to this end.

Having defined profession generically, Kenney proceeded to assess whether real estate brokerage measured up. First, he noted, brokers participated in disseminating a body of knowledge. During their annual convention in 1911 the men of the national association had "very ably and comprehensively discussed" such topics as city planning, taxation, uniform laws, good roads, organization, and ethics. Clearly, America's real estate men were no longer "devoting their time and attention to cheap booming and boosting with an eye single to immediate financial returns." Instead, they were "systematically and carefully going about the great business of carefully and properly planning, developing, building and beautifying towns, cities, counties and States." Applying broad "scientific knowledge" to the practice of selling real estate was the hallmark of the professional real estate broker. The high-class real estate men who belonged to real estate boards affiliated with the national association were "professional men of no uncertain and doubtful status."[30]

Thus, Kenney argued, real estate brokerage was indeed a profession, at least as practiced by the members of the national association, and it stood to reason that brokers were entitled to legal recognition in the form of professional licensing, like other professions. The criteria for granting licenses should include "certain definite evidences of good character" and demonstrating "some reasonable acquaintance with the chief duties, and rights of real estate brokers." An applicant could satisfy the first requirement with an affidavit from the county judge or some other prominent person qualified to testify to his character. The second qualification would be determined objectively from a test given by a state real estate commission. It would be unethical for professional real estate men to allow "ignorant and unscrupulous men" to hold themselves out as members of the profession when, "as a matter of fact," they had neither the "character, standing nor intelligence to properly attend to this most important kind of business in a proper way." Thus, licensing laws must empower a "competent state board" to administer entry to the profession.[31] Of course, the state board would itself be composed of experienced real estate men. Kenney's view was the "establishment" position, as represented in the *National Real Estate Journal*, as well as in most local board publications and the real estate pages in the major daily newspapers.

There was, however, articulate opposition from the ranks of local boards to the very idea of licensing. To J. J. Kenna, president of the exclusive St. Paul, Minnesota, board, it was immaterial whether brokers called themselves professionals or not. He strenuously objected to the idea that any outside agency should decide upon his qualifications or those of his colleagues to do business. There was only one measure for brokers, success, as defined in the competitive marketplace—"if the balance is on the right side of the ledger on the first of January." Entrepreneurial masculinity spoke loudly and fervently.

For the opponents of licensing, a worthy real estate broker "excelled in the art of influencing men," and "the greatest of all crafts, salescraft." If real estate professionalism meant some bookish application of "theoretical" knowledge, Kenna and his allies wanted nothing to do with it. He avowed that no truly self-respecting businessman would want to place himself in "that class." What disturbed the dissenters most was the subservient and unmanly implications of the pro-licensing argument. Kenna was nonplussed that his fellow real estate men, "members of the great National Association," seriously considered petitioning state governments to "please enact laws restraining us from doing a dishonest act." Kenna had a point: If brokers emphasized that they needed to be watched and were naturally dishonest, how could they expect the public to have confidence in them? The pro-licensing argument was a serious affront to Kenna's sense of honor. "There is not one single man in the whole St. Paul Real Estate Board who has not the confidence of all the other members," he wrote passionately. "Papers, documents, moneys are exchanged freely among such members without any fear or favor. We do not allow a questionable man to become a member of the Board, neither do we allow a man who is guilty of a questionable act to remain a member of the Board and we are not licensed either."[32] To Kenna it was obvious that members of local boards, men whose character had been verified by their peers, were in a better position to detect a "questionable" man than appointed bureaucrats on a state licensing board.

The pro-licensing forces would not only make a government agency the occupation's gatekeeper but would also compel brokers to pay a fee for obtaining a certificate that they would be compelled to display in their offices. Kenna found it "personally obnoxious" that real estate men "ought to be licensed to insure their honesty and to protect the gentle public and thus secure its confidence." Displaying such a license for all to see only exacerbated the humiliation. If the public could be educated to deal only with real estate men who belonged to a "properly conducted Real Estate Board," it would need no further guarantee of honesty and efficiency. In sum, pro-licensing forces were traitors to the occupation. "To have real estate men come out openly and demand they be licensed on these grounds," Kenna concluded, "is an admission of their own weakness and a claim that they have not confidence in their own fraternity."[33] Problems were to be solved internally, at the level of the "fraternity" itself, and not by appeal to outside entities. Opponents of licensing perceived anything less as an attack on the virility, the self-reliance, and the character of real estate men as a group. Tests, licenses, affidavits, and state regulatory boards were necessary only for those lacking in self-control, the defining premise of the sort of artisanal and entrepreneurial masculinities exemplified by Hannan and much of the older generation.

Fittingly, in 1918, the year of Hannan's death, the annual convention ratified a model licensing law, and many states enacted it almost verbatim over the course of the 1920s. In 1922 the U.S. Supreme Court upheld the constitutionality of real estate licensing laws, and by 1923 about thirteen states had some sort of licensing law in place. By 1950 forty-eight states had adopted licensing for brokers.[34] The model law, drafted by the national association's counsel, the prominent Chicago attorney Nathan William MacChesney, represented a compromise, and it incorporated many of the dissenters' concerns. While it called for the establishment of state licensing boards and proposed a fee for licensing, the fee was practically symbolic, generally around $25—far less than the initiation dues or annual fee for membership in a major real estate board. More importantly, the licensing process involved demonstrating one's impeccable reputation, not technical competency. Just as a broker would apply for membership in a local real estate board, he—or she, since no states restricted licensing by sex—would have to verify character to obtain a license. In most states, an applicant needed to provide affidavits from two or more "prominent" personages from his or her hometown who would vouch for the applicant's integrity and creditworthiness. In the early years, licensing was little more than a bureaucratized version of an application to a local board, with two caveats—there were no gender exclusions and the approval rate was far higher from the state than by a typical local real estate board.

State licensing boards rarely denied or revoked real estate licenses. Typical reasons for denial included a revelation that an applicant had misrepresented his or her past on a license application or the exposure of some sort of fraudulent activity. Wisconsin created one of the nation's first functioning state licensing commissions, the Wisconsin Real Estate Brokers Board, in the summer of 1919, and Governor E. L. Phillips appointed three members of the national association to serve on the panel.[35] Initially, the Wisconsin board was disposed to hold hearings on virtually every questionable license application, but with the increasing volume of applications in the mid-1920s, it decided to streamline the application process. The board's members realized that they were "personally acquainted with leading lawyers and real estate brokers in practically every county in the State whose recommendation with respect to applicants would be dependable." They therefore concluded that because these local eminences would have reliable local knowledge of the applicants, "their recommendations would be as dependable as would information obtained by members of the Board by informal hearings." Thus, the board decided to reserve the hearing process primarily for those cases in which a complaint had been brought, saving both time and money.[36] In its first year, the board's secretary reported that of 4,456 applications received, it granted 3,586 brokerage licenses and 693 salesman's licenses. It investigated forty-six cases, of which it denied brokerage licenses in twelve.[37] The board generally denied licenses in the face of evidence of a prior conviction, usually relating to fraudulent brokerage practices, or on strong evidence of debased character.

Assessing the efficacy of various state licensing laws in the mid-1920s, MacChesney preferred the Wisconsin model to the available alternatives. In California, for example, a single salaried commissioner handled enforcement, while in Michigan real estate licensing was folded into the other responsibilities of the securities commissioner. In a system modeled after the "dollar-a-year" voluntarism of wartime, three practicing Wisconsin real estate men recused themselves from business for a specified period of time to serve on the board at the request of the governor. MacChesney favored real estate commissions composed of three or more experienced real estate men willing, "for the good of the cause," to devote part of their time to proper enforcement of the law, rather than a full-time, salaried commissioner. This was partly because he preferred voluntarism to careerism, but he also argued on pragmatic grounds that only experienced real estate men understood "what is good practice in this business." Only practicing men in touch with current realities were capable of appreciating "the delicate kinks and quirks" by which the dishonest broker misled the customer. "The line of demarcation between honest, conscientious representation and dishonest misrepresentation is frequently so indefinite as not to be easily recognized" except by the experienced real estate man. Critically, MacChesney asserted, only experienced real estate men could discern the subtle forms of misrepresentation that occur in real estate practice. Misrepresentation "consists not so much of *what is said*, but of the *manner of saying it*, and of the *impression* which the broker *knows* he is creating in the *mind of the client*."[38] Only an experienced man possessed sufficient mastery of the subtle psychology of brokerage to discern the thin line between legitimate practice and chicanery. Ironically, one of the founding members of the Wisconsin board was himself stripped of his license for fraudulent real estate practices, less than a year after his term expired.

MacChesney stopped short of calling for objective competency testing, preferring to leave licensing decisions to the discretion of honorable men. It was not only for the dissenters' passionate objection or MacChesney's preference that the model law neglected to include proof of expertise in the license application process. Wisconsin led the way in real estate regulation. It was one of the first states not only to create a license commission but also to require literacy in English and passage of an examination; these provisions were not introduced until the late 1920s.

The elegant rhetoric marshaled in favor of competency-based licensing obscured a fundamental lack at the center of the enterprise. Kenney and others grossly exaggerated the coherence of real estate as a field of practice. Assessment of technical aptitude presupposed a systematized body of knowledge from which to draw examination questions, for example, and textbooks to provide a common base of understanding. Real estate knowledge circa 1918 was composed almost entirely of localized rules of thumb and aphoristic "tips for success." The list of books published by the Cleveland broker Stanley McMichael's Realty Book Company at the time is illustrative: *How to Sell Real Estate, Practical Real Estate Methods, Practical Guide in the Purchase of Business Property*.[39] While academic economists had just recently begun to define a subfield called "land economics," few if any practicing real estate men had had any training in it. A field of knowledge called "real estate practice" developed only in the mid-1920s, when the national association formed a federation with the Institute for Research in Land Economics at the University of Wisconsin and the education division of the Young Men's Christian Association to produce textbooks and promote a standard course in real estate. Before this development, of course, it was logically and practically impossible to incorporate technical competence into the licensing process.

The Name Is the Thing: "Realtor"

In the midst of the acrimonious licensing debate, Charles N. Chadbourn, a broker in Minneapolis, devised an ingenious solution to the underlying problem of differentiating ethical member-brokers from the unethical, run-of-the-mill curbstoner. As Chadbourn told the story years later, he was on his way to a meeting of the Minneapolis Real Estate Board in November 1911 when he was confronted by a newsboy "peddling a sensation sheet" bearing the headline "Real Estate Man Swindles a Poor Widow!" The "real estate man" in question was not, Chadbourn quickly realized, a member of his board, but only "an obscure speculator with desk-room in some back office." Nevertheless, his actions had "besmirched every real estate man" in Minneapolis, including all the members of the board. This led to an epiphany: "Why should not Real Estate Board members adopt some name by which to call themselves, which would distinguish themselves from such rascals? Why could we not adopt a title [that] would designate our members, would imply that we are vouched for by our Board as well as qualified and responsible and would confirm the confidence of the public in them?" A month later, after much ruminating, Chadbourn hit upon the title "Realtor," arguably the most successful, and almost certainly the first, attempt by a trade organization to give its members a brand name.[40]

By 1915 membership in the National Association of Real Estate Boards, already "a recognized means of identification of the competent," was good, but it was not enough. In the "high consciousness" of what their new code of ethics meant, the "men of 1913 and 1915" wanted to mark those pledged to that code "as clearly as a chevron marks a soldier's sleeve."[41] The word would be a success only insofar as it remained associated exclusively with the national association, and as the national association, in turn, achieved wide recognition as reputable.

The convention at New Orleans in 1916 gratefully accepted Chadbourn's gift of his word to the national association, though behind the scenes at the midwinter board of directors meeting, there had been doubters. A regional vice-president took exception to the notion that inventing and promoting a new name would change either the behavior of real estate men or the public's perception of their vocation. He argued that heavy promotion of the new name might have unintended consequences. For example, it might make real estate men seem more conscious about their appearance than about the underlying reality, which could further undermine public confidence. Despite reservations, however, the board voted to endorse Chadbourn's proposal, and its recommendation was ratified without discussion by the convention at New Orleans the following March.[42]

In 1917 the word "Realtor" appeared in the addendum to *Webster's International Dictionary*. A Realtor, according to *Webster's*, is a "real estate broker who is a member of a local board having membership in the National Association of Real Estate Boards, an organization incorporated in 1908 for the advancement of the interests of real estate brokers and the protection of the public from unprincipled agents or brokers."[43] With the definition published in black and white in one of the country's most respected dictionaries, the organization was in a relatively strong position, legally speaking, to defend the word from unauthorized use. The national association's president, Walter Collins Piper, appointed Chadbourn to head a Realtor Committee charged specially with disseminating and defending the word. Similar committees proliferated at the local level.

In 1920, the Realtors won their first test of the word's legal standing when the District Court of Hennepin County, Minnesota, decided in their favor in a case against a telephone directory publisher that had indiscriminately used the word in listings. The complaint filed by the national association's counsel Nathan W. MacChesney asserted that the word "had never been used in any way whatsoever until so invented" and thus only those duly licensed by the National Association of Real Estate Boards were eligible to use it. Use by others was "fraudulent and states facts that are not true," causing harm to the national association and its members. The court agreed with the plaintiffs, and ordered the Northwestern Telephone Company to recall the directories and remedy the harm, listing only those brokers on the national association's membership roster under the heading "Realtors." Until the Lanham Acts of 1948 changed federal patent regulations to allow protection for registered collective marks, the national association fought and won sixteen cases on the local and state levels to protect its symbolic property.[44]

Local Realtor Committees took up their task in earnest, and vigilantly policed the use of the word in popular culture. Frank Ward O'Malley misused the word in 1920 in a story in the *Saturday Evening Post* satirizing the travails of a young, home-seeking couple.[45] He was swiftly informed of his error by William H. Wilson, district vice-president of the national association and president of the Philadelphia Real Estate Board, who dispatched a letter to the *Post* editor, George Horace Lorimer, informing him of the dictionary definition of the term. Wilson noted pointedly the decision by the Minnesota court. Lorimer apologized publicly to the Realtors, affirming the word's remarkable circulation in just four years. "Probably nine men out of ten" would be willing to place a wager upon their "ability to give a correct definition of the word . . . yet eight of them would lose their bets." The proper definition was not obvious—"for though all Realtors are real estate brokers, not all real estate brokers are Realtors by a long shot." The editor praised the real estate men for having "hit upon an exceedingly clever and ingenious device to assist them in the achievement of their aims" to become recognized as professionals.[46] In 1921 the secretary of the national association advised the relevant officials in each state of the meaning of the word "Realtor" and urged that states prohibit corporations from using the term in their names.[47]

So popular was the word "Realtor" among the rank and file that by 1922, fifty-five member boards had changed their name to include it. However, MacChesney worried that because of the diversity in local board structure, this proliferating usage might endanger the legal status of the term. He advised the board of directors of the national association to ask the local boards to cease this practice, and they did so. In 1937 the national association changed its bylaws to explicitly permit local boards to use the word in their names, and by the 1950s more than half of member boards resumed using it.[48]

Though the Realtors won on both the legal and the popular culture fronts, intellectuals and élites deplored the symbolic innovation. The term particularly irked the caustic critic H. L. Mencken of the *Baltimore Sun*. Commenting upon the lofty rhetoric of the Realtor's code of ethics, Mencken wrote, "In the conduct of business a *Realtor* is bound by much stricter rules than incommode an ordinary business man; in fact, he is cribbed, cabined and confined in a way that almost suggests the harsh working conditions of a justice of the Supreme Court or an archbishop." In a letter to the *Philadelphia Inquirer*, the renowned Philadelphia lawyer J. B. Townshend declared the word an "etymological mule," a "meaningless jumble of letters," since the suffix "-or" was to be used solely for the transformation of a verb into a noun, and no such verb as "real" or "realt" existed. Another gentleman of the same city declaimed, in apparent exasperation, "few of us know how [the word] came to be jammed into our vernacular." Robert J. Nash of the Philadelphia Real Estate Board rushed to defend the term on both populist and pragmatic grounds. "Many useful words . . . were not reared in cultured circles," he noted. Ubiquitous words in the everyday lexicon of the 1920s, such as "booze" and "jazz," were not inventions of the cultural élite. Nash contended that "the woods are full of words which grow up like Topsy," and that Realtor, short for real estate operator, "saves time and printer's ink," and thus "serves a useful purpose."[49]

Mencken was not satisfied, and he proposed an etymology for the term. "Realtor," he quipped, was "derived from two Spanish words, *real* meaning royal, and *toro*, a bull," and thus connoted "*royal bull*." Chadbourn replied, apparently without irony, that "*Real estate* originally meant royal grant. It is so connected with land in the public mind that *Realtor* is easily understood, even at a first hearing. *-Or* is a suffix meaning a doer, one who performs an act, as *grantor, executor, sponsor, administrator. Realtor*, a doer in real estate."[50] Chadbourn thus subtly connected the practical value of the word as a short form with the subtextual association between brokerage and active, manly work. "Realtor" quickly became generic, though its meaning remained somewhat vague. Yet it was clear even to the satirists that the national association's right to the word was to be respected. In 1922, when Sinclair Lewis published his classic novel *Babbitt*, featuring the Realtor George Follansbee Babbitt as the archetypical middle-class American male, he was careful to use the word properly to refer to a member of a local board affiliated with the national association.

The spectacular spread of the word and the ire and ridicule it provoked in highbrow circles suggest that Chadbourn's creation solved some of the real estate men's professional problems. By the early 1920s the members of the national association claimed enviable name recognition, and the generally positive coverage of the national association's activities in the press counter-balanced the satirical barbs of Mencken, Lewis, and others. However, there was a potential drawback to the acceptance of the term as generic, used in everyday conversation to describe any and every real estate broker. Hence-forth, fraudulent acts would be associated not with a generic "real estate broker," but with a "realtor." The word was a double-edged sword: it could just as easily attract praise as ridicule.

Whither Real Estate Education?

The adoption of the term "Realtor" notwithstanding, fundamental profes-sionalization issues remained unaddressed. Toward the end of the First World War many leading real estate men were calling for real estate education and acknowledging the inadequate state of the existing literature on real estate brokerage. The debate over the form and content of real estate education echoed the character-versus-competency argument from the licensing de-bate. Some Realtors argued that education was a local issue, best conducted by local boards, and ought to consist primarily of moral guidance by example. Others urged the national association to design and promote a uniform and systematic course of real estate instruction, including a series of standard texts in real estate practice. Unlike in the licensing debate, however, this time there would be no compromise. After a lengthy struggle, the proponents of system-atic education came away the victors.

The initial discussions of real estate education revolved primarily around instilling proper ethical values in men with a reputation for moral laxity. Addressing the annual convention in New Orleans in 1916 concerning a course in real estate sponsored by the Detroit Real Estate Board and his city's YMCA, Harry T. Clough began by condemning the "lack of knowledge" upon which the real estate profession, "so-called," was based. He expressed doubt that another endeavor "directly interests the masses to the extent that the transfer of real property does," about which there was "such dense igno-rance." Clough mocked the apostles of real estate education, quipping that "a little knowledge is a dangerous thing" but "no knowledge is a still more dangerous thing." Without their own field of knowledge, real estate men suffered from not only reduced credibility but also their particular bugbear, lack of autonomy. Clough noted that the real estate man required legal counsel on virtually every question pertaining to land, his own alleged area of expertise. "Must we go on for the succeeding generations and never do anything to ameliorate our dependent condition?"[51] The real estate man without his own base of knowledge, without his own disciplinary jurisdiction, could never achieve self-reliance, the bedrock of middle-class manhood.

Nevertheless, Clough's address focused not on devising a plan to build a knowledge base to remedy the situation, but on the vital importance of moral guidance to the profession. He admonished the "able and successful" men attending the annual convention to recognize that they "do not by long odds constitute the rank and file" of real estate men. The average broker was equipped with far less knowledge and experience, and, more important, possessed a far smaller modicum of good business sense and moral fiber. As the "cream" of the occupation, the men of the national association had an obligation to do their part to "direct[] into the right line of thought and action" those who "drift (and drift is exactly the word we want to use) into the business each year." The educational program run by his board in Detroit aimed not only to train prospective real estate men but to impart ethics to a large class of men every six months by "bringing before them for examples, as it were, the cream of our Board members, successful and well established business men." In its first few seasons, the Detroit board's course consisted of "little but a recounting by members of the Board of their business methods," but the content of the course was almost beside the point. Education for Clough and others had less to do with conveying substantive information or teaching fundamental principles than with instilling what he called "common business sense" and ethics. Clough recognized the insufficiency of this approach in the long run, conceding that "ours is a business calling possessing little of a written character, and much of the little is of questionable value." He hoped that eventually someone would produce a textbook, "something of a substantial character," but he clearly felt that the "wholesome" moral guidance provided by experienced businessmen outweighed the need for any sort of systematic program of instruction, at least from the point of view of 1916.[52]

The discussion at New Orleans spurred the leadership of the national association to create a Committee on a Uniform Real Estate Course, with B. L. Lambuth of Seattle as its chairman, as well as a Committee on Text Books. Lambuth's report to the convention at Milwaukee in 1917 echoed Clough's earlier emphasis on the inadequacy of the literature and the poor state of real estate knowledge, but his proposal was vastly different, and represented a frontal assault on Clough's notions of education. Lambuth's committee urged the national association in the strongest terms not only to sponsor the preparation of textbooks on real estate practice but also to create a standard, national curriculum. This position was a significant step away from the far more voluntaristic approach to education advocated and practiced by local boards across the country. His committee proposed to centralize authority over knowledge in the national association, to create a standard and systematic field of practice, and to eliminate dependence on the goodwill and free time of local real estate men for education. Lambuth championed modern system and science against old-fashioned moral guidance and common sense.

A nationalized curriculum had manifest advantages for both the development of the profession and the influence of the national association. Lambuth's committee proposed creating a number of centers under trained students of real estate conditions to observe the "laws of city land value" and analyze the rules of the local real estate market. Further, Lambuth urged the national association to provide adequate real estate training for individual brokers "who stand in need of the touchstone whereby their potential wealth of undeveloped possibilities may be transmuted into dynamic professional ability and power."[53] The national association stood to gain control over the development of the field by creating cadres of brokers trained according to its methods, thereby ensuring steady membership growth and fealty to its principles. Thus, the plan represented not only an educational agenda but also a strategy for creating a far more powerful and effective national organization.

Lambuth's committee also rejected as repetitive, overly detailed, and disorganized the "compound system" of instruction prevalent among local boards, such as that of Detroit, in which a number of experts gave lectures on their area of specialization. The ad hoc system of lectures was "obsolete," tending to contribute to the "superficial training" of real estate men. Steeped in modern pedagogical ideas, Lambuth called for a single, authoritative instructor teaching a course carefully developed in one "central plan," designed around textbooks written specifically for the course. The committee earnestly recommended that the national association sponsor such a course only once a satisfactory text had been written. The course itself would consist of two parts, "general principles" and "practical treatment of local conditions." Lambuth insisted that his committee would only endorse a text in the name of the national association if it were a "scientific treatment of the subject,"

designed "to build a solid groundwork of real estate knowledge in the valuation and care of property, and to develop the fundamental possibilities of the
practice of brokerage."[54] For Lambuth and other educational modernizers,
the choice was clear: either superficial preparation for active practice (that is,
mere vocational education) or else development of the "fundamental possibilities" of a true profession.

Thus the Committee on a Uniform Real Estate Course aimed to create
exactly the sort of school that Clough had rejected for turning out prospective
real estate men. Not surprisingly, the committee's plan met with opposition
on the floor of the convention. Several men who had taught just the sort of
local, voluntaristic, "superficial" courses that Lambuth disparaged took issue
with his call for standardization and nationalization. S. M. Peep of Minneapolis, a self-identified former real estate instructor, acknowledged that the
committee had done good work, but chafed at the plan's implication that
instructors must use a particular text or follow a specified course outline.
Further, Peep argued that there should be choice among texts and that instructors, as in other subjects like sociology and economics, should have the
freedom to choose. He doubted that "any compelling influence" could be
"brought to bear to compel the use of a certain text book."[55] The convention
did not adopt the committee's report directly, but referred it to the incoming
Executive Committee for further action. The educational modernizers eventually acquired powerful allies both within and outside the national association, and Lambuth's plan would eventually come closer to fruition than even
he probably imagined possible at the time. However, both the educational
modernizers and the traditionalists had got ahead of reality. Choice among a
variety of textbooks on real estate practice was a fantasy in 1917, since no
single textbook on the subject had yet been published. As the Committee on
Text Books noted at the same convention, it had not been able to find or
develop a single text that would cover the whole field of real estate knowledge.[56]

A textbook such as that envisioned by Lambuth presupposed the existence
of a definite, coherent, differentiated body of real estate knowledge, something like a science of real estate practice. Such a field was emerging, fortuitously for the Realtors, and its apostle was in Madison, Wisconsin. Richard
T. Ely, a renowned economist at the University of Wisconsin, had a grandiose
vision of establishing a national center for research in the subfield of land

economics, which he had founded just before the First World War. Ely imagined that in the national association he would find men broadly supportive of his agenda who would lavish upon him the support he desired. Within a year of the Milwaukee convention, Ely began a concerted effort to recruit the Realtors to his cause.

CHAPTER FOUR

Applied Realology: Administration, Education, and the Consequences of Partial Professionalization in the 1920s

Cities are hand made. Whether they are physically bad or physically good, is the responsibility of the Realtor. We cannot claim that our business is a profession unless we constantly endeavor to improve the product of our hands . . . Laboratories of research are needed in the real estate profession. "Realology" should be as much an established science as geology and zoology.

—J. C. Nichols, Realtor, 1925[1]

Leading Realtors knew that their occupation required at least two things to become a true, modern profession: an uncontested field of specialized knowledge underpinned by scientific authority, and an efficient organization that would serve the interests of its practitioners and define the terms of entry. In the 1920s, fortunately for the Realtors, the social science enterprise was expanding rapidly; many academicians sought greater cooperation with businessmen, driven by the progressive impulse to apply knowledge for social betterment as well as more practical financial considerations. The Realtors entered into a marriage of convenience with the renowned economist Richard T. Ely and his new Institute for Research in Land Economics that lasted for much of the 1920s—until the real estate bubble burst late in the decade, shattering many of the promises that social science would ameliorate business practice.

Richard T. Ely and the Realtors

Early in the national association's history, leading brokers had realized that their vocation, if it was to become a profession, needed an educational curriculum. Yet there was no coherent body of literature, or even a well-structured textbook. The Publication Council was founded in 1916 to rectify this problem, and by 1920 its members understood that lack of books was only the tip of the iceberg. An educational curriculum worthy of a modern profession presupposed a well-defined field of knowledge and relative consensus as to what real estate practice entailed and how it was to be taught. Until the field was defined, any discussion of producing a corpus of literature was premature.

Fortuitously, as the Realtors were becoming aware of their occupation's epistemological deficiencies, a group of economists led by the renowned professor Richard T. Ely at the University of Wisconsin was establishing a new academic discipline, land economics. The new field purported to deal with land use, land valuation, and land ownership from an "impartial" and "scientific" perspective. Reports began to reach the national office that Professor Ely had been giving talks at local real estate boards on "real estate as a profession," and had spoken of transforming American real estate brokerage into a true profession. Like many leading Realtors, Ely saw the professionalization of real estate as a precondition to fulfillment of the American promise of universal property ownership. Ely and the Realtors shared a new exceptionalist dream of conquering historical time and preempting class conflict through widespread possession of property, scientifically utilized.[2] There was a happy coincidence between the Realtors' demand for a science and the academy's supply.

Ely began his "crusade" to professionalize the real estate business in 1918.[3] After many years of refusing opportunities to give public lectures—no doubt the lingering fallout from his chastening experience with publicity during his infamous academic heresy trial in 1894[4]—he sought invitations to speak to major real estate boards to impart his message, and to activate his vast network of former students employed as land agents across the country. Apparently unaware that the leaders of the National Association of Real Estate Boards had already embarked independently on the same path, he aimed "to start an organization of real estate men who are doing business on a high plane and want to cooperate in the effort to make it a real profession."[5]

In his initial contacts, Ely treated the Realtors as potential students—that is, as junior participants in the educational process. "I think all the real estate men of the better class are beginning to appreciate that they are injured by those who do a dishonest business," he confided to a former student employed in the U.S. Department of Agriculture. He noted that he had received a "good response" to his talk at the Cook County Real Estate Board in Chicago, although he did "not mince terms in speaking about dishonest practices."[6] He would later modify his professorial, paternalistic stance—particularly when it came time to raise funds and write textbooks—and came eventually to exhibit a great deal of respect for the Realtors, particularly their administrative leadership.

Ely began corresponding in 1918 with Thomas Ingersoll at the national association as well as with several prominent men in large local real estate boards, including those in Chicago, Milwaukee, St. Louis, Madison, and Minneapolis. He quickly and accurately surmised that the impetus to professionalize real estate brokerage emanated from established boards in the Midwest. Well versed in the history of American settlement patterns, he understood that real estate boards were most powerful and effective in the more recently and rapidly developed regions. In the newer regions of the country, brokers and developers could be credited or blamed for land use patterns, and thus, it was in the heartland that professional standards and control were most needed. Whereas the East was old, crowded, and haphazardly overdeveloped, Ely's science could potentially salvage the new Midwest and West. Thus Ely aimed to implement his agenda swiftly, to prevent further social harm from ill-conceived, unscientific land use. Unlike in many countries in Europe, in the United States the free alienation of land combined with weak state controls meant that land policy was essentially made by those who bought and developed the land. From colonial times through the twentieth century, expansion across the continent was rapid but haphazard, leaving the burden on modern progressives to make order out of chaos.

Ely's social theory of property provided the intellectual fuel for his crusade. In his massive tome *Property and Contract* (1914), Ely had dismissed the deeply held Lockean notion of private property as a pre-political, "natural" right. He argued that property relations were a matter of political decision and therefore were historically contingent. It followed that there was no such thing as absolute private property, no unrestricted right to use or own property according solely to individual preference or perceived self-interest. However, neither could ownership be considered entirely social. There were two facets to private property in Ely's account, the individual side, "property-as-commodity," and the social side, "property-as-propriety."[7] The social aspect was not exceptional or epiphenomenal but an essential part of the institution itself, meaning that any deterioration in the social side of property threatened the demise of private property as an institution. The state, as society's agent, was therefore obliged to enforce the social side with regulations pertaining to use, eminent domain, taxation, and so forth. On the individual side, it was incumbent upon owners to avoid waste and nuisances, misuses of property that impaired its social side. Here again the state was enjoined to devise regulations to enforce individual compliance. In Ely's mind, any program of education for real estate professionals had to begin with the social theory of property, since real estate brokers were in effect the executors of American land policy.

Encouraged by the warm response his ideas received in Chicago in 1918 at his inaugural talk on real estate as a profession, Ely began to solicit invitations from other boards. Perhaps the most important contact he made in this regard was with the young secretary of the Minneapolis Real Estate Board and future executive secretary of the national association, Herbert U. Nelson, who invited him to Minneapolis in May 1918. Accepting the invitation, Ely began to demonstrate personal identification with the Realtors' project: "I feel that at the present time it is possible for us to take a great step forward in putting this business on a higher plane." After his lecture in Minneapolis in May, Ely wrote to Nelson of his plan to "establish a Bureau of Research in connection with the real estate boards of the country."[8]

Ely believed that his work was of millennial importance. As he repeated to countless audiences, only the science of land economics could rescue the country from the catastrophic boom-and-bust cycles that had characterized American history from settlement through the early twentieth century, from the financial and moral ravages wrought by short-term, greed-driven, unplanned development. Speculative and indiscriminate building by unscrupulous and untrained men had created urban slums and rural ghost towns, wasting enormous financial, natural, and human resources. Correct land use policies that were built upon scientific knowledge were the nation's highest ethical priority and were fundamental to social peace and welfare.

Unlike the single-tax followers of Henry George, who wanted essentially to do away with private property in land, Ely wanted to broaden the base of ownership. Ely's fundamentally Jeffersonian message resonated with many audiences. Perhaps Ely's most important early endorsement came from the Farm Mortgage Bankers Association (FMBA). which pledged its strong support after Ely's speech at its national convention in 1920. The farm mortgage bankers contacted the National Association of Real Estate Boards and proposed to the Realtors that the two organizations share the costs of underwriting a research bureau. E. D. Chassell, secretary of the FMBA, made it clear that business organizations could use a respectable academic veneer. "The organization which Dr. Ely suggests," Chassell wrote to the president of NAREB, Frederick E. Taylor, "would be entirely independent of every line of business," would "work in the interests of truth and not be biased by the claims of investors, borrowers and consumers." As a consequence, its findings would carry "greater weight with the general public." Most important, Chassell argued, the publications put out by Ely's research institute "would not be discounted in advance as is the case with arguments put forth by Associations like yours and ours, because of a suspicion of bias in their own interests."[9]

In 1920 Ely drew together some prominent former students and devoted friends, among them John Finley of the *New York Times* and Albert Shaw of the *Review of Reviews*, and formed a board of trustees for the Institute for Research in Land Economics. At this time he also began to correspond directly with officials of the National Association of Real Estate Boards. President Taylor gave him great encouragement and suggested that he direct his efforts at the Publication Council, composed largely of strong professionalizers. Irving Macomber, a Realtor from Toledo who had led the committee in 1921, expressed broad support for Ely's agenda. "Naturally, I believe that the immediate need in the real estate field is for a more fundamental knowledge of first principles, and a better perception of vital relationships," Macomber wrote, echoing Ely. "The real estate field is almost entirely unorganized, and in these critical times, it is nothing short of a calamity that no organized and dependable data is available." Yet Macomber hesitated to support Ely's institute at the expense of developing the association's own competence in research. "There is no reason why the National Association . . . cannot develop basic data in its own field, and at the same time render material assistance in support of the splendid work you have so ably outlined."[10] Macomber and Taylor proposed a compromise: the national association would build its internal capacities while at the same time supporting independent research. However, the association had limited resources.

Becoming aware of the politics within the association, Ely began to seek ways to sell his idea to the membership at large. He contacted J. B. Mansfield, the editor of the *National Real Estate Journal*, which by 1920 was reaching a wide audience within and outside real estate circles, as the national association's membership rolls swelled to 12,500, a threefold increase in five years. Ely hoped to influence prominent rank-and-file members directly and requested Mansfield's help in arranging a conference in Chicago. However, Mansfield was rather discouraging. Though he was strongly interested in "the economics of land ownership," he had discovered that many leading real estate men were not, and he reported to Ely that his efforts had been rebuffed. Mansfield informed Ely that a forthcoming issue of the *Journal* was to publish an outline of Macomber's research plans, but these were along "purely practical lines."[11] Ely, not to be deterred, asserted his practical business experience with real estate, noting that he had "organized companies and bought and sold a good deal of real estate" on his own account, and thus was able to "combine practical knowledge with theory."[12]

Ely was most concerned with the nature of his institute's prospective relationship to the National Association of Real Estate Boards, and thus the place of objective, academic social science in the real estate men's professionalization project. He persistently attempted to convince the Realtors that an independent research organization was necessary, with proper "equipment" to conduct studies on crucial questions, the results of which could then be applied in everyday practice. Armed with the latest scientific knowledge, Realtors could become true professionals; that is, executors of the public trust in their sphere of expertise, land use. Ely appealed directly to the technocratic masculine impulse driving the professional project.

In his scramble to find funding for the institute from individuals, associations, and foundations, he quickly ran into the typical catch-22 of new organizations: to make a persuasive case for funding, an organization had to show results, which of course were unattainable without adequate funding. In the institute's case things were even more difficult, because the field that Ely attempted to capture was new, and the clientele for his services seemed so clear: real estate men, mortgage bankers, and eventually public utility companies. If these groups were not willing or able to underwrite his activities, why should a foundation? And should foundations spend their money on research ostensibly for the use of profit-seeking businessmen?

Ely insisted that he did not intend for his institute to provide information for businessmen's profit, but rather to perform "epochal" research in land economics that would allow humanity to improve its relationship to the land and thereby to itself. Time and again Ely became exasperated when a prospective individual or institutional donor failed to grasp the importance of the institute's work for the human condition. Land use questions were simply about human relations, pure and simple, as far as Ely was concerned. "The problems of land economics," he professed, "reach to the ends of the earth and to the minutest detail of economics interests." For this reason, the institute's slogan was "Under all, the land."[13]

Ely soon realized that the exigencies of finance would force him to devise ways to make the institute marketable to a broad audience, particularly among businessmen. His pitch to the Realtors had three main themes. First, he emphasized the absolute necessity for a modern business organization to have impartial, objective, accurate facts at its disposal for members and for the public at large. Such information was crucial in the fight to secure rational public policy in the interest of landowners, for whom the national association purported to speak. Since land economics was a new field, and since he and his associates essentially had this niche of the academic market cornered, the Realtors were obliged to support the institute—there was no alternative source for this information. Second, Ely proposed a members-only information bureau, analogous to the services offered to subscribers by the Harvard Business School, to provide current data on market trends, land prices, and other information pertinent to the operation of a high-class real estate office. And third, appealing to the Realtors' nascent sense of professional pride, he proposed that the institute be a credentialing institution, along the lines of the English Surveyors' Institute, which awarded a certificate to members after completion of a course of study.[14]

A longtime academic empire builder, Ely was surprised and more than a bit frustrated by the hesitance on the part of men who he presumed would have a great deal of authority and influence in the organization. Ely expected the national association's leaders to possess sufficient authority simply to dictate to the membership the terms of cooperation with his institute. Things turned out to be more complex and democratic in the world of organized business than the academician, a Progressive acolyte of "expertise," imagined. Ironically, Ely boasted that he ran his own organization as efficiently as a business, when in fact he had far more personal authority than the businessmen who ran trade associations.

As Ely feared, during its meeting in spring 1921 the board of directors of the national association decided to establish its own research bureau. Disappointed but not completely discouraged, Ely intensified his lobbying efforts, and garnered an invitation to speak before the board at its meeting in Des Moines in November 1921. In a letter to a colleague a few days before the meeting, he assessed the situation, noting in his characteristically Manichean fashion that there seemed to be two groups among the members of the national association. One comprised those "who have a strictly scientific point of view and desire research absolutely without any limitations or trammels of any sort and description." In this group he included the NAREB president, Irving B. Hiett, and its executive secretary Tom Ingersoll, who both "see that this is in their interests as well as in the public interest." Unfortunately, there was a "less advanced group of Realtors who feel that the Board should do its own researches, or at any rate, they should be conducted by employees of the Board and reach desired results." Ely was confident that his personal intervention would make all the difference.[15] He often conflated the leadership and membership of the national association, assuming that the leaders' opinions with regard to research and education mirrored those at large. However, there were many Realtors, even among the most prominent, who saw no use for "scientific" research and had no compunction about appearing self-interested.

Ely's oft-noted powers of persuasion did not fail him in front of the board of directors. " 'Veni, vidi, vici,' " he gloated privately to a colleague. "That was my delightful experience at Des Moines . . . Between sixty and seventy were present from all parts of the United States. I carried them for my proposition unanimously and enthusiastically." As he had predicted, those with the "professional point of view" triumphed at the meeting, and the finance committee was instructed to arrange an appropriation for the institute of $5,000 per annum for five years. "I scarcely see how we can fail now, but, of course, until we actually get the appropriation of money some unexpected snag may be struck."[16] From late 1921 onward, Ely used the unanimous endorsement of the board of directors in virtually every fund-raising appeal he made. He was now able to show the philanthropic agencies that the putative beneficiaries of his institute's work were solidly behind him. Pleased that Ely's reform message was reaching its intended audience, the Carnegie Corporation soon approved an appropriation of $62,500 for the institute, payable over five years.[17]

Ely quickly learned that pledges in the business world were, at least in the world of trade associations, not always reducible to cash. Apparently there was some confusion about the precise nature of the commitment made at the board meeting in 1921. Paul Stark, a Realtor and devoted Elyite from Madison, Wisconsin, forwarded a letter from President Irving Hiett regarding the national association's financial condition and the sheer impossibility of funding the institute at the levels that Ely proposed. Ely had asked for $12,500 for 1922, to be increased to $25,000 in 1923. The latter was an impossible sum, representing close to 25 percent of the national association's total annual revenue, and even the smaller sum well exceeded the salary of the executive secretary. Further, the NAREB leadership was under the impression that "for $6,000 Dr. Ely could prepare the necessary information for a Bulletin on various subjects to go out monthly," and additionally that "the Dr. was securing information that would enable him to prepare some books on property interests." For an appropriation of $4,000–$5,000, President Hiett thought "a start could be made that would bring tangible results, quickly, and without increased dues." Nonetheless, the leadership of the national association was committed to establishing ties with Ely's organization. "I know that most all of the men at the Convention were impressed with the practical way that the Dr. talked," Hiett assured Stark, and, "personally, I am convinced that if some arrangements can be made, as I suggest, we can get quicker results than otherwise."[18] Hiett was expressing a common sentiment among practical businessmen: demonstrate the institute's cash value first, and the national association would dole out the cash.

Fearing that opportunity was on the verge of slipping away, Ely immediately reverted to persuasion. "I have now a very clear idea of what you need, and I am sure I can render the service . . . If your organization would only trust me, I am sure that the beginning of our work for the National Association of Real Estate Boards will mark an epoch in your history, and of which everyone concerned will be proud." Ely shifted his appeal from pride to practicality, reminding the Realtors that the institute was the nation's only research organization concerned with real estate, the "only group that has given very careful and prolonged scientific attention to the subject," and the only group capable of doing the work well in order to ensure "the largest returns." Finally, he appealed to fear: "you know that real estate has a great many enemies, and it is important that the work be of the highest grade."[19] Without a scholar of his reputation conducting their research, any information published on behalf of the Realtors would undoubtedly be tainted by the appearance of bias, providing fodder for the foes of the industry, the enemies of private property.

Yet there were many men within the real estate world who failed to see the value of "scientific" research. In late 1922 Ely met with a group of brokers from Chicago and was stunned to discover that many considered land economics an enemy of real estate. An acclaimed study published by George Arner, an urban land economist at Columbia University, had demonstrated that land values in New York City had been rather stable over the long run, contrary to popular opinion. Arner and Ely interpreted this finding as demonstrating the sound conservatism of real estate as an investment, as a powerful counter to the criticism that real estate had a tendency to boom and bust. To many real estate men, however, these results seemed "calculated to injure the real estate business." One broker in Chicago went so far as to suggest that Arner's work, "if more generally known, would kill the real estate business." This encounter led Ely to think that perhaps the institute "must come up with some other lines of work first" and "educate" its "constituency" before embarking on studies of land values, which could easily be marshaled by investment bankers to demonstrate the higher returns attainable in securities other than land. "I think almost any other line of work would be better calculated to educate them than the study of values," he confessed.[20] This presented a dilemma, since one of Ely's main appeals to local boards for funding had involved offering a member of his staff to conduct a historical study of local values. Nevertheless, many if not most leaders of local real estate boards perceived Ely as a valuable ally, praising his "services to real estate interests generally" if occasionally quibbling with the results of his institute's research.[21] Ely put his associates to work on a survey of real estate activity and other practical reports, the first of which was published in 1923.

Educating the Realtors

Despite the uncertain financial relationship between the national association and the Institute for Research in Land Economics, Ely and Stark forged an educational alliance that would turn out to be the more important and enduring outcome of the board meeting of November 1921. The board had voted to make the institute its official "reference organization," enlisting Ely as its "adviser for Research and Education." Always on the lookout for an opportunity to raise funds for the institute, Ely immediately suggested that his publisher, Macmillan, a "firm of high standing," be given the exclusive rights to any reference materials or textbooks produced in the partnership between the national association and the institute. "Do you appreciate the potentialities of this?" he asked the vice-president of Macmillan, in the course of one of his many entreaties for an increase in royalties. "At present they have 16,000 members and the number is rapidly increasing." Ely promised Macmillan huge sales of textbooks from real estate courses that the institute would devise. The Realtors, the most progressive real estate men in the country, demanded "thorough-going courses," at a variety of levels, something more than "salesmanship, advertising, etc. which constitute the old-fashioned courses," Ely insisted.[22]

Ely was anxious to put his imprimatur on the educational program of the national association, and he forged ahead in developing course materials. During the spring and summer of 1922, he began to compile the *Outlines of Land Economics*, a collection of the seminar lectures he had given in Wisconsin that he hoped would be the foundational textbook for a comprehensive real estate curriculum. He aimed to get the *Outlines* together quickly to show the national association some tangible results of the institute's work. Initially he solicited comments on the manuscript from Realtors, among them Stark, with whom he had become acquainted through business dealings. Stark's firm managed Ely's property in University Heights in Madison, and the men had long exchanged ideas on real estate matters. As he did with many others with whom he became personally acquainted, the professor exercised a great deal of moral authority over Stark, who was much younger. At first Ely adopted his typical paternalistic stance, but by 1922 or so Ely realized that he might learn a few practical things from Stark. A successful businessman with intellectual curiosity, Stark became Ely's exemplar of the possibilities for professionalism in the actual world of real estate practice. "A man like Mr. Paul A. Stark" became a stock phrase in Ely's correspondence.

Ely seemed rather surprised, though not unpleasantly so, to receive six pages of considered criticism from Stark on the chapters of the *Outlines* dealing with the real estate business. Though Stark had found the *Outlines* generally stimulating and useful, on the whole he felt that the text was too laden with academic jargon for the average Realtor and that it overemphasized rural land issues. In Stark's judgment, the social losses due to shoddy rural land practices paled in comparison to poor urban and suburban land use. He urged Ely to include a few paragraphs on the possibility of incorporating proper subdivision practices into licensing laws, something that was under consideration in Wisconsin. Stark also encouraged him to place greater emphasis on the importance of credit, by drawing the connection between technological change, particularly the spread of the automobile, and the need for larger investment capital on the part of subdividers. The latter, as a matter of course, now had to include sewers and roads in their plans, and increasingly had to make provisions for access to financing for homebuyers. In this way, subdividing was becoming a more specialized business, one that required a more highly developed organization and better sources of funding. Finally, Stark recommended that Ely explain the origins of the word "Realtor," and link development of the word to the broader trend toward professionalization.

William E. Shannon, a prominent Realtor in Washington, similarly advised Ely that the practicing real estate man needed "more concise statements of the fundamentals with direct practical conclusions based upon them." Realtors were busy, important public men, and they desired succinct and practical texts, not dense volumes crammed with superfluous facts and arcane jargon. The Realtor was no different from the lawyer, "who in the law school has been trained in the theory of law" yet in practice "turns for his further knowledge and assistance to the actual cases decided from day to day." Realtors needed ready reference books, not multivolume anthologies of academic "theory." Criticism of the *Outlines* also came from other quarters. Henry S. Pritchett of the Carnegie foundation, the institute's primary sponsor, echoed Stark's and Shannon's sentiments, opining that the *Outlines* were of a "pronounced academic character," far too verbose and arcane to be particularly useful to the "intelligent businessman."[23]

As Ely was preparing the *Outlines*, Stark conveyed some relatively good news about funding. In July 1922 Samuel S. Thorpe argued strenuously to the board in favor of centralizing all research functions within the confines of the national association. None of the members of the board were willing to oppose Thorpe, a venerated founder of the organization, but neither would anyone make an unequivocal commitment to his proposal. Fearing bureaucratic deadlock at best, Stark had intervened with an extended speech in favor of funding the institute, noting that Ely was under the impression, and rightly so, that the national association had made a pledge. Would the board honor that commitment or not? Stark forced the question, cutting across lines of advocacy by invoking the organization's honor. The newly elected president, Nathaniel J. Upham of Duluth, agreed that the board had already gone on record in support of an appropriation, and that this obligation must be met. As Stark described the dramatic moment, "this request of Mr. Upham settled the matter as all of them felt that they wanted to support the President in his new administration," and the board voted an appropriation of $3,000. Apologetic to Ely for the apparent indecisiveness on the part of some members of his organization, and modest with regard to his own considerable achievement in defeating the imposing Thorpe, Stark assured Ely that the national association's support was solid.[24]

Stark and the Publication Council, with the enthusiastic support of Herb Nelson, began to discuss the creation of a standardized course in real estate. Much to Ely's delight, Nelson immediately set about compiling a library at the national association's headquarters, by now permanently located in Chicago. He requested of Ely and others bibliographical information and any materials they had available, to be reviewed by a committee for inclusion in a standardized course. Ely responded with a didactic missive on how to proceed. "If the real estate business is to become a profession," he began, "its basis must be far broader than that found in many real estate courses, such as those you find offered by various YMCA's" or local boards, many of which offered some sort of instruction. Loosely organized courses taught by untrained instructors would "never make the real estate business a profession." First, he besought his new friend, "we have got to get down to underlying principles, and that is what we are trying to do" in the *Outlines*. "After we have got the foundation, then we can build up and take special applications." Speaking from his professorial perch, he told Nelson, "This is the way we do [things] in a modern university."[25]

Ely was, however, aware of Nelson's dilemma. "You have very unequal preparation in your clientele. Some men have had scarcely a high school education, and others have gone through college." Although Ely was firmly committed to a four-year, collegiate model for real estate education, it seemed likely that any viable program would consist of at least two tiers, one for those already engaged in the business and another for those yet to enter it. The national association indicated its commitment to an Elyian program, at least in spirit, when it lured Ernest M. Fisher away from the Institute for Research in Land Economics to serve as director of education and research. At first Ely was "inclined to be pugnacious" in keeping Fisher, "one of our choicest men," but "on further reflection" he realized that it would be to the advantage of both the national association and the institute for Fisher to relocate to Chicago. Ely admired Nelson's "insight and quickness in picking out the best man we have for your purposes."[26]

With his man firmly in place on the national association's staff, Ely had Fisher announce an educational conference to be held in Madison in April 1923. The publicity spread quickly. An official of the United Schools of the Young Men's Christian Association wrote to Herb Nelson asking how the YMCA might aid the Realtors' efforts. Noting that the YMCA had a long-standing interest in aiding the development of the "commerce professions," he suggested that the United Schools sponsor the course. Nelson, who recalled Ely's judgmental views on the YMCA approach to real estate education, thanked the YMCA for its offer, at the same time making it clear that the Institute for Research in Land Economics had primary responsibility for the academic content of the curriculum. Just to make sure the message was clear to everyone, Ely staked out his turf in a letter of his own, in which he assured the YMCA official that his vision of real estate education, built on solid scientific foundations after many years of study, was guiding the preparation of the course. "The task of doing this work properly is one of the utmost importance to this country and indeed it is not an exaggeration to say to the world. We are dealing with the most fundamental problems of our time," he intoned. A task of such moment called for "something far more than courses of a commercial character; not that I mean to disparage these courses."[27]

Ely was thrilled to see his vision of standardized, national real estate education coming to fruition with such rapidity. The joint commission, comprising representatives from the institute, the national association, the United YMCA Schools, and the American Association of Business Colleges, approved a textbook series and a two-year curriculum during the meeting in Madison in April 1923. Ely got nearly everything he desired, including editorial control over the entire list of twelve textbooks, the "Standard Course in Real Estate," to be published by Macmillan as the "Land Economics" series. Demonstrating a newfound flexibility, induced partly by the promise of large royalties, he agreed that it was unrealistic to expect active businessmen to read more than a single 350-page book in a sixteen-week course. Massive, jargon-filled tomes like the *Outlines* were out of the question. Ely commissioned Fisher to write the first book in the series, *Principles of Real Estate Practice*, and to his son-in-law-to-be, Edward W. Morehouse, he assigned the task of radically condensing the three-volume *Outlines of Land Economics* into a single volume, *Elements of Land Economics*.[28] Ely and the Realtors had come to a consensus on a rigorous course of study, grounded in academically sound research, but designed for the busy, practical businessman.

In less than six months, Ely, Nelson, and Fisher had created the rudiments of a national, standardized real estate educational program. Ely was characteristically unrestrained about the achievement in a letter to the president of the Carnegie Corporation, predicting that the results of their efforts would "be felt a hundred years from now."[29] One member of the joint commission, Ralph E. Heilman, dean of the School of Commerce at Northwestern University, presented the educational program to the huge gathering of Realtors at the annual meeting in Washington in 1924. He explained that in the prescientific era, training for the professions, such as law, was purely practical. "The young man, for example, who aspired to enter the practice of law was apprenticed to an old-fashioned country lawyer or judge where he swept out the office, cleaned the spittoons and read the law until he was finally regarded as being qualified to be admitted to the bar." In modern times, before a young man can enter "any of those important callings," he must "submit himself to a rigorous course of study . . . of the organized and the analyzed and the assembled and the systematized experience of others."[30] Here again Heilman invoked core precepts of technocratic masculinity: rigor, organization, system, analysis.

The "calling or vocation" of the Realtor was now, Heilman continued, in the transitional period from the first to the second stage of development—that is, in the midst of a shift from an old middle-class to a new middle-class notion of a calling. The Realtor of yesterday was forced to learn in the "school of hard knocks," while the Realtor of tomorrow would be able to learn from the "organized experience" of others, as codified in the "forthcoming literature." This prospective body of knowledge would eventually be disseminated through an ambitious educational program. A vocational component constituted the first phase, already under way in the United YMCA Schools, a two-year program designed to enable currently practicing Realtors to get a "fuller understanding of the business" and "increase their capacity."

Heilman, as a university dean, was more excited about the second phase in "the education and training of the Realtor of tomorrow," a regular four-year university course culminating in a "major in real estate." As of 1924 only Ely's university, Wisconsin, Heilman's, Northwestern, and the University of Michigan had implemented the curriculum, but Heilman expected many more to join the bandwagon. He identified a very significant new tendency in American higher education, away from pure devotion "to thought and contemplation with regard to subjects which were of very little concern to the world," and toward "those problems which are of great importance in the workaday world." He understood that the university—once an "institution primarily apart from the world," attended "primarily by the sons and daughters of the well to do" for the purpose of obtaining a "sort of personal culture" or to prepare for "entering the so-called learned professions"—was becoming a place dedicated to training "young men for leadership in every single important field of human activity." And, he submitted, "there is no field of human endeavor which is more important to . . . mankind than that which has for its purpose the promotion and the development of the utilization of our land and our land resources." The university was obliged to educate the Realtor of tomorrow, just as in the previous generation or two it had taken on the function of educating the physician, the lawyer, and the engineer.[31] The university in the 1920s aimed to broaden its role as a mechanism of social reproduction, to play a part in the development of a new middle class, distinguished by credentials rather than social background.

To round out the educational program, a third and final phase would emulate the work of Ely's institute, establishing centers of research and advanced study that would produce competent faculty to teach real estate, train men and women to staff government agencies, and generate new knowledge. As Ely explained to the convention in 1925, while there would always be a distinction between real estate education and land economics, it would be like the distinction between medical practice and the science of medicine. Just as the physician could be a competent practitioner only after a course of study of principles, and could maintain competence only by keeping abreast of new developments in medical science, the Realtor of the future would be fit to practice real estate brokerage only after a study of the fundamentals of land economics, and would be obliged to keep himself informed of the developing science through continuing education. Ely envisioned a series of certificates and degrees to reward diligent Realtors.

Since "scientific achievement comes largely through laboratories," Ely declared, he was proud to announce to the Realtors at their convention in 1925 that the institute now possessed two "experiment stations" of its very own. The first, a rural operation called the Fairway Farms Corporation, consisted of a series of farms designed to test "standards and methods where-by men may become farm owners." The second, Sunnyside, a development under construction by the City Housing Corporation on Long Island, aimed to devise standards and methods for proper suburban land use. The institute, Ely noted, "participates in the formulation of policies to be applied in these laboratories and uses the results of these experiments for the establishment of standards and methods." Here again was the medical metaphor: the institute would provide the clinical setting for research that would generate the advances in knowledge and technique about "land systems," as Ely now called them; the business schools would produce the clinicians to design and conduct the experiments; and the United Schools would train the rank-and-file practitioners in diagnosis and prescription.[32] The vision was complete.

From "Off Hand Knowledge" to the Standard Course

Before the pedagogical alliance between the institute, the United YMCA Schools, and the national association, the typical real estate course was a local affair. Taught at the YMCA, a proprietary business college, or a real estate board, or through a university extension division, the typical course consisted of a series of informal lectures given by self-styled local experts in particular areas of the business. An appraiser might share his methods of assessing property value one week, a sales "wiz" might give a snappy talk on the psychology of selling the next, and a successful subdivider might impart the secrets of his craft the third. Without an underlying theoretical framework to lend coherence, this was a buffet approach to education. Written instructional materials usually consisted of compilations of lecture notes or a series of pamphlet-length disquisitions on individual subjects.

In 1921 John B. Spilker and Paul G. Cloud, Realtors as well as real estate instructors at the University of Cincinnati, claimed to have produced the first synthetic treatment of the "real estate business as a profession." They organized the contents of their slim tome, *Real Estate Business as a Profession*, departmentally, like the modern real estate office. Suburban, city, subdivision, management, auction, appraisal, insurance, salesmanship, advertising, finance —each had a chapter. The authors sandwiched various departments between short summaries of general knowledge: a "historical" chapter on the evolution of the business, a discussion of legal terms and documents, a very brief section on real estate law, glosses on taxation and zoning, and finally a discussion of ethics. Aimed at busy practicing real estate men enrolled in adult education courses, the eighteen chapters each averaged four pages in length in the first edition.[33]

Spilker's and Cloud's book was typical of the real estate texts of the period, lacking any sort of integrative, systematic understanding of "real estate practice." Or more precisely, the implicit notion of "real estate practice" embedded in these texts was the ad hoc, rule-of-thumb, idiosyncratic logic of the artisan. No recognizable hierarchy of concepts structured the texts, no theoretical framework lent coherence. Early texts offered a purely instrumental, pragmatic approach to a definite end: maximizing income through selling real estate.

The books in the Standard Course in Real Estate, endorsed by the national association, represented a fundamental break with the real estate literature of the past. The first three books, published as part of the "Land Economics series" edited by Ely for Macmillan Press, appeared in 1923–24: Ernest M. Fisher's *Principles of Real Practice*, *Elements of Land Economics* by Ely and Edward W. Morehouse, and Frederick A. Babcock's *The Appraisal of Real Estate*. The series, which included nine additional volumes published between 1925 and 1930, was characterized by an underlying unity—namely, the new field of scientific knowledge called land economics. The Standard Course represented the culmination of Ely's work since the publication of his opus *Property and Contract* in 1914, and the fulfillment of the research prospectus he laid out in 1916 during a roundtable at the annual meeting of the American Economics Association.[34]

"While the present work is simple and elementary in character," Ely wrote in the introduction to Fisher's text—tacitly acknowledging his past aversion to communicating his ideas succinctly to laymen—"it is scientific and lays a proper foundation for the work that is to follow." But what exactly did Ely mean by "science" and "foundation"? To Ely the scientific enterprise was a multifaceted endeavor requiring close connections between theory and practice, the ultimate goal of which was the discovery of "basic causes" that operate within institutional contexts. His approach to social science research was influenced by the late-nineteenth-century German "scientific clinical" school. He rejected monocausal and reductionist explanations for complex phenomena, repeatedly scorning the solutions that flowed from such methods as "panaceas" and "palliatives." He emphasized linking "book knowledge" and practical experience. "Just as in medicine, a man has to have an

internship, after completing his medical work," Ely later wrote in his autobiography, "in the social sciences a man should have practical experience to
test his theories." Thus did Elyian land economics share with nineteenth-
century medicine the idea that the body—in this case the body of relationships that constituted landed property—was a "system of dynamic inter-
actions."[35] This conception of science pervaded the work of his students such
as Fisher.

Fisher organized the table of contents of *Principles* departmentally, with
chapters on the real estate business as a profession, office organization, renting and leasing, insurance, selling, advertising, valuation, building operations,
finance, law, subdividing and city planning, taxation, the role of the state,
professional relationships, and "requisites to success." Intended for both the
man "who expects to enter the real estate business without experience" and
the man "who is already in the business but wants to make his work more
effective," the book aimed to increase "uniformity in real estate practices."
Each chapter began with a series of structuring questions and proceeded to
address them systematically. Every subject was given equal treatment, and
each question was intended to integrate the text's teachings into a coherent
field of professional knowledge.

Fisher began by precisely delimiting the field of activity of the real estate
broker. The specialist in real estate had several basic functions. He was a
source of information and counsel on "matters connected with the value,
transfer, improvement, and use" of real estate. (Methods of purchasing or best
utilizing real estate were obscure to the "uninitiated" but "second nature" to
the real estate man.) The real estate man "created" a market for real estate, by
bringing together seller and purchaser, saving both valuable time and effort.
He acted as an information conduit, helping to create a more nearly perfect
market—that is, closer to the ideal in which all sellers meet all buyers. He
actually made sales, and salesmanship did indeed matter. The role of the real
estate salesman was cast in clinical terms: he was responsible for "diagnosing
the needs of his prospects and matching those needs in the minds of his
prospects with the goods he has to sell." He also created real estate itself as a
developer, by subdividing new "additions," constructing buildings, and settling farm lands. Some real estate men even created an "idealistic home
environment," building "homes for the families that are the hope of the
nation." Real estate men also managed, appraised, insured, and secured credit

for the purchase of property.³⁶ Each function fulfilled a socially necessary task, the crucial connective tissue in the Elyian social science epistemology.

The text proceeded with a detailed exposition of each function. Unlike that of Spilker and Cloud, however, it did not aim for comprehensiveness but aspired merely to introduce the student to each subject, assuming that the student would pursue further study. *Principles of Real Estate Practice* was intended merely as an introduction to brokerage, a "bird's-eye view" map of the entire, broad field. Fisher entreated the reader to seek in-depth knowledge of one or more of the enumerated subfields. As director of education for the national association and a member of the joint committee that outlined the entire course, Fisher was well aware of the other offerings available to the prospective professional broker. Thus he possessed a vision of the entire horizon of real estate practice, of the possibilities for specialization, and of the various types of knowledge that each specialty might require. Fisher knew that the joint committee had approved courses on general economics, real estate law and finance, transfers and conveyances, salesmanship, building construction and design, principles of land economics, property management, and valuation and appraisal.³⁷ This view of the entire prospective field undoubtedly lent coherence to his text, allowing him to strike a balance between too little and too much coverage of any particular topic.

As in the work of Spilker and Cloud, the idea that real estate was, or could be, a profession is central to *Principles of Real Estate Practice*. Unlike the earlier text, however, Fisher gave content to the concept, and he related professionalism integrally to the larger purposes of the book. For Fisher, a profession had three principal characteristics. Naturally, the first prerequisite was an accepted body of knowledge, "obtained by long experience and consist[ing] of generalizations made from the observation of many cases." In a self-referential nod, Fisher suggested that a marker of a profession-in-the-making is the accumulation and systematization of this knowledge in textbooks and courses of instruction, whence it may be conveyed to the "novice." Echoing Abraham Flexner, whose studies for the Carnegie Corporation from 1910 to 1920 established important benchmarks for modern professionalism, Fisher asserted that the second defining feature of a profession was "group consciousness." This "feeling of unity," Fisher indicated, arises naturally from similar work experiences and similar training, and the Standard Course consciously purported to inculcate group spirit among real estate brokers. Finally, group consciousness extended, in a true profession, to self-enforcement of norms of conduct, often entailing rules intended to circumscribe strictly self-interested behavior and presuming some notion of public interest. Real estate, the author contended, truly is a profession-in-the-making, having made substantial progress with regard to each of these criteria.[38] Fisher's text worked particularly hard to demonstrate that real estate brokerage served the public interest. While the older texts also asserted the socially beneficial function of the real estate man, they appeared to do so to compensate, in a sense, for the manipulative, self-interested behavior that they simultaneously promoted. Moreover, previous texts failed to provide any conceptual linkage between brokerage practice and the public good. Fisher's text was, by contrast, thoroughly steeped in Ely's social theory of property, to which a compelling conception of the "public interest" in regulating land use was intrinsic.

Principles of Real Estate Practice likely performed its most important cultural work by identifying the emerging professional real estate man as a social type with shared, if not primary, responsibility for conducting land policy under American conditions of private property. While the state had a compelling interest in regulating his conduct and establishing constraints on his freedom of action through zoning and planning ordinances, the real estate man was, and ought to be, the primary executor of American land policies, the "instrumentality through which the land resource of the nation reaches its highest use," in the words of the Realtors Code of Ethics. Here the analogy to private practice in medicine was quite direct: the state sanctioned a particular definition of "medicine," licensed persons called "physicians" who embodied that definition, and regulated the conditions under which they operated, all in the public interest—which, to complete the tautology, demanded qualified physicians.[39] In Fisher's text, underwritten by Ely's social property theory, the American system of private property itself virtually demanded the professional real estate broker, a private practitioner subject to social control. It remained to be seen if the social type called forth by the text—a scientifically informed and public-spirited broker who deftly balanced his own interests with those of society—could exist in pure form under American conditions in the 1920s.

Appraisal, Scientific and Racist

In the third text in the Standard Course, *The Appraisal of Real Estate*, the prominent Chicago appraiser Frederick M. Babcock systematized appraisal knowledge and made a strong case for his specialty as a profession within the profession. Appraisal as practiced through the early 1920s relied on "offhand" opinions and "empirical" methods, and Babcock aimed to reorient the field around logical, statistically sound, scientific techniques. His ultimate goal was not so much to create a separate appraisal profession—an appraiser, in his opinion, required brokerage experience—but to make scientific appraising a specialized aspect of professional brokerage and, eventually, to create a separate credential that a broker could obtain after additional education. In Elyian fashion, Babcock wanted to combine the "business man's knowledge and observation" with the "scientific method of thought and analysis."[40]

The real estate market relied heavily on the work of the appraiser. Buildings and parcels of land were bought and sold based on their appraised value. Value determinations were crucial for mortgage underwriting, real estate bond issues, and establishing rents for residential and commercial leases. Appraisers played a key role in determining the share of taxes owed, rates for public utilities, and benefits and awards in connection with public improvements, as well as the obverse, impairment of value for damage suits in the case of value destroyed by public projects. In general, the appraiser's task involved determining the "best utilization of a property."[41]

To Babcock, the appraiser was the diagnostician and the prognosticator, the clinician who often analyzed the "value of a site under several assumptions as to its future utility," indicating "which of the uses will be the most productive over a reasonably long period of time."[42] Thus, his expertise was in some ways at the center of the strong professionalizers' vision of the field. Appraisers performed the analyses upon which brokerage decisions rested; only with competent appraisal could the Realtor fulfill his ethical obligation to protect property values. If anyone required rigorous training in land economics, the professionalizers believed it was the appraiser—and Babcock's book was the first rigorous attempt at providing it.

A professional appraiser needed three distinct skill sets. First, he needed to know how to "investigate and secure data," and what elements constituted "evidences of value." An appraiser needed to mine all possible sources of data, such as public records, other brokers, and newspaper accounts of sales and transfers. Second, the "properly equipped" appraiser must be "capable of relating evidences of value and weighing them by consistently organized logical reasoning," and therefore he must have a strong command of mathematics, particularly statistical techniques. Third, the appraiser must have brokerage experience and preferably should be a practicing broker, because the value of real estate was "a market phenomenon" and only constant "contact with the real estate market" would keep him abreast of market trends. Aside from concrete skills, the appraiser, like all professionals, needed to possess more than the average share of discretion and judgment, and a sterling reputation.[43] His signature on an appraisal report would be meaningless without the latter intangible qualities; like a doctor with adequate training but terrible bedside manner, he would likely find himself without a clientele.

All appraisal methods ultimately consisted in "finding a true value of a property to a typical real estate user and the correction of the true value for market influences." Appraisal began with a determination of "fair cash market value" under "normal and typical conditions": that is, the "price which a seller who is willing and able but not compelled to sell will accept for his property from a purchaser who is willing and able but not compelled to buy." These conditions rarely obtained, but they served as a useful baseline, a necessary assumption in statistical analysis. The "base value" was an abstraction that applied in a fictitious "static city," in which population remained constant, prices reached "that Utopian state where supply and demand are in perfect equilibrium," rent levels would not change, and construction would be for the replacement of worn-out buildings only. At this point all land would be at its "highest and best use," defined as its most remunerative use over a long period. Under static conditions, scientific appraisal assumed a principle of uniformity, which asserted that values tended to settle into roughly homogeneous districts, interrelated and graded, each site in a district tending to be used to its highest and best use. A behavioral uniformity principle underpinned the entire calculus, namely the principle that man generally acted "rationally and uniformly so."[44] However, as Babcock would later demonstrate, *homo economicus* could act non-rationally, particularly where race was concerned.

After calculating the static base value, the appraiser introduced dynamism into the equation. Districts constantly mutated in character. They "slid" as businesses grew, "died" when they did not. A "dead" district might be "jumped" over by a developer, another might "burst" when there was no room for further growth within its boundaries. The analyst needed to include attempts by cities to regulate movement through building codes, planning, and zoning restrictions in the dynamic equation. Babcock's language, particularly in the sections on dynamism, clearly conveyed the real estate man's agency in shaping the city, building on the image put forth in Fisher's text.

Yet Babcock was aware that "in the final analysis," large-scale social forces circumscribed the Realtor's range of action. Values of real estate ultimately depended on "people and the movements of people." Industrial site values were affected by labor supply, commercial site values by access to buyers, residential values "by racial and religious factors." The appraiser's task was to base values on anticipated changes, and predicting social flux produced complex statistical formulations. Of course, these "predictions" themselves formed a powerful narrative about the future of a district or a city, and often became, as scholars of blockbusting and redlining have shown, an odious, self-fulfilling prophecy. Applying the abstract uniformity principle that "like attracts like" to residential neighborhoods, Babcock asserted that "the desirability" of a neighborhood rested "primarily on its [racial, ethnic, and class] homogeneity." If the "wrong" "element of value" infiltrated a district, the rational Realtor, working on behalf of his client, would have to declare it "dead" and possibly "jump" over it.[45]

While Babcock paid only minimal attention to "racial and religious factors" in determining value in *Appraisal*, a few years later he would become the chief appraiser of the Federal Housing Administration and would draft the appraisal guidelines used to evaluate properties for federal mortgage support. As many scholars have noted, federal housing policy during the New Deal codified racial segregation. Babcock's work forms the link between the federal sanction for such practices as redlining and the Realtors Code of Ethics.[46] In 1924 the Realtors Code of Ethics was substantially revised, and continued membership in the national association was made contingent upon adherence to the code. Under loose cover of paying heed to scientific zoning, land use, and appraisal doctrine, Article 34 of the code essentially elevated racial discrimination to the status of an ethical and scientific principle. It intoned that a Realtor "should never be instrumental in introducing into a neighborhood a character of property or occupancy, members of any race or nationality, or any individuals whose presence will clearly be detrimental to property values in that neighborhood."[47] Professional practice demanded keeping things in their proper places.

It is tempting to dismiss this element of the code as a mere reflection of the tendencies of its time. The economic boom of the First World War produced a massive wave of migration of African Americans from the Jim Crow South to northern industrial cities like Chicago and Detroit, and racial tensions were at historic highs in the urban North. Local board policies like the amendments of the Chicago Real Estate Board to its Code of Ethics in 1917 were designed to keep African Americans out of "white" neighborhoods—in the process, formally recognizing residential segregation by race. The war exacerbated racism and nativism, and by the early 1920s there was overwhelming popular support for the restrictive Immigration Acts of 1924. At the same time, the eugenics movement enjoyed renewed popularity, and its assumptions of racial hierarchy were shared by the Realtors and even by ostensibly enlightened intellectuals like Richard T. Ely, who had written in 1918 about the natural inferiority of "Negroes" as a basis for his defense of tenancy as preferable and "natural" for certain groups.[48]

On the other hand, this provision of the Code of Ethics remained in force for two and a half decades, and ample evidence links its racist ideology with the discriminatory redlining and blockbusting that became the focus of public attention in the 1950s and 1960s. At the very least, Article 34 transmuted into something self-fulfilling, the common belief that ethnic and racial segregation was a natural phenomenon and that people innately preferred to live among "their own kind." The provision also helped to bring racial discrimination in housing into the mainstream. The upper classes always had had the option of discriminating by writing restrictive covenants into their deeds, and of course by pricing "undesirables" out of their neighborhoods altogether. But after 1924 such discrimination became a normalized practice among the middle class, perhaps even a defining feature of it. Realtors—and later, federal housing officials—now had a codified principle, supported by the "science" of real estate appraisal, upon which they could justify racially exclusionary practices. Article 34 must share culpability for the destruction of perhaps billions of dollars of property values, precipitated by white flight. When the Realtors revised the Code of Ethics in 1950 they removed the phrase "members of any race or nationality." Nevertheless, the ideological and structural conditions that it symbolized linger to this day.[49]

The Politics of the Textbook

The textbooks in the Standard Course aimed to imbue the prospective professional broker with state-of-the-art knowledge of the field. This goal posed
unusual dilemmas in the case of real estate brokerage. In a well-developed
field, a textbook author would draw upon a wealth of monographic literature, and likely would present controversies in the field explicitly, allowing the
student to get a sense of the processes by which professional issues were
typically resolved. This served in established professions the important function of creating a professional metanarrative, so to speak, about the proper
relationship between theory and practice and between pure science and applied science, as well as highlighting the appropriate mechanisms for adjudicating disciplinary disputes and negotiating boundaries.

However, real estate practice was a completely new "applied science" in
1923, and so too was the "pure science" that Fisher and Ely claimed for its
foundation. Moreover, the epistemological basis of Elyian land economics—a
notion of science inextricably bound to addressing practical, social concerns—
meant that controversies about theory would almost inevitably devolve into
political questions directed at the very legitimacy of the field. An attack on the
social theory of property, for example, was tantamount to an assault on the
entire enterprise of professional real estate brokerage, as conceived by the
strong professional program. Similarly, preemptive categorical statements
aimed at antithetical conceptions of property, at the "vulgar Lockeanism"
underlying the single-tax position or at the Ricardian rent theory of marginal-
ist economics—which peppered the Fisher and Morehouse and Ely texts in
particular—revealed anxiety about the tenuous basis of the field.[50]

Thus, the texts reflected the state of real estate practice itself. Realtors
were not unified behind Elyian land economics and the practical prescriptions
that flowed from it. Real estate proved unable to suppress theoretical hetero-
geneity. Realtors remained lukewarm at best about the need for formal,
university-approved credentialing as a marker of their professionalism, and
thus Ely's dream would be only partially realized. The Realtors would become innovators in the modern "credential society," ultimately creating a
scheme of designations and certifications awarded outside the formal university structure.[51] Their skepticism about the value of formal education for
businessmen was consistent with long-standing tendencies in American culture: ambivalence about social control versus freedom of action, about the

social side of property versus putative absolute rights to free alienation of property, and about expertise versus entrepreneurship—in short, widespread ambiguity about the bases of middle-class identity.

The Sound of Paradigms Clashing

The 1924 version of the Realtors Code of Ethics drew directly from the writings of Richard T. Ely, formally and publicly committing Realtors to his vision of the profession, and made them responsible, in a sense, for the behavior of the real estate market.

> Under all is the land. Upon its wise use and widely allocated ownership depend the survival and growth of free institutions and of our civilization. The Realtor is the instrumentality through which the land resource of the nation reaches its highest use and through which land ownership attains its widest distribution. He is a creator of homes, a builder of cities, a developer of industries and productive farms. Such functions impose obligations beyond those of ordinary commerce; they impose grave social responsibility and a patriotic duty to which the Realtor should dedicate himself, and for which he should be diligent in preparing himself.[52]

The esteemed Realtor and "community builder" Jesse Clyde Nichols was the most outspoken advocate of establishing the real estate profession on these Elyian grounds. When Nichols preached to his Realtor brethren of their accountability for the shape of American cities, about half the members of the congregation were converts.[53] Nichols knew that many brokers, even some men legally entitled to call themselves Realtors, were not worthy of the name "professional," at least as far as he understood it. He admonished his audience, "If we simply serve as a medium for the mere exchange of real estate, we are not a profession; the world does not recognize any calling as a profession unless its members intelligently work to add knowledge and betterment to the world." It was incumbent upon men worthy of the profession to devote their efforts to creating and stabilizing property values, improving living conditions, making cities "more efficient, economical, and practical, better planned, more beautiful, cultural, orderly." Nichols appealed to his fellow brokers to support "laboratories of research" in real estate. "Realology," he asserted, should be "just as much an established science as geology and zoology."[54]

For Nichols, educated at Harvard, "Realology" comprised a wide field of knowledge, including city and regional planning, architecture, housing reform, demography, sanitation engineering, and road surveying. Thorough study of Realology would naturally lead the Realtor to follow Nichols's own example in building planned and picturesque communities well adapted to their natural surroundings, complete with street layouts that recognized topography and main lines of traffic that considered the long-term perspective. In short, the Realtor should "surround[] our people with uplifting influences for greater citizenship."[55] A true professional Realtor had many tools at his disposal, including deed restrictions, zoning ordinances, building codes, and landscape architecture, and the science of real estate would help him master them.

Thomas Shallcross Jr. of Philadelphia, a former president of the national association, agreed wholeheartedly with Nichols. In the midst of a heated struggle among Realtors in his city over a proposed zoning ordinance in 1926–27, Shallcross argued that zoning represented the intelligent use of police power and would have a "beneficial, stabilizing effect" on the real estate business. Zoning not only made it easier "to arrive at fair market value" but also made financing real estate less difficult. He divided opponents of zoning into three categories. First was the "selfish" class, who objected to any government regulation of anything. "This is the same clan," he noted sarcastically, "that objects to parking regulations, one-way traffic, and other prescribed interferences with their own free will to do as they please, and of course there is no real answer to their wail." Second were those "really honestly concerned as to whether such zoning regulations . . . really come within the police power of the State, using the argument that it is a 'taking without compensation,' all of which of course has merit."[56]

In rebutting this traditional argument, Shallcross quietly invoked the march of historical time, averring that "we are in a changing world . . . Many of the regulations and restrictions that we are now living under and take as a matter of course were undreamed of in the time of our fathers, and are as subservient of the rights of the individual to the general will of the community as is zoning." Finally, the third class of objectors was troubled by the creation of another regulatory agency, and was concerned that a zoning commission would become too political. To this Shallcross replied, "I would rather take this chance than go without benefit of regulation and protection." Invoking the language of republicanism to ground his argument, he concluded that it "would seem . . . to be a denial of the thoroughly accepted theory of the American form of self-government, to say that a community, no matter how small or large, cannot set up for itself a program of orderly development and mutual protection."[57] In this remarkably rich passage, Shallcross both admitted the inevitability of historical change and proposed zoning as an updated version of the classical republican solution to controlling the impact of change. Zoning could save the Republic from its own excessive dynamism and maintain some semblance of balance within progressive change.

There were dissenters from this agenda even within the ranks of prominent Realtors. Shallcross's fellow Philadelphian Albert M. Greenfield was a "free-market" advocate who opposed planning and zoning as "socialistic." Greenfield, known by the 1920s as "Mr. Philadelphia" for his incredibly profitable dealings in West Philadelphia and Center City property, invoked notions of professionalism linked primarily to "vision" and initiative rather than the sort of science that spawned planning. In fact, Greenfield embarked on a career in real estate after leaving law school because he was disillusioned to discover that law was not a "science."[58] For Greenfield, the right of individuals to own and transfer property was inviolable, part and parcel of the Lockean natural-law tradition against which Richard T. Ely had inveighed in *Property and Contract*. For Greenfield, property was largely and almost exclusively a commodity to be alienated freely.

Greenfield's opposition to zoning placed him primarily in Shallcross's second category of opposition, occasionally in the third. The city council "would be adding another anchor to Progress were a zoning ordinance to be passed to clutter up the municipal statute books," he wrote in a letter to the head of the Philadelphia Chamber of Commerce. "Every man of ordinary experience knows," he continued, "that the value of property is dependent upon the demand for it." The price for the site of a building, he asserted, must be "determined by the anticipated revenue." Zoning would limit property values "by limiting the uses for which it might naturally be put." Under such conditions, "it would take longer for the property to increase to the value which it would probably attain much sooner in the course of natural development." Greenfield, who had largely built his fortune on often risky, speculative ventures, saw comprehensive zoning regulations as overly restrictive, a threat to his business practices, and built upon a theory of real estate valuation that ran counter to natural law.[59]

Horace Groskin, a member of the board of directors of the Philadelphia

Real Estate Board, joined Greenfield in criticizing zoning on natural-law grounds. Proponents, he argued in an anti-zoning tract in the mid-1920s, admitted freely that zoning would reduce property values in certain districts for the benefit of other districts: "Now, I would ask, by what right has a zoning commission to set itself up as the judge and the distributer of property values? To take the value away from one property owner and give it to another, or not to give it to anyone but to destroy it entirely for the imaginary benefit of the community, strikes me as coming mighty close to Socialism. To me, zoning means the most serious Socialistic gesture ever attempted in this country."[60]

Moreover, to Groskin this "socialistic gesture" flowed directly from a faulty understanding of economics. "The locations selected by the Zoning Commission are not always the BEST ADAPTED locations according to the natural economic law, and it is THIS law that has made Philadelphia the great city it is today."[61] In sum, to Greenfield and Groskin real estate was a commodity, albeit a very socially important commodity, and as such it was subject to the same natural economic laws as any other commodity. Interfering with the workings of the "free market" was tantamount to interfering with nature, and thus with Progress itself. The invisible hand of the market and not a bureaucratic, political zoning board was the best arbiter of land use.

There was a fundamental cultural conflict associated with the economic interests at hand. In one camp, J. C. Nichols expressed disgust at the sight of the "disorderly, littered roofs" he saw from his office window, and so he and Thomas Shallcross sought a remedy in the sciences of social control. In the other camp, Albert M. Greenfield saw his home city grow "from a wooded wilderness to the third largest city of the world in two and a quarter centuries, following the natural course of development," and thus he and Horace Groskin had faith in the natural workings of the free market. The old-stock, native-born Protestants, Nichols and Shallcross, intended to bring social order to American life through planning, while the Russian Jewish émigré Greenfield and his German Jewish compatriot Groskin saw themselves as "modern day explorer[s] like Columbus and Magellan," using their creativity to take entrepreneurial advantage of the opportunities of American capitalism. Perhaps in unconscious reaction to the stereotypical association of Jews with Bolshevism, Greenfield and Groskin vociferously condemned socialism and proclaimed their Americanness. Ironically, Nichols was well ahead of his time in permitting Jews to buy property in his exclusive suburban developments.[62]

Greenfield spoke the language of entrepreneurial masculinity, explicitly invoking Theodore Roosevelt and Benjamin Disraeli as models to emulate. He selected individualistic traits like "vision," character, diligence, ability to persuade, and imaginative craftsmanship as keys to success.[63] Nichols privileged the social responsibilities of the Realtor, linking professional practice and success not to personal achievement but to community welfare. For Nichols technical skill and scientific knowledge—"Realology"—were assumed to guarantee a socially beneficial result. Technocratic masculinity ascribed social responsibility to the Realtor through scientific practice. For Greenfield, the invisible hand of the market would produce similar results, and the masculine entrepreneur feared not taking the risks of letting the market pick winners and losers. Nichols's notion of science-as-control became the official orthodoxy of the national association, yet it never achieved unquestioned hegemony. Men like Greenfield and Groskin constantly mobilized their ideas of true American values to prevent the passage of zoning laws, and to weaken those that did pass. The articulate opposition to key elements in the strong professionalizers' agenda of prominent Realtors like Greenfield—who proudly used the term "Realtor" and considered himself a "professional"—virtually ensured that the field would not unify around a coherent doctrine.

In short, part of the profession operated according to Ely's social theory of property, and the other adhered to natural-law conceptions of land as a commodity. The clash echoed that of the previous decade over licensing, but with important differences. Unlike in the previous decade, the strong professionalizers' vision carried the day, at least within the officialdom of the National Association of Real Estate Boards, dominated by community builders like Nichols. Yet men like Greenfield and Groskin had the numerical advantage. The two groups coexisted uneasily within the profession.

An Undisciplined Profession?

In a keynote address before the national association's convention in 1928, Glenn Frank, president of the University of Wisconsin, likened the Realtor to the pioneer of the American frontier. However, Frank's pioneer was not an altogether noble figure. The pioneer, he observed, "cleared the forests to create farms [while the] Realtor is clearing the farms to make cities." To this extent, he argued, "the job of the pioneer and the job of the Realtor seem the same." Yet "candor compels us to admit" that the Realtor "has sometimes done his job in much the same way that the pioneer did his." The pioneer, he continued, "was an exploiter":

> He got while the getting was good and then moved on to fresh fields of exploitation . . . He left us denuded and disorderly landscapes. He left us something worse—the pioneer willingness to tolerate denuded and disorderly landscapes. The pioneer left behind him a double heritage of ugliness and impermanence . . .
>
> The Realtor rises to the dignity of a professional man only as his methods cease to be dominated by the mind of the pioneer, that is, until he becomes more than an exploiter of site values, leaving behind him, as did his pioneer predecessor, a trail of ugliness and impermanence . . . The Realtor has not always been free from these sins of the pioneer . . .
>
> American civilization is flinging this challenge to American Realtors: Can the Realtor bring beauty and permanence into a civilization to which the pioneer bequeathed ugliness and impermanence?[64]

In a few short years, optimism about the Realtors' mission and their ability to prevent human misery and promote human happiness had turned to pessimism. By 1928 the speculative fervor of the mid-1920s had come to an abrupt halt, first in Florida in 1926 and then elsewhere, as large developers went bankrupt and annual residential housing starts plummeted from close to 900,000 in 1926 to a trough of 100,000 in 1933. The Florida banks lost 40 percent of their deposits over the course of a year.[65] In the late 1920s the real estate market collapsed, followed closely by the entire economy.

Could the most progressive elements in the national association possibly have gained enough control over the field by the mid-1920s to curb the speculative tendencies that would cause such devastation? Ely ascribed primary causality to inadequate national land policies. While he did not explicitly indict the Realtors for their failure to fully professionalize, his relationship with the national association had been based entirely on his belief in the importance of real estate professionalism and the pivotal role of the Realtor as the practical executor of American land policies. Though he did not blame the Realtors explicitly, he was undoubtedly disappointed that his efforts and those of the strong professionalizers in the national association did not forestall the catastrophe.

Some of Ely's associates were less circumspect. His disciple Morton Bodfish—chief executive of the United States Savings and Loan League—referred directly to the greed and shortsightedness of the men in the real estate business and the tendency of the business toward "dramatic production and overselling in prosperous times" and "growing weeds" and "rotting stakes" in other times. Bodfish noted that the real estate business, particularly subdividing activity of the sort that led to the Florida debacle, did not usually attract "the type of entrepreneurial skill which is responsible or permanent." But real estate should, he argued, "become and remain an industry attractive to men of ideals and ideas."[66] It clearly had not arrived yet as a profession.

During the 1920s the national association transformed itself from an ineffectual and unfocused men's club into a distinctive, effective, modern hybrid of a trade association and professional association. It standardized real estate education across the country. It could legitimately claim responsibility for the passage of numerous licensing laws, zoning ordinances, and city planning acts. It successfully created and defended a distinctive professional appellation, "Realtor," which its members bore proudly (and its critics pilloried mercilessly). By the same token, Ely's new field, land economics, was established, the textbooks his institute had written disseminated his "Realology" to thousands of prospective brokers, and his students were found in land economics faculty and research positions at universities around the country, and in major governmental agencies concerned with land use policies.

Yet the national association had not achieved anything close to a disciplinary monopoly over real estate brokerage. Among Realtors, there were many who either rejected the Elyian ethical imperative to place public service ahead of profit or accepted it in theory but not in practice. Like other members of the new middle class, many Realtors became adept at espousing platitudes about professionalism and ethics and the virtues of science, while at the same time, and without exhibiting signs of cognitive dissonance or moral qualms, acting in ways thoroughly self-interested and even rapacious, reflecting the double consciousness of the middle class. Thus the tragedy of the 1920s: real estate brokerage had in fact become more professional, more rooted in research and education, better organized, and effective institutionally and politically; at the same time, speculative, "unscientific" behavior on the part of many brokers was reaching critical mass, paving the way for a devastating collapse.

Some of the roots of the real estate debacle were endemic to the professionalization effort itself. The national association's formal commitment to

Elyian social science, particularly its medical model, had built-in disadvantages. On the one hand, it promised to diagnose ailments and prescribe treatment; on the other hand, it implicitly cast real estate brokers in the role of physicians, committed first to "do no harm" and second to take affirmative steps to promote the health of the patient. The medical model thus established definite—and virtually unattainable—standards by which it could be judged, even under the heroic, and false, assumption that the entire field was unified behind the agenda that it represented. At the same time, the historical economics of Ely's generation were in decline, and the rest of the economy was operating largely according to neoclassical, speculative principles.

Thus the partial professionalization of the field may have exacerbated the worst tendencies of both profession and market. As aspiring professionals, the Realtors took public responsibility for the "health" of the land system, as called for in the Realtors Code of Ethics in 1924. Would it have been plausible to expect the Realtors to cure the boom-and-bust cycle in their first decade as a profession? Even if the strong professionalizers' agenda had prevailed completely, it probably would be unfair to blame them alone. The nation's economic collapse resulted from a confluence of tendencies in the American political economy, many related to speculation. Real estate undoubtedly contributed heavily to the severity of the crisis, particularly in its destabilizing impact on the banking system. There was, however, a narrow break in the very dark clouds looming at the end of the 1920s. Despite the economic crisis, and the partial culpability of real estate for its severity, the Realtors had an ally in the White House, Herbert C. Hoover. Considering how far the reputation of real estate had fallen between 1924, when it was the subject of accolades from Calvin Coolidge, and the late 1920s, Washington would prove remarkably amenable to the Realtors' proposals for transforming federal land and housing policy in the 1930s.

CHAPTER FIVE

The Realtors Go to Washington:
Enshrining Homeownership
in the 1930s

In my own business I expect a better year in 1930 than in 1929. If I do not have it, I will blame myself, and not conditions. Business is there for those who will go out and get it.

—L. Reaume, president of NAREB, 1930[1]

Thus far we have focused primarily on the internal development of the real estate brokerage field, the ways in which real estate men invented a field of practice, promoted it by inventing a trade name, Realtor, and attempted to define and police disciplinary boundaries through the law and the creation of a social science subfield. We have seen how gender, particularly what we have called technocratic masculinity, has been central to the professional project.

In this chapter, we will turn our view outward to explore the ways the Realtors use their self-styled status as professionals to embark on a cultural crusade in the 1920s to make homeownership central to middle-class identity and then, through strategic political work, to enshrine their ideas about homeownership in national housing policy in the 1930s. Despite the acknowledged role of the real estate industry in exacerbating the severity of the economic downturn of the 1930s, the Realtors played a central part in writing federal housing policy. By the end of the 1930s, homeownership had become a taken-for-granted public good, in some respects a compensatory project for the damage wrought to American manhood by the Great Depression, a goal heavily favored in national policy despite vigorously pursued alternatives.

Housing and the Economy

By the mid-1920s residential real estate had become one of the most important sectors in the national economy; construction of non-farm dwellings constituted nearly 40 percent of net capital formation in the entire economy. The Great Hurricane that struck Florida in 1926 and led to the implosion of its super-speculative land development bubble precipitated a devastating downturn in real estate activity across the nation. Local savings and loan banks collapsed under the weight of bad mortgage debt, fatally weakening the financial sector and setting the stage for the Great Depression. Real estate values plummeted 25.1 percent between 1930 and 1940, along with membership in the National Association of Real Estate Boards, which fell 53 percent in the same period.[2] By the early 1930s the heady days of the mid-1920s were nearly forgotten: a time when the dominant voices among the Realtors saw themselves nearing the top echelons of American professions, from which they would scientifically manage land use for the good of the nation.

The collapse of the housing market in the late 1920s and early 1930s, and the connections that many pundits and policymakers drew between the real estate crisis and the deepening Depression, might have provided an opening for the construction of at least a semblance of a noncommercial housing sector along European lines. Yet this option did not materialize. The public, not-for-profit housing sector eloquently advocated by "modern housers" like Catherine Bauer was and would remain an underfunded, highly politicized second tier of American housing policy.[3] The centerpiece of New Deal housing policy, the National Housing Act of 1934, institutionalized the vision shared by Herbert Hoover and the Realtors, in which the free-standing, owner-occupied, single-family home in the suburbs became, if not the reality, at least the aspiration of every (truly) American family. The act established a system of mortgage insurance and standardized homebuilding procedures, solving the private real estate market's two major long-term problems—the scarcity of finance capital and the rising costs of construction. The Realtors deployed the political influence they had accrued during the 1920s to shape housing policy in the 1930s, putting in place levers of federal power that would greatly privilege homeownership of a particular sort. The claims to expertise advanced by their professionalization project, inflected with technocratic masculinity, certainly added value to this effort. The mobilization for the Second World War would create enormous pent-up demand for housing, and the Realtors would emerge in the mid-1940s poised to reap the benefits of their extensive labors during the 1930s.

Only Your Own(ed) Home Is a True Home

From about 1915 through the 1920s, the Realtors collaborated with various government agencies and civic groups to promote single-family homeownership. Their goal was to reinforce the idea of the home as a privileged consumer durable, worth sacrificing (and going into debt) for. These campaigns helped to authorize homeownership as a central element of middle-class identity. They were freighted with gendered images urging men to "make her happier, build a home first," a slogan promoted heavily by commercial interests and the Department of Labor at the end of the First World War.[4]

Wartime restrictions on building beginning in late 1916 forced the Realtors to abandon the "Buy a Home" campaign they had launched in 1914. In the period directly after the war, the national association and various agencies within the U.S. government collaborated, albeit loosely, on the first of several major campaigns to promote homeownership. Immediately after the armistice in 1918, the Information and Education Service of the Department of Labor and the national association's Own-Your-Own-Home Committee launched a massive campaign to revive the construction industry and thereby to enhance the country's "capacity to absorb labor" as the economy made the transition from war to peace. The national association and other interested trade organizations, such as the Southern Pine Association, coordinated the campaign, which was conducted by numerous local Own-Your-Own-Home committees. It hammered away at a central message: only an owner-occupied single-family home is a true home.

While the pre-war campaign had commanded Americans to "buy a home," after 1918 the message became the less authoritative "own your own home." The shift indicated a change of strategy to a more psychological, persuasive approach, one less blatantly a promotional tool of the real estate industry—or so its strategists reasoned. The Own-Your-Own-Home campaign employed the associational techniques of modern advertising, attempting to draw subtle connections between the "good life" and homeownership. At the same time, officials in the Department of Labor and the businessmen who orchestrated the campaign imagined themselves on a moral crusade akin to the mobilization for war. "It is as much a patriotic duty to build [a home] now as it was to render service and to make sacrifices in all possible ways during the war," read a pamphlet written by Paul Murphy, a Realtor from Portland, Oregon, and distributed by the Department of Labor.[5] In this spirit, the emissaries of homeownership also employed many of the frequently proven techniques of wartime propaganda, including recruitment of numerous local and national civic and business leaders to speak on behalf of the cause.

The Own-Your-Own-Home campaign was built around an article of faith, namely that the long trajectory of American civilization would finally achieve its preordained goal in the twentieth century. The mission to make America into a land of universal homeownership was merely the culmination of a long republican tradition linking civic virtue to property ownership. The American republic would be able to save itself from the degenerative ravages of historical time, class struggle, and urban corruption by providing all citizens with a home of their own in healthful, natural surroundings: American civilization would develop in space rather than in time.[6]

But the intensity of the Own-Your-Own-Home campaign and the evangelical zeal of its leaders suggest underlying tensions. There was a palpable fear of social unrest from about 1915 through the early 1920s that triggered a general reactionary wave against radical labor and foreigners. This distress was itself part of a more diffuse response to what some historians call the "modernist historical crisis" triggered by the First World War, a yearning for orderly, scientific solutions to the chaos of a world in rapid and bewildering flux.[7] "The more immediate the resumption of business and commerce," a pamphlet of suggestions for the homeownership campaign produced by the Labor Department asserted, "the sooner the unemployment menace, with its unrest and incipient disorder, will fade before such demands for labor as will be incidental to an era of unprecedented prosperity and industrial activity."[8] "Incipient disorder" was a threat; business, especially the real estate industry, must provide the solution. Yet business had to be conducted properly. The war had provided a context in which many businessmen, Realtors included, had allegedly taken advantage of the crisis for selfish ends. There was a rising tide of criticism of wartime rent profiteering, and Realtors and other business leaders apparently felt the pressure. Thus virtually every appeal to civic leaders made by the National Own-Your-Own-Home Committee was qualified with a proclamation of the "purely educational," nonprofit, and non-mercenary motives of the campaign.[9]

Adding to the urgency of the campaign was the sense that the country had crossed a demographic threshold. The Bureau of the Census reported in 1920 that for the first time, more Americans lived in "urban" than "rural" settlements. This development was disturbing to many people who pinned their hopes for the integrity and stability of the American republic on the maintenance of a solid agrarian foundation. City dwellers were much more likely to rent than to own their homes, far less likely to live in single-family, detached homes than rural or suburban families. Richard T. Ely directed a study for the Census Bureau that showed a small decline in homeownership in the first decades of the twentieth century, noting in particular the very low rates of homeownership typical of cities.[10] The handwriting was on the wall, and these findings set off a veritable panic in some quarters.

Ely's study also pointed to another trend, ominous to some, of steadily increasing mortgage indebtedness. In the period from 1900 to 1920, rates of homeownership remained statistically flat at about 46 percent, yet the terms of ownership changed considerably. Between 1890 and 1920 the number of mortgaged homes increased from 27.7 to 38.3 percent, the number of home mortgages grew by 350 percent, and aggregate mortgage debt soared sixfold, to $6 billion. On the one hand these figures were a sign of structural change in the mortgage underwriting industry—an indication that more finance capital was available for housing because there were more institutional lenders willing to lend for mortgages. The increasing size and efficiency of large-scale developers meant that Realtors were increasingly involved in financial matters. On the other hand, with the growth of indebtedness many more people were tied into a relatively unregulated mortgage banking system in a very substantial way.[11] In either case, more Americans were willing or able to incur long-term debt to own their own homes.

But borrowing money for buying a home in the period 1910–30 was complicated and risky, particularly for those of moderate means. Generally, a prospective homeowner needed to have a fairly large share of the total cost of constructing a house in hand before beginning the arduous process of procuring a lot, engaging a contractor, and purchasing building materials. First mortgages—available from institutional lenders such as savings and loan banks, commercial banks, and insurance companies—generally covered no more than 50 percent of costs. The "lump-sum" mortgage predominated, meaning that the borrower typically had either to repay the entire amount upon maturation, or refinance, at additional cost. In addition, since mortgages were rarely extended for periods longer than three to five years, terms often had to be renegotiated several times during repayment. In the interim, of course, land values or interest rates (which were generally high for mortgages before the 1930s) might have changed dramatically, increasing the cost of financing, not to mention commissions and other refinancing charges attendant upon a new loan. To cover the remainder of the costs of construction, the home buyer would be forced into the much less predictable "junior" financing market to procure a second mortgage, generally from a mortgage bank.[12] In sum, buying a home in the early twentieth century for the family of moderate income meant involvement in a complex and precarious array of credit arrangements.

The Own-Your-Own-Home campaign provided no solution to the problem of financing homebuilding. Its organizers mainly aimed to stimulate what they perceived to be flagging demand for homes, and trusted in financial markets to supply solutions. The Labor Department received numerous complaints about the scarcity of financing, and these were invariably dismissed as problems to be dealt with by the local business community, not the government. Aside from emergency wartime contingencies, the role of the state in the housing market in the years following the First World War was almost exclusively exhortatory.

The ideology of the Own-Your-Own-Home campaign assumed the absolute moral and civic necessity of homeownership. At the same time, the campaign's stridency revealed anxiety among the élites about whether this belief was shared by all Americans. The decision to buy a home could not be made on purely economic grounds, the campaign asserted. The moral aspect of homeownership was said to be in need of reinforcement, particularly in the context of the sharp postwar economic downturn and rising labor militancy. The central tenet of the movement—that only an owned home is a true home—gained cultural authority from the environmental determinism characteristic of the Progressive era. For the middle-class managers of the campaign, it almost went without saying that better home surroundings and a better metropolitan environment would create better citizens and a better society.[13]

The reams of propaganda produced by the various business organizations collaborating with the Labor Department on the campaign were saturated with messages about class, gender, and homeownership. The Retail Service Bureau of the National Lumber Manufacturers' Association, for example, published an "Own Your Home" Campaign Handbook, the frontispiece of which featured a picture of a model home and two well-dressed young boys, one of whom proclaims to the other, "That's Our Home—My Dad Owns It." The booklet, produced for local lumber retailers, combined organizational information cribbed from the Department of Labor's pamphlets with language connecting business and moral principles. The reader was told that the U.S. Department of Labor "fathered" the national Own Your Home campaign "as a means of encouraging and stimulating building of homes," and that the campaign required the "support of all good citizens." With the increased demand for homes must come renewed activity in the building trades, leading to "Prosperity, Happiness, Comfort, and Contentment." The sole purpose of the Own Your Home campaign was "to sell the one Idea, Home Ownership," an idea that once sold would naturally increase demand for lumber products.[14] The Own-Your-Home handbook suggested campaign slogans, most of which —like "Own a Home for Your Children's Sake," "Don't Promise a Home to Your Sweetheart and Then Ask Her to Live in a Rented House," and "Make Her Dreams Come True by Owning Your Home"—attempted to reinforce distinctions between "house" and "home" and to create associations between family, proper gender roles, and homeownership.[15]

Local campaigns made concerted efforts to link gendered notions of domesticity and possession with class. Most of the promotional materials deployed overt appeals to gender norms, occasionally working at cross-purposes with the implicit class project. The Southern Pine Association's publicity cut (figure 2) featured the slogan "Make Her Happier, Build a Home First" and depicted a stylishly dressed, ostensibly middle-class woman in two images. In the lower image she stares pensively and bites the nails of one hand, while she grasps a floor plan (of the dining room and kitchen) that she has just completed sketching. The image of "Her Greatest Desire," "a home of her very own . . . a place of comfort, contentment and harmony . . . practical, convenient, beautiful," floats in a dream-bubble. In that bubble the same woman, now with an assured, satisfied visage, is shown embracing the "Home of Her Dreams." This representation, which might be termed "Satiating Feminine Desires through Home Ownership," was circulated in mass-market magazines such as the *Saturday Evening Post*, *Ladies' Home Journal*, *Literary Digest*, and the *American Magazine*.

The advertising campaign draws subtle links between sexuality and ownership. The woman in the Southern Pine Association poster can only be

FIGURE 2. "Make Her Happier . . ." Southern Pine Service Association promotional poster, box 455, Records of the Real Estate Division, Records of the U.S. Housing Corporation (USHC), 1917–52, Record Group 3, National Archives II, College Park, Maryland.

fulfilled by homeownership. There seems to be a tension between the ad copy and its own aims—to sell homes, to produce consumer desire—in that the woman's creativity is foregrounded and her desire is shown as originating within her own psyche. The ad offers homeownership as the fulfillment of her particular imaginings. She "thinks," "sketches," and "pictures" the house in a way that masks its very status as commodity. The ad also invokes a different model of masculinity: the man of the companionate family. It addresses the man as patriarchal "provider," but also as domestic partner and, in a surprisingly sentimental turn, as the fulfiller of an autonomous female desire. There is also an appeal to more traditional models of masculinity: a man can only be a real, self-assured man if he owns his own home, if he "pays rent to himself" rather than to a landlord—in short, if he is not a dependent vassal. If there was any doubt about the intention of the campaign to appeal directly to masculine anxiety and pride, a Southern Pine Association campaign guidebook (evidently directed at employers) counseled that the "family man who does not own his own home" should be made to feel "as uncomfortable as possible."[16]

Philadelphia conducted its "Own Your Home" campaign from January through April 1919. The Realtor Philip N. Arnold led the coordinating committee, and from September 1918 through January, he worked with thirty-eight district directors, mostly Realtors, to make sure that "every nook and cranny" of the city would be reached by the public relations onslaught. Unsurprisingly, owing to the overwhelming role of business in the campaign, every effort was made to assure the public of the selflessness of the movement. As the official history noted in rather convoluted phraseology, "as good business men [the Realtors and bankers] would not have been guilty of the folly of conducting such a Campaign for profit." The immense public relations effort—"systematically and scientifically planned" and a "masterpiece of sequential and convincing logic on the value of home ownership"—had one sole aim: to appeal to the "great class of Philadelphians who, if they were not jarred out of their lifelong habits of thought, probably would go on from generation to generation as renters of their homes." The campaign was "purely educational—to teach the advantages of home ownership"—in other words, to save the "great class" (read: the working class) from its own patterned ignorance.[17]

Although the campaign prepared materials, available on request, that compared the costs of renting and owning, economic arguments were not central to the campaign. Rather, the focus was on moral, civic, and political virtues that flowed automatically from homeownership. Each advertisement presented a scenario of happiness attained through homeownership, many using gender to make their appeal. "How glad I am that I agreed with John when he proposed that—we 'Own Our Home'!" broadcast one ad, the fictitious happy housewife standing before her husband and son, both seated in comfortable chairs, reading. In the text of the ad, she reflected back on the "worries and discomforts that were always with us when we rented our house." She expressed amazement at how easy it was to put down four hundred dollars in cash, borrow the rest of the money, and pay it back in monthly installments. Another ad, the masculine counterpart to the first, depicted the stark image of a man in jacket and tie, his face half in the shadows: "The Man Who Owns His Home—is a better Worker, Husband, Father, Citizen, and a *real* American." The ad appeals to masculine virtue, exhorting men that it "should be a matter of personal pride to own your home. Pride—in your proved ability to give your family a home of their own. Pride—in the ownership of real property, an ownership that places you among the bigger men of your community." In an interesting oblique reference to the changing realities of the postwar world, the ad continues, "Give your wife an opportunity to show you that she can be a business woman and a loving wife and mother at the same time," ostensibly by managing her family's home.

The campaign culminated in an "Own Your Home" exposition in the Philadelphia Armory. An estimated thirty thousand visitors came to examine twenty thousand square feet of displays by manufacturers and dealers of building supplies and home appliances and furnishings. To "make the exposition attractive to the public," organizers provided musical entertainment and raffled off a small house at the end of the week. Similar local efforts were held in other cities: a particularly fascinating campaign took place in Portland, Oregon, in 1918. Also run primarily by Realtors and other business groups using similar propaganda techniques, the effort culminated in a wedding held in the living room of a model bungalow, in which a chosen couple listened to a sermon on the virtues of homeownership.[18] Religion, business, and the state made for a powerful combination, and the organizers declared the campaign a success.

Secretary Hoover and Better Homes

In 1919 the federal government scaled back its involvement in housing, dissolving the United States Housing Corporation (USHC) and selling its assets. At the same time, the Labor Department severed its connections with the Own-Your-Own-Home campaign. In 1921 the new secretary of commerce, Herbert C. Hoover, got approval to incorporate into his office the coordination of national housing policy. Hoover deeply believed in the primacy of homeownership, and his wartime experience had convinced him that the proper role for the state was to promote cooperation among private actors to bring about socially desirable ends. He founded the Division of Building and Housing (DBH) in 1921, initially to coordinate a standardization and waste-elimination campaign for the housing industry. Within a year of the founding of the DBH, Marie Meloney, editor of the mass-circulation women's magazine the *Delineator*, wrote to Hoover suggesting a cultural mobilization for "better homes in America." Meloney proposed using her magazine to activate the nation's women and other groups so as to start a true grassroots movement. Hoover perceived the movement as an ideological complement, so to speak, of the cooperative ventures he had planned among business leaders in the enormous but chaotic housing sector.

The self-proclaimed aim of Better Homes in America was to "educate the American people to higher standards of home life," and to help the population realize the "inestimable values" that "lie in the true home." Hoover realized quickly the enormous potential of mobilizing women for his cause, and he drew the movement into the nexus of the associative state. Meloney was encouraged to institutionalize the campaign and broaden its base of support—that is, to convert it from a movement into an organization. In 1923 Better Homes in America was incorporated as an educational foundation, Meloney agreed to take a more limited advisory role, and James Ford was "borrowed" from Harvard University to run the organization full time. The foundation opened a central headquarters in Washington, a block from the White House, and began producing prodigious amounts of written material, including guidebooks on organizing local Better Homes Demonstration Weeks, civic awareness, furnishing a small home, home music and home play, and how to become a homeowner, among other topics.

Better Homes Week was a huge success from its first year. In 1923 more than 1,000 demonstration houses were built. In 1926 nearly 3,000 houses were built by local committees; in 1938 there were more than 5,000. The demonstration homes aimed to enlighten the community to all modern means available to homemakers, "to show the best that each community is doing to promote and strengthen the wholesome, normal family life." The demonstration house was the focal point of the Better Homes movement, the concrete monument to the new American middle-class family, focused on combining technology and thrift to "make a sweet wholesome home life available to all."[19]

As in the Own-Your-Own-Home movement, local committees conducted campaigns their own way, although with far greater coordination during the Hoover era than in the past. Caroline Bartlett Crane, the upper-middle-class chairwoman of the Better Homes Committee in Kalamazoo, Michigan, wrote a book describing the planning and construction of her city's demonstration house, "Everyman's House." The house was awarded the first prize by the national organization in 1924. Built "around a mother and her baby," the house was "designed, built, furnished, and exhibited to nearly twenty thousand people as a modest-cost plan of comfort and convenience for a mother of several children, including a baby" and, as in most American households in the 1920s, "a mother who does all her own work." Crane was inspired to share her experience for the sake of "the thousands of people who long to build a home of their own, but fear they cannot afford to," as well as for those undecided as to the type of house they wanted.

Everyman's House exemplified "the possibilities of comfort, of convenience, and of beauty" in a "space-saving, step-saving, time-saving, money-saving small house," in the idiom of scientific household management then in vogue, "built around the mother and baby of an average American family." The home as woman's workspace, the "factory in which twenty million American women toil every day," was central to the Better Homes vision of technocratic improvement for the woman's sphere, a feminine counterpart to Hoover's myriad campaigns for standardization and elimination of waste in industry. If only the home could be standardized both as a commodity and as a site of production and consumption, Hoover envisioned savings enough to drive housing costs to levels in reach of nearly every family.[20]

Crane's story of the construction of "Everyman's House" was a parable of civic participation in which Realtors played a foundational role. The house did not "happen," but was built as a result of the "premeditated" efforts of sixty thousand people, a collective response to the "idea that nothing can prosper if the home does not prosper." The construction and furnishing of the house was a textbook example of small-town American cooperation, albeit in a medium-sized city. Virtuous "public-spirited business men" provided furnishings and supplies, Realtors procured the site, a contractor supplied labor for constructing the house, an architect drew up the plans without charging a fee, and various other local artisans (including a plumber, electrician, decorator, and landscaper) donated labor and materials.

Crane ended with a message to less affluent prospective home builders, encouraging them to persevere and build a home, even if it fell short of the ideal created by the committee. "It is curiously hard," she noted sympathetically, "to renounce perfection in a house we are about to build, even though we put up comfortably enough with recognized defects in our own persons and character. Yet we must begin by recognizing the fact that it is not always possible for people to embody the most suitable materials and the best workmanship in creating a house, any more than in creating a costume—or a physique—or a character. *We have to work with what we have to work with.*" Homes, like children, were precious enough to demand patience, compassion, and even total self-abnegation, despite the apparent physical shortcomings. It does not require too much reading between the lines to understand that Crane was referring to, and possibly commiserating with, her predominantly female readership when she added, "Compromises, painful sacrifices, even, may have to be made in order to build a home at all." The sacrifices would be worth it, however, because homes were the "roots of the future."[21] We can almost see Crane extending her gloved, feminine hand across class lines.

While national-level publications of the Better Homes movement were conspicuously silent about class, *Everyman's Home* attempted to dispose of the issue quite neatly. "And who is Everyman?" Crane asked rhetorically, noting that the reflexive answer from the newspapers and the general public was that Everyman was "the wage-earner." Crane immediately countered that Everyman's House was intended "not any more for the wage-earner than the grocer, or the photographer, or the doctor, or the lawyer." The idea that the wage earner was "in special need of our philanthropic assistance causes a smile," she noted, since such "wage-earners" as the plumber and the electrician drive cars "more expensive than that driven by the professional man who will pay them." Crane adroitly shifted the subject away from the proletarian factory worker, the focus of most discussions of the "wage earner," and toward the presumably self-employed craftsman. The plumber might have been paid on an hourly scale, but more likely than not he owned the tools of his highly skilled and well-paid trade; and in any case, he probably did not identify with the industrial proletariat. Better Homes of Kalamazoo did not intend to ignore "the difficulties and struggles of the business man and the professional man" in favor of the working class. Crane lashed out at classism, asserting, "We must never be satisfied with any scheme of things which assumes that there is any class or cross-section of our people who 'of course' cannot hope to be 'home-owners.' " She ended her defensive sermon on class by avowing "the everymans" were "about 90 percent of all of us."[22]

A particular conception of femininity suffused the publications of the Better Homes movement, one that worked to reinforce a distinct notion of taken-for-granted middle-classness. In a chapter revealingly, perhaps ironically, entitled "Occupation, None," Crane explained that it was really the home and the women's work of homemaking that made all other productive activities worthwhile, even possible. Homemaking was "*the* productive business which alone makes barns and stock and factories and mines and railroads and churches and schools and governments and all other human institutions worth anything at all." Stopping short of calling for remuneration for women's unpaid domestic labor, Crane asserted that the home should be treated as a productive enterprise, analogous to the family business, a capital investment necessary for "raising and cultivating" the family's "crop of children."[23] Here we see starkly the Hooverian conflation of ethics and efficiency, of social obligation and productivity: the home as moral economy. Hoover often included this moral economy vision in his addresses, asserting in an article in 1926 that the home was "the mold in which the character of the next generation is formed." At the same time, the home was a basic productive unit, characterized by a "primary division of labor" that "still lies within the family"—the "breadwinner who is employed outside in our vast organized economic structure and the home-maker who keeps house, prepares food, and attends to other personal wants." Hoover also noted the crucial function of the home as a site of consumption. The home "is basic in our economic system because it is the principal point at which men and women consume the final products of our farms and mines and factories."[24]

By acknowledging woman as an important economic element in the family and by extension in society, yet carefully circumscribing her productive role to the unpaid domestic sphere, this ideology served to fortify the old middle-class patriarchal ideal of the family. The "breadwinner" primarily operated "outside" and the "homemaker" inside, Hoover asserted. However, we can interpret the intensity of the Better Homes movement in part as a tacit acknowledgment of the waning cultural power of this ideal—a response not only to the housing crisis but to the gender confusion exemplified by the New Woman, as well as the class problem alluded to in Crane's quick dismissal of the "wage earner." The story of "Everyman's Home" embodied the cultural tensions of the 1920s.

Thus by the mid-1920s the dominant notion of "home" in America was a detached, single-family dwelling, which became a home not merely by virtue of habitation or character but by virtue of *ownership*. The discourse of homeownership portrayed the new middle-class homeowner as the contemporary equivalent of, in the words of one influential proponent, "the landed barons of King John . . . the squirearchy and yeomanry of England . . . [and] the makers of the American Revolution." The so-called everyman, tied to a quarter-acre plot and a 30-by-25-foot house by a mortgage, was lionized as a cousin of "the men who have preserved the civil liberties of the English-speaking peoples," men "with a stake in the soil."[25] Homeownership was equated with full membership in American society. Yet lurking beneath these texts was the stubborn fact that homeownership rates had actually remained stagnant in the first decades of the twentieth century. Universal homeownership was more mythical than real. Under Hoover the Commerce Department, working with the National Association of Real Estate Boards and other organizations, attempted in earnest to realize this promise through cooperative associationalism. With firm footing established in the Commerce Department, the Realtors were in position to work their way into the federal policy arena.

The Development of a Washington Strategy

The Realtors first came to Washington in 1917 to serve the war effort. Henry P. Haas, president of the National Association of Real Estate Boards during the early phase of the mobilization, sent a telegram to the secretary of war, Newton D. Baker, volunteering his members' expertise "in securing locations or sites for mobilization camps." Haas informed Secretary Baker: "By reason of our knowledge of properties in different localities we believe we might assist you to make proper selections. We feel that this is a time when all good citizens should do what they can for our country."[26] Haas's successor, William May Garland of Los Angeles, the first president from the West Coast, established the Realtors Washington Committee.

Numerous prominent Realtors took positions in Washington and elsewhere as dollar-a-year men, most helping to provide appraisals, negotiate transfers of property, and commandeer housing for war-related purposes. One future president of NAREB, for example, John Weaver of Washington, served during the war on a committee that "undertook the curious and unprecedented task of commandeering housing in Washington for federal purposes." The committee boasted of "returning all properties to owners without a single dispute reaching the courts," an achievement that Weaver attributed in part to the experience Realtors had accumulated mediating disputes at the local level through arbitration and ethics committees. Another future president of NAREB, Frederick Taylor of Portland, Oregon, handled the appraisal and purchase of property in Bremerton, Washington, for the U.S. Housing Corporation. Thomas Shallcross of Philadelphia, a past president of NAREB, served as an official negotiator and commandeering officer for the USHC over a territory that extended from Boston to Norfolk.

The work of the Realtors was mostly lauded. President Woodrow Wilson thanked Garland and the Realtors for their "fine spirit of unselfish co-operation." An editorial in the *Boston Transcript* noted that the national association helped the government "buy real estate without being swindled," and that "to the real estate men themselves should go the credit" not only for devising the system "to protect the Government against the rapacity of local sharks" but also "for following it with a thoroughness and loyalty which are beyond praise." The editorial acknowledged that "the professional real estate world at large" deserved credit for its "hearty cooperation" with federal officials. It was estimated that "millions of dollars were saved by the participation of Realtors of skill and integrity in the government's large scale real estate operations." Garland personally was commended at a National Affairs Banquet held in his honor by Senator Robert Owen of Oklahoma and Representative William Borland of Missouri.[27]

Of particular note among wartime collaborative efforts between Realtors and the federal government was the USHC's Real Estate Division, formed in 1917 to provide housing for workers in the defense industries. The Real Estate Division was the U.S. government's first direct intervention in the nation's housing market. Not only did the USHC construct the first federal public housing, it also experimented for the first time with a government-backed mortgage program to encourage private industry to build moderately priced housing for war workers. It promulgated rent control laws, passed in Washington and elsewhere, which endured through the early 1920s—when the courts declared that in the absence of a wartime emergency, there was no longer a constitutional basis for them.

USHC's construction projects, begun less than a year before the armistice, were never completed. Initially, the actual building was to be done through privately controlled local development companies. But USHC was unable to find sufficiently "public spirited" firms willing and able to do the job. It turned out to be simpler for USHC to plan the developments and supervise the contractors itself. At the end of the war, the federal government held the titles to over fifteen thousand houses it had built. These projects demonstrated state-of-the-art community building and architectural techniques for low-cost housing. Senator William Calder of New York sponsored legislation—strongly backed by the National Association of Real Estate Boards—to get the government out of the house-building business, and the homes were sold to private buyers. Although the federal government got out of the housing enterprise as swiftly as it had gone into it, the wartime programs had shown that the government could do the job reasonably well if need be—a lesson drawn upon in the 1930s by the "modern housing" movement.[28]

When a sharp postwar economic downturn in 1920–21 focused attention on the urban housing shortage created by wartime population movements, various proposals for remedies circulated on Capitol Hill, including revisions to the tax code and the ending of wartime rent controls. Congress held hearings in 1920 on real estate mortgage taxes. Realtors and mortgage bankers testified that the government had exacerbated the housing crisis by interfering with the workings of the market in at least two ways. First, rent control had undermined incentives to develop new rental properties in cities by nullifying the law of supply and demand. Second, by exempting war bonds and other securities from taxation, the government had unnaturally diverted investment capital out of the mortgage market. In the industry's view, the housing shortage was due largely to a lack of available mortgage funds.

The National Association of Real Estate Boards was split over the prospective role of the federal government in the housing market. At their board meeting in November 1921, leading Realtors had a particularly heated debate about the Calder Report, which called for expanding the role of the Federal

Reserve to include providing home loans, for tax-exempt bonds to establish land banks, and for tax exemptions for mortgages. Senator William Calder of New York had presented his proposal in July 1921. The national association proposed a positive form of federal "interference" in the form of tax exemptions for mortgages, while the U.S. Savings and Loan League put forth a related proposal to create a secondary mortgage market modeled on the Farm Land Bank System. In 1920 the association supported Congress in its passage of legislation enabling the mortgage interest deduction, one of its first legislative victories. The Realtors also backed the unsuccessful Calder-Nolan Bill, which called for the establishment of a Home Loan Bank patterned after the Land Bank of New York State.[29] John Weaver, the past president of NAREB, favored Calder's proposal, arguing that the proposed federal intervention would merely restore the natural working of the laws of supply and demand. J. Willison Smith of Philadelphia argued from a more Elyian point of view that the health of the real estate industry was a vital "public issue," and thus deserved special treatment in the tax code. Smith had said as much in testimony before the House Ways and Means Committee in 1920. Members of Congress, while perhaps sympathetic to the underlying sentiment, were not particularly amenable to what they saw as a federal subsidy for private enterprise. As Representative William A. Oldfield of Arkansas put it in response to Smith's request for support, "it seems that everybody's business is hurt."[30]

The debate within the national association about federal intervention devolved, interestingly, from an argument about whether working-class families would buy homes even if mortgage money were readily available, and was cast in classed and gendered terms. John Maguire of New York City, member of the board of directors of the national association, argued passionately that "working men do not want to own their own homes . . . do not want to build their own homes . . . do not want to borrow the money wherewith to build those homes." The housing shortage flowed from rent control and the high cost of labor and materials, he asserted. But Maguire really questioned whether self-respecting Realtors wanted federal help: "Do we want Federal interference . . . in the housing situation in this country?" Maguire's indignation rose as he questioned the implicit premise of unmanly dependency that he saw lurking behind proposals for federal help. If working-class men were not responsibly frugal and manly enough to work hard, save money, buy a lot, and build homes for themselves, there wasn't much the Realtors could or should do about it, Maguire implied: "Have we reached a condition where we must ask for Federal subsidy or Federal exemption, or whatever you may wish to call it, in order to get houses for the community? Now you know, and I know, we all know, that the very beginning of this great democracy was a man who was able to build his own house and own it, and he did not require anything from the Government, nor from the state, nor from the munici- pality, and I take it that if this association makes any recommendation toward Federal interference or Federal subsidy in the question of producing houses for the populace, you are going to make a very great mistake for this reason— you are going to attract Federal regulation."[31] The image that Maguire evokes, of the self-reliant man, the pioneer on the frontier hewing logs to build his own home on his own land, was a romantic nineteenth-century vision shared by the new secretary of commerce, Herbert Hoover. In his view Realtors must not advocate a policy that abetted the workingman's depen- dency by making homeownership less of a manly sacrifice. American democ- racy itself was at stake.[32]

Realtors' concerns notwithstanding, in the early 1920s members of Con- gress bent on returning to "normalcy" after wartime experimentation and a major increase in the size of government expenditures balked at the idea of further tax exemptions and far-reaching new programs. In the mid-1920s the Calder-Nolan Bill was revived and again defeated. Nevertheless, the ideas would incubate internally, and resurface during the policy debates of the early 1930s. The Realtors did not yet possess the political clout in Washington needed to turn back the tide of postwar fiscal conservatism in Congress.

Realtors were divided about maintaining an active presence in the nation's capital. From one point of view, doing so made sense because the war had increased the scope of the federal government and Washington had demon- strated its capacity for active engagement in issues of direct interest to the profession. The pre-war tax codes and the Federal Reserve Act failed to provide the same support for real estate finance as they did for other se- curities, and some Realtors argued that the national association's lack of a Washington presence was partly responsible. However, much of the leader- ship was opposed to anything "in the nature of a lobby, as undignified and not worthy of the ideals of our Boards and Association."[33]

But in 1920 the board of directors created a Division of Information, hired Robert B. Armstrong as its director, and sent him to establish an office in Washington. The bureau was to be "for information only," Armstrong told the board, and was not "in any sense a lobby." Within a year, Armstrong was fed up with Washington and recommended shutting down his post in the capital, which he saw as hopelessly corrupt and politicized. "My judgment is too many people are trying to rob the dog in Washington," Armstrong testified—presciently, in light of the recent inauguration of Warren G. Harding, whose administration would later be consumed by scandal. "I personally will not be connected with anything that looks like a lobby," he continued. "I do not think this Association will gain friends or make progress by maintaining the bureau in Washington." At root it was a question of dignity, Armstrong implied. "You will be on a par with the other two hundred and forty nine organizations, and I do not think that will be to your credit."[34]

The most ardent professionalizers saw the national association as a professional group that should remain strictly apart from the politics of policymaking. These men believed that the national association ought to extend an open offer of its expertise to the government but should refrain from attempting to influence the hopelessly debased political process. Another group believed that the Realtors, as professional *businessmen*, did their clientele (property owners) a disservice if they abstained from advocacy for policies favorable to real estate interests. They endorsed the establishment of a permanent Washington bureau with representatives who would "educate" members of Congress and relevant officials about the Realtors' point of view on issues of concern. These men in particular saw the government moving in the wrong direction, failing to act in the interests of real estate. When Herbert U. Nelson became executive secretary in 1922, those in favor of an active Realtor presence in Washington gained a reliable ally.

During the 1920s, a new approach to relations between business and government would emerge, defined by neither strict self-help individualism nor direct governmental intervention. Secretary Hoover extended to their logical extreme the ideas of Theodore Roosevelt about using the government to induce and coordinate cooperation among the leading elements in business, civic, and technical and scientific life—a sort of "administrative progressivism."[35] Hoover began a crusade for standardization and simplification, using the resources of his department to promote cooperation among trade associations, with the aim of eliminating waste in industry from the top down in order to maximize productivity and thus increase the standard of living. Deriving many of his ideas from the scientific management doctrines of Frederick Winslow Taylor, Hoover formed the Division of Simplified Practice. It aimed to bring together businessmen and engineers under the auspices of the federal government to coordinate efforts at reducing the staggering (and, it was believed, inefficient) variety of goods produced by American business. From the perspective of the strong professionalizers among the Realtors, Hoover's associationalism offered an attractively "clean" administrative answer to their qualms about the taint of corruption implicit in lobbying Congress.

Hoover quickly established a standard operating procedure. He would choose an industry that he wished to reform, convene a conference of representatives from various trade associations, and instruct his staff of efficiency experts to work with the leaders at producing an agreement on industrywide standards to be codified in a set of Simplified Practice Recommendations. Leading firms would voluntarily adhere to the guidelines, and smaller firms would find it economically unfeasible to resist. Hoover established the federal government as a standard setter by mandating that firms desiring federal contracts would have to abide by the SPRs.[36]

In addition to having an engineer's passion for maximizing efficiency, Hoover was also fervently committed to the notion that American civilization depended upon widespread homeownership. "One can always safely judge the character of a nation by its homes," he asserted in 1922. "For it is mainly through the hope of enjoying the ownership of a home that the latent energy of any citizenry is called forth. This universal yearning for better homes and the larger security, independence and freedom that they imply, was the aspiration that carried our pioneers westward."[37] Hoover was quite concerned that the nation, and specifically the real estate industry, was not doing all it could to realize this "universal yearning." Very early in his tenure as secretary of commerce, Hoover petitioned and won backing from President Harding for a $50,000 appropriation to set up the Division of Building and Housing. Hoover called on John M. Gries, a housing specialist from the Harvard Business School, to head the new division. He called for a voluntaristic, yet efficiently coordinated response to the postwar housing shortage. Hoover initially perceived the cause of the shortage to be a decentralized and disorganized industry, incapable of meeting its *obligation* to provide American society with suitable shelter at a reasonable cost. Viscerally opposed to statist solutions, Hoover preferred to use the resources of his office to establish a cooperative program of modernization to lower construction costs by achieving economies of scale through standardization. To Hoover, business (no less than government) had social obligations at least equal to its selfish concerns. The real estate business, in Hoover's view, had a particularly vital social role to play.

From the beginning Hoover realized that the National Association of Real Estate Boards could be either a vital ally or a major obstacle in the crusade to combine his most important causes, elimination of waste and the promotion of homeownership. In his keynote address before nearly five thousand delegates to the annual convention in Chicago in July 1921, he expressed his pleasure with the professionalizing trend in the field. "I view with great satisfaction the real estate men from all parts of the United States endeavoring as they are to codify the practice and elevate the ideals of the profession." It was up to Realtors to "bring[] the home within the purchasing power" of consumers. "Is it not a great mission for your association," Hoover inquired, "to provide the assurance of the million new homes needed by our people?" The secretary acknowledged the "most far-reaching" influence of the Realtors, and the potential for the national association to become "a great moral as well as a business force in the nation." He urged the Realtors to rise to the challenge of their obligations, particularly that of "protect[ing] the homes which they have sold from encroachment," by helping to pass zoning and planning laws, and protecting the equity of the homeowner by keeping fees, commissions, and bonuses to a reasonable level. "I know of no greater mission for the whole of the realtors," Hoover concluded, "than that they should definitely undertake to organize in each local community the forces that bear on this problem for its constructive solution." Hoover urged the Realtors to use their well-developed organization to help marshal the forces that would ameliorate the housing crisis.[38]

The Realtors reacted with thunderous applause, consummating a warm relationship. Representatives of the Commerce Department regularly attended meetings of the national association. Correspondence flowed steadily between the national association and the Department. Commerce staff often submitted articles to the *National Real Estate Journal*, beginning with John Gries's piece in November 1922, "The Home Buyer and His Problems." The Realtors also become active promoters of the Better Homes movement. The department regularly called on the expertise of Realtors, particularly after Nelson reorganized the association into functional divisions in 1923, which Gries hailed as an "unquestionable" step toward a "greater sense of responsibility to the public" on the part of the Realtors.[39]

However, of all the industries that Hoover attempted to organize, housing was perhaps the most daunting. How could economies of scale be realized in a field in which the average producer built but a few houses a year, a field dominated by very small, localistic enterprises, in which even among the biggest high-class subdividers like J. C. Nichols there was not even a rough facsimile of a Henry Ford? How could a commodity that was defined in part by its uniqueness be standardized?

True to form, Hoover proposed a housing conference in 1922 to deal with two aspects of the housing problem, financing and standardization. He delineated the problem for President Harding: "We have mobilized the commercial capital of the country through the Federal Reserve Banks. We have mobilized the farm mortgage capital through the Farm Loan Bureau . . . The country badly needs a mobilization of the home building capital based upon our building and loan associations, insurance companies, and savings banks."[40] The administrative methods that were Hoover's stock in trade might work well for attacking the problem of standardization in construction, but the financial problems would prove far more complex. Bringing order to the sprawling and chaotic American banking system would require more than voluntary agreements on standards. However, Harding did not give approval for the conference; it would not be held for nearly a decade, until 1931—after the real estate industry had collapsed, partly because of structural weaknesses in the system of real estate finance.

Despite the lack of a master plan, Hoover's Division of Building and Housing began its work in earnest to develop standards at the local level. Gries organized a series of "advisory committees" to devise and publicize model building codes, standardized contract specifications, and better zoning laws. The zoning initiative produced a primer, and a plan of action for local civic groups to use in mobilizing forces to pass zoning laws. Zoning spread rapidly in the 1920s, and many municipalities cribbed their ordinances directly from the primer. Hoover attributed the success of the zoning initiative largely to the widespread exposure it received from organizations that distributed the zoning primer, including the American Institute of Architects, the American Civic Association, Better Homes for America, and the National Association of Real Estate Boards.[41]

The national association had come of age by 1923 as a "legitimate trade association," an important element in Hoover's overall scheme of business-government cooperation. The leadership of the national association was clearly pleased with the enhanced reputation that was sure to result from its connection with the revered secretary of commerce. In a letter to local real estate board secretaries that accompanied packages of zoning primers, Don Goss, NAREB's publicity director, nervously announced that this was "by far the most important publicity ever released from this office and should be handled with great care." Goss requested that board secretaries use their contacts among real estate editors to publicize the zoning standards in the local press.[42]

However, there was articulate dissent on the zoning issue within the ranks of Realtors. The leadership of many local boards was caught between pressure from national headquarters to take an official position in favor of zoning and the need to maintain cordial relations within the board among pro- and anti-zoning factions. In Philadelphia, for example, an acrimonious propaganda battle ensued between several prominent zoning opponents, including Albert Greenfield, and the leadership and old guard of the Philadelphia Real Estate Board, most of whom favored zoning. The opponents managed to prevent the leadership of the board, which generally favored zoning, from officially endorsing a state enabling act, a factor that contributed to the long struggle for zoning both in Philadelphia and statewide.[43]

The Zoning Advisory Committee provides an object lesson in the ways in which Hooverite associationalism drew the Realtors into a nexus of organizations that made policy in the 1920s. The committee, which operated from 1921 to 1934, brought together a number of men who had previously worked together at the USHC and other wartime agencies. It comprised a veritable Who's Who in the planning and housing fields: Lawrence Veiller of the National Housing Association; the eminent landscape architect and planner Frederick Law Olmstead; J. Horace McFarland of the American Civic Association; Nelson P. Lewis of the National Conference on City Planning; Morris Knowles and John Ihlder of the Chamber of Commerce of the United States; Edward M. Basset, counsel of the Zoning Committee of New York; and Irving B. Hiett, president of the National Association of Real Estate Boards for 1921–22. These men all shared a belief in zoning as a means to achieve urban order, so as to prevent and correct the "stupid, wasteful jumble" that unregulated building had wrought. It was, in the words of the *Zoning Primer*, "the application of common sense and fairness to public regulations governing the use of private real estate. It is a painstaking, honest effort to provide each district or neighborhood, as nearly as practicable, with *just such protection* and *just such liberty* as are sensible in *that particular district*." One committee

member, John Ihlder, summed up the perfectly Hooverian—or Elyian—
balance between social control and individual property rights that zoning
represented. At the same time, the coordinated, cooperative methods used to
promote zoning also exemplified Hooverite ideology.

By the mid-1920s the national association was therefore embedded in the
associational state, and the associational state had made its impact on the
Realtors. The organization had imbibed fully the Hooverite spirit. This was
reflected in the *National Real Estate Journal*, in articles about standardizing
practices for title closings and standardizing forms. Realtors wrote about the
"great sifting process" of "discarding practices that are useless" and about
"attaining uniformity," about using stopwatches to increase income on business property, about standard tests for real estate. Stories were told of Realtors
who succeeded through "amazing" feats of organization. Writers advised the
salesman to create a personal time evaluation system, because "time is his
capital." In an address on real estate organization in 1925, the president of the
national association, Charles G. Edwards, recapitulated the associational vision, writ small. "Each type of real estate organization," national, state, and
local, "has its function to perform in the big plan." The national association,
he asserted, was a "clearinghouse," the "instrument through which we formulate our broad national policies," and a "mechanism by which we can
organize and launch" national campaigns. The cornerstone of the entire
edifice was of course the local real estate board, the "chief instrument
through which we hope to accomplish our aims."[44]

In fact, the true cornerstone of the Realtors' growing influence was the
organizational structure that Herbert Nelson had devised in 1923. The functional divisions both attracted and created cadres of expert policy advocates, a
ready pool to be drawn upon by the federal government and by the association itself for promotional and lobbying efforts. Of particular importance to
policy issues were the divisions on mortgage and finance and for home
builders and subdividers. The latter division worked with the American Institute of City Planning and the National City Planning Conference at the
request of the Commerce Department to devise controls on community
building, particularly on the edges of urban areas. The Realtors invited the
city planners to their annual convention in 1925, and as the Florida land boom
was reaching its frenetic peak, the Realtors and planners established a Committee on Subdivision Control. Irenaeus Shuler, head of the Subdividers Division and chairman of the new committee, conducted a study for the national

association on subdividing activity in a score of cities and concluded that uniform planning standards were needed, on a regional level, particularly with regard to arranging street layouts. It took nearly two years for the Realtors and the planners to agree on the details. Among other things, they disagreed on whether developers ought to be required to donate land for parks or rather should merely be encouraged. In the end, however, the joint statement of principles promulgated in 1927 was, according to one historian, "so influential that it formed the basis" of the Commerce Department's Standard City Planning Enabling Act, a landmark guide that affected state and local planning for decades.[45]

A final nexus between the Realtors and federal policymaking emanated from Richard T. Ely and the Institute for Research in Land Economics. Research by Ely and the numerous land economists he trained made lasting and important contributions to national housing policy, particularly in institutionalizing his "homeownership vision" through mortgage insurance during the New Deal.[46] The influence of the "dean of American economists"—as Herb Nelson often referred to Ely—was profound, both on the Realtors and on the administrative apparatus responsible for land use policy, broadly construed, at the national and state levels. Ely's student Ernest M. Fisher was the first director of the national association's Department of Education and Research from 1923 to 1926, resigning from that post to join the faculty of the University of Michigan, where he occupied the first full-time professorship in real estate at an American university. In 1935 Fisher was hired as the director of the Economics and Statistics Division of the Federal Housing Administration. Frederick A. Babcock, whom Fisher and Ely had commissioned to write a text in real estate appraisal in the mid-1920s, became head of the FHA's Underwriting Division. Babcock wrote the FHA's influential *Underwriting Manual*, infamous later because of its impact on residential segregation by race and ethnicity. Arthur J. Mertzke, another Ely student, replaced Fisher at the national association and later worked for the Committee on Finance during President Hoover's Conference on Home Building and Home Ownership in 1931. Coleman Woodbury, a scholar at the institute, went on to become executive director of the National Association of Housing Officials, a spinoff of NAREB, in the 1930s, and an administrator of the National Housing Agency in the 1940s. H. Morton Bodfish, also affiliated with the institute in the late 1920s, was head of the Society of Residential Appraisers, chief executive of the United States Savings and Loan League, and a member of the original Federal

Home Loan Bank Board appointed by President Hoover. The city planner Harland Bartholomew did a stint at the institute and consulting work for the National Association of Real Estate Boards, and headed the influential Committee on Subdivision Layout at the President's Conference.[47] Thus by the beginning of the 1930s, the Realtors were well positioned in Washington, poised to take advantage of the crisis brought on by the deepening Depression. The logic of their professional project had almost inexorably interjected their ideas and personnel into the policymaking process.

Commodifying the Home

The combined cultural campaign of the Better Homes in America movement and the relative standardization of practices brought about through cooperation achieved its goal of building more houses and made the home a bona fide consumer good in the 1920s. Americans began to treat mortgage debt much the same way as they treated other forms of consumer debt. In retrospect, of course, this was unfortunate, as the instability of the mortgage lending market contributed heavily to the collapse of the banking system in the early 1930s. Pent-up wartime demand, the massive movement of people during and after the war, and an acknowledged housing shortage in the immediate postwar period all contributed to the building and borrowing frenzy, which came to an abrupt halt in the early 1930s. It would be nearly two decades before such prolific residential construction activity would resume, spurred again by the lifting of wartime restrictions, but under the very different structural conditions of New Deal housing programs. The Federal Housing Administration and the Home Owners Loan Corporation essentially made it safe for real estate developers to build speculatively, but FHA rules ensured that ventures were more or less feasible.

The Great Depression profoundly called into question the Realtors' accomplishments in the 1920s. The structural changes implemented to the field of real estate practice and the concerted efforts made to establish what the Realtors perceived to be sound public policy in real estate were not nearly enough to prevent the speculative fervor that provided the conditions for the Depression's severity. In failing to fully professionalize—that is, to organize the entire field around a coherent doctrine of land utilization and ethical real estate brokerage and development practices—or to purge short-term speculative builders from their ranks, the Realtors were forced to accept some culpability for the Depression.

Nevertheless, when Hoover became president, with the Depression looming, he turned to the National Association of Real Estate Boards and their allies for help in solving the housing crisis. The White House Conference on Home Building and Home Ownership, at which the national association had a strong presence, set the parameters for governmental intervention in the American housing market. Although Hoover's voluntaristic associationalism could not stem the Depression, the Roosevelt administration picked up more or less where Hoover had left off, using the strong New Deal state to solve the real estate industry's collective-action problems. Thus, the central thrust of New Deal housing policy bore the distinct stamp of the Realtors, particularly the community builders who led the association in the 1920s.

As Gail Radford has argued, a "small political space" was opened by the collapse of the real estate market in the late 1920s and 1930s for "people committed to a new kind" of "modern" American housing. But to stretch her metaphor, it was a very low-value piece of property in the midst of a large and lucrative subdivision already owned and occupied by the Realtors. While the Realtors were committed to traditional forms of American housing, they certainly were not opposed to pursuing novel forms of federal intervention in the private housing market. The foundation that the national association laid in the 1920s, particularly its associations with Ely and his numerous students and Herbert Hoover's Department of Commerce, combined with the limits of cultural possibility with respect to housing that the Realtors, among others, helped to establish in the years following the First World War, virtually overdetermined the outcome of the policy struggles of the 1930s in favor of the single-family home and in opposition to high-density housing along European lines.[48] The Realtors would play a central role both in organizing federal housing policy to favor the private sector and in opposing attempts to develop more robust public-sector approaches to low-income housing. In both aspects of this effort, the Realtors mobilized their cultural authority as professionals and defenders of middle-class values.

Chastened by their failure to stave off the housing crash, the strong professionalizers in the national association nevertheless continued to pursue their agenda. Paradoxically, the Depression provided conditions quite conducive to the implementation of their program, albeit through the instrumentality of the state rather than the profession's disciplinary mechanisms. The national association's profession-building and political work during the 1920s paid off. Realtors, along with Elyian land economists, became key figures in formulating the land use policies of both the Hoover and the Roosevelt administrations. In a sense, the Depression made it possible for the Realtors to accomplish, through federal policymaking, what they could not achieve voluntaristically: disciplining brokers into behaving more or less professionally. At the same time, however, some of the Realtors' more pernicious ideas, such as the belief that market value was contingent upon the racial and ethnic homogeneity of neighborhoods, were written into federal policies with social implications down to the present day. The Realtors also used the wartime emergency to solve their own collective-action problems, and in the long run this was propitious for the national association. After the Depression, the proportion of brokers belonging to the organization increased markedly. The "homeownership vision" promoted by the Realtors, Richard T. Ely, and Herbert C. Hoover became the centerpiece of American housing policy in the 1930s and beyond, while the modern housing vision was relegated to the margins.

Hoover's Housing Conference

By the beginning of 1930 the Realtors were beginning to admit the need for significant federal intervention in the housing market. Even the normally sanguine president of the national association, Leonard Reaume, was willing to acknowledge the existence of a housing problem, telling a National Building Survey Conference, "Our industry is not wholly prosperous."[49] Herbert Nelson sent a short note to Walter H. Newton, an old acquaintance from Minneapolis who had served in Congress and in 1930 was working as President Herbert Hoover's personal secretary. The note was attached to a copy of a long letter from Nelson to Julius Barnes, president of the U.S. Chamber of Commerce, which offered Nelson's analysis of the decline in real estate activity. Nelson called on the chamber to join the Realtors in attacking the "primary cause" of the housing problem: the high costs of real estate construction and finance. "I am told," Nelson wrote, "that the average income in the United States for 85 per cent of its people is $2,000 a year or less." A "very modest modern home" in a major urban area costs at least $7,000, and the costs of financing and taxes entailed an annual expenditure for homeownership of about $1,000. "It is not remarkable that people cannot buy or build their homes as they used to, or keep them if they do."[50]

With housing starts plummeting and the economy going into free fall, Hoover finally announced a White House Conference on Home Building and Home Ownership, to be held in December 1931—at least five years too late for it to have any immediate impact on the real estate market. The Realtors were hopeful that a consensus would emerge from the conference reflecting their preference for federal intervention in the area of home financing, rather than more radical involvement along the lines of wartime government-built housing, as advocated by some proponents of "modern housing" after the European model. As the starting date of the conference approached, economic conditions worsened. Foreclosures increased rapidly and housing starts continued to plunge, falling below 300,000 for the first time since 1920. Housing prices declined as much as 30 percent from their values in 1926, wiping out the embodied savings of millions of middle-income families.[51] Hoover addressed the opening session of the conference on 2 December 1931 with words intended to ease anxieties among the assembled leaders of business and civic life, yet aimed at keeping the delegates focused on long-term, structural solutions to the problem. Acknowledging the "emergency," he swiftly emphasized that the purpose of the conference was to "consider [the matter of housing] in its long view." He asserted that "the sentiment for homeownership is so embedded in the American heart that millions of people who dwell in tenements, apartments, and rented rows of solid brick have the aspiration for wider opportunity in ownership of their own homes." As if to keep his audience convinced, he repeated the assertion several times throughout his two-thousand-word address.[52]

Hoover's goal for the conference, shared by the Realtors, was not to "set up government in the building of homes" but to "stimulate individual endeavor and make community conditions propitious" for the resumption of home building by private enterprise. The means he proposed were his stock in trade: to "coordinate the national intelligence," to devise means for achieving maximum savings from maximum efficiency and thus to "stimulate individual action" rather than legislation. The conference did not entertain emergency solutions along the lines of wartime construction of homes with public funds. But local lending institutions had demonstrated their inability to create favorable conditions for reviving home building. Housing was a core sector of the economy, and its decline had major ripple effects: thus the massive wave of foreclosures sweeping the country presented a massive problem in need of a swift solution.

The Realtors had long called for a system of home loan discount banks that would provide similar mobility for mortgage capital as the Federal Reserve provided for commercial transactions, the agricultural banks for farm credits, and the stock exchanges for industrial credit. Surely, Hoover opined with some disdain, in a nation that had "established [credit] mobility for the sale of automobiles and radio sets and fur coats on the installment plan, where 20 and 25 per cent cash payments are gratefully accepted," some way could be found to finance homeownership on similar terms. "Our chief problem in finances," he continued, "relates to those who have an earnest desire for a home, who have a job and therefore possess sound character credit, but whose initial resources run only 20 or 25 per cent." Clearly, left to its own devices the private sector had not yet been able to accommodate the needs of the average family. His goal was to "make a home available for installment purchase on terms that dignify the name credit," rather than through the unsavory, loan shark–like aspects of the junior mortgage market.

The conference's final recommendations comprised much of the Realtors' long-standing agenda. First, on the financial front, the conference endorsed the creation of a federal mortgage discount bank to facilitate the widespread use of amortized, long-term mortgages, and the reduction of taxes on real estate. Seven months later, the Federal Home Loan Bank Act would create a federally coordinated network of mortgage lenders with a common credit pool and uniform lending standards. Though the law adopted during Hoover's presidency was gravely flawed and ineffective—it granted loans only in very low-risk situations and contained no provision for bailing out foreclosed homeowners—it nevertheless represented a critical turning point in the policy debate. After 1932 it was no longer a matter of whether the federal government had a role in home finance, but what it should be.[53]

Second, and crucial for understanding the form of the American landscape in the long run, the conference sanctioned the "neighborhood unit" principle of subdividing, an idea long promoted by the Subdividers Division of the National Association of Real Estate Boards. The Conference's Committee on Subdivision Layout aimed to replace piecemeal speculation in land with stable community development, an unsurprising recommendation given that the committee chairman, the city planner Harland Bartholomew, often served as a consultant to the national association, and that the majority of the members were large-scale community builders and members of the strong professional faction among the Realtors. The conference explicitly approved "large-scale housing operations" to take advantage of economies of scale. This recommendation would be incorporated into the policies of the Federal Housing Administration, thereby giving favored status to large planned developments for securing government-backed financing. The era of the tract-home development was dawning.[54]

Third, the conference reiterated the Realtors', and Hoover's, long-standing support for zoning and city planning, and the desire to ensure well-built houses irrespective of family income by devising rigorous building codes. Fourth, in the controversial area of "slum clearance," the conference agreed with the Realtors that the government could play a role, "unless the problem can be met by private enterprise." This provision led to the creation of the Reconstruction Finance Corporation and to controversial policies of neighborhood demolition and rebuilding "in accordance with its best usefulness to the community"—often narrowly construed. Finally, the conference called for the development of research and educational services, in order to crystallize and expand public support for the "promotion of home ownership and better homes." In his concluding remarks, Ray Lyman Wilbur, secretary of the interior and a conference co-chairman, reiterated the master theme of the Hoover era's approach to housing: that the promotion of homeownership was "the prerogative of all civic leaders and of citizens."

The Realtors were quite pleased with the outcome of the conference. Edward MacDougall of New York, who had served on the City Planning and Zoning Committee, reported proudly to the national association's midwinter board meeting in January 1932 that the proposal for home loan banks to "nationalize first mortgages"—the conference's "high spot"—was based on the Realtors' "definite and specific recommendations."[55] The Realtors' organizational, political, and cultural work of the 1920s had materialized in a set of influential recommendations that would establish the parameters for American housing policy for generations to come. While the actual policy changes implemented under Hoover were undoubtedly too timid and came too late in the crisis to make much of an impact on the housing market in the deepening Depression, they established the ideological and political parameters for the much more ambitious programs of Roosevelt's New Deal.

New Deal Housing Policy: Hooverism + The State

The leadership of the National Association of Real Estate Boards waxed enthusiastic about the Roosevelt administration's housing program in the first hundred days—not surprisingly, since it incorporated the key elements of their own agenda. The Realtors' successes in the policy arena augmented their own authority as middle-class professionals at the same time as they embedded a particular notion of home into the fabric of the political economy. "Real estate is on the way up," declared the association's president, William C. Miller, a few days after the creation of the Home Owners Loan Corporation (HOLC). The Realtors found Roosevelt's strident pro-homeownership rhetoric particularly heartening. Excerpts from FDR's speeches peppered the pages of the *National Real Estate Journal* in the first months of the new administration. Introducing the HOLC legislation, Roosevelt had proclaimed to Congress, "The broad interests of the Nation require that special safeguards should be thrown around home ownership as a guaranty of social and economic stability, and that to protect home owners from inequitable forced liquidation, in a time of general distress, is a proper concern of the government."[56] From the beginning, Roosevelt was as committed to homeownership in word and in deed as was his predecessor.

The Realtors welcomed the FHA, despite the massive government presence that it assured in the real estate market, both because it promised greatly enhanced general demand for housing and because the agency was run largely by Realtors and their allies in the banking world. The FHA more or less solved the collective-action problem that had plagued real estate since the first stirrings of professionalization in the 1890s. For one, it was a major victory for the large-scale community builders, some of the most strident professionalizers among the Realtors. Drawn almost directly from recommendations of the Subdivision Layout Committee of Hoover's conference of 1931, the FHA's *Operative Builders Guide* stated flatly that the government sought to "encourage the type of builder who . . . assumes responsibility for [the production of homes,] from the plotting and development of the land to the disposal of the completed dwelling unit." To make this goal concrete, FHA devised a "conditional commitment" that promised to underwrite mortgages for buyers in developments meeting the agency's standards. With the FHA seal of approval on a plan, a developer could readily obtain financing and rest assured that the homes would sell. FHA underwriting had many strings attached, but they were conditions that large, vertically integrated operative builders had long desired.[57] FHA underwriting rules essentially enshrined in federal policy the proposals long advocated by the Realtors' Home Builders and Subdividers and Mortgage and Finance Committees.

The impact on the housing market was immediate and profound. Housing starts jumped 40 percent in 1934, 70 percent in 1935, and 50 percent in 1936, when a nearly normal long-cycle annual rate of 300,000 was again achieved. Except for the wartime building freeze in 1942–45, housing starts would never again fall below 300,000 per annum.[58] By imposing exacting standards for approval, the FHA reinstilled confidence in real estate development among lenders. At the same time, the FHA's clear biases toward "privately controlled and coordinated development of whole residential communities," composed of mainly single-family housing on low-cost land on the periphery of cities, shaped the American landscape to a degree that is difficult to overstate. On the one hand, the FHA reduced the costs of building and financing, making possible a huge expansion in homeownership, particularly for families of moderate income. The FHA raised construction standards greatly—again, especially at the lower end of the economic scale. On the other hand, the FHA's policies of favoring low-cost land and new construction over rehabilitation undoubtedly contributed to the decline of cities and massive migration to new suburban subdivisions.

On a more subtle cultural level, the agency's aesthetic agenda in its formative years—informed by the Better Homes ideal of the modest bungalow on a standard-sized tract of land, each house set back from the street by a standard distance—effectively abolished a wide range of housing and neighborhood forms, thereby overdetermining the monotonous post-Depression landscape of the American suburbs—the quintessence of middle-class America. Statistics on housing starts, disaggregated by type of structure, demonstrate the impact vividly: from 1900 to 1933, 66 percent of new private nonfarm residences built were single-family houses. From 1934 to 1953, single-family houses constituted nearly 84 percent of new dwelling units built.[59] The Realtors shaped the policy agenda, the built landscape, and metropolitan racial geography. In short, they helped level the class distinctions embedded in architecture at the same time as they helped ensure residential segregation by race. The Realtors' political work in shaping federal housing policy would effectively create a broad new white middle-class haven in the suburbs, while leaving behind the upper class and the poor in cities increasingly polarized by race and wealth.

As the federal government reoriented housing policy according to the Realtors' agenda, the "modern housing" movement struggled for survival. A variety of public works housing projects were proposed, and a few were actually built. The Greentown Program, run by Rexford Tugwell's Resettlement Administration, was perhaps the best known.[60] In 1937 a much more extensive and enduring public housing sector was created in the form of the U.S. Housing Authority, but it too was circumscribed by the new consensus. The modern housing proponent Catherine Bauer helped craft the legislation that created the agency, the stated purpose of which was "to construct, and aid in the construction, of modern large-scale housing, available to those families who in good as well as bad times cannot afford to pay the price which will induce the ordinary and usual channels of private enterprise to build such housing." The proposed legislation aimed to give USHA a mandate to build directly, as well as to make loans and grants to local housing agencies or noncommercial, nongovernmental housing organizations. To avoid politicization, USHA was to be funded by bonds rather than by direct congressional appropriation. As initially submitted, the bill creating the USHA embodied the modern housing advocates' ideas about high-density development, about housing as a public good, and about the absolute value of energetic participation on the part of residents in the governance of federally funded housing.

The Realtors and other business groups, empowered by the victory for their point of view represented by the FHA, lobbied vigorously against the bill. In the end, the bill was eviscerated, its more radical elements removed. Limits on unit costs written into the final legislation were particularly ruinous to the aims of the modern housing movement to develop new architectural models for urban residences. The resulting Wagner Housing Act, named after the senator from New York who became the bill's chief sponsor, established a means-tested housing program intended essentially as a stop-gap: a measure to provide cheaply built housing for people assumed to be temporarily incapable, but ultimately desirous, of partaking in the American dream of home-ownership.[61]

Real Estate and the Second World War

The mobilization for war that began in 1940 dramatically affected the real estate market in most major cities. The massive influx of defense workers increased demand for housing, and severe shortages led to calls for federal intervention. Public housing advocates struggled with real estate groups over the type of housing to be provided and the means to be used. The advocates perceived the war as an opportunity to revisit the policy struggles of the New Deal, a second chance to use the power of the federal government in a national emergency to reconfigure the housing market. Some of them, such as Nathan Straus, head of the U.S. Housing Authority, saw a historic possibility to expand his agency's mission of providing decent and affordable housing to poor urbanites. Straus and others wanted to take advantage of the war to build permanent low-income communities that would endure beyond the emergency.

But the public housing movement's agenda met with fierce opposition, not only from predictable quarters such as the national association, which had long articulated its opposition to government-built housing as socialistic, but also from important leaders in Congress and the president himself. Roosevelt's deep belief in the value of homeownership led him to choose administrators for the defense housing program accordingly. To coordinate the provision of shelter for war workers, Roosevelt chose Charles F. Palmer, a Realtor from Atlanta with a record of public-private cooperation. Though considerably more progressive than most developers, particularly on issues like race, Palmer was no radical, and he stuck diligently to Roosevelt's mandate to use the federal government for coordinating private initiative and for supplementing private construction only if absolutely necessary. In sum, Roosevelt aimed to use the basic New Deal policy framework of government aid for private enterprise to handle defense housing.

Following the pattern established during the First World War, many Realtors became involved in the administration of federal property issues on the local level. When the government sent three thousand federal employees to Philadelphia, the Philadelphia Real Estate Board was asked to help find them housing. The rapid migration of defense workers into industrial cities created enormous demand for housing, and the large number of African American workers led to some particularly nasty racial tensions, revolving largely around housing. Serious race riots rocked Detroit in 1942 as black families moved into the Sojourner Truth public housing project, foreshadowing the deadly riots of the summer of 1943.[62] Because of both the seemingly intractable problem of racial prejudice and cost concerns, Palmer chose to build housing for black workers on vacant land at the urban fringe rather than attempt to insert blacks into existing inner-city neighborhoods. Because racial segregation in housing was the norm in the United States, reinforced by the Federal Housing Administration's redlining policies, and because the American federal system of government left most decisions in the hands of local housing authorities, racial segregation was actually exacerbated by wartime housing programs. Nevertheless, the degree of segregation in public housing projects declined significantly, from two-thirds before the war to 42 percent during the war.[63]

Palmer resisted the public housing lobby's arguments about the need for the federal government to build low-income communities that would endure after the war, declaring that "sociology was no part" of his job. This brought him into direct conflict with Straus of the USHA, for whom Palmer's decision to rely on private builders for defense construction was a sign that the survival of public housing in the postwar period was at stake. In a sense, Straus and Palmer talked past each other: Palmer remained tightly focused on the specific task of providing defense housing expeditiously and inexpensively, while Straus was more concerned with the impact of wartime building on postwar housing. Straus and the public housing lobby were at a disadvantage to begin with, however, since President Roosevelt and most of his key advisers favored homeownership over public housing.[64] The lack of clear bureaucratic control over defense housing at the national level was compounded by the American tradition of delegating tasks to local agencies, where business forces could exercise greater influence. Thus wartime housing policies only reinforced the American approach to housing: public subsidy for private enterprise, biases toward homeownership, more deeply entrenched social conventions like racial segregation.

At the end of the war, federal subsidies for rental dwellings under the Federal Emergency Housing Act were scaled back, and insurance programs for mortgages on single-family homes were greatly expanded under the G.I. Bill. The impact of this abrupt change was profound. William Levitt, later known for his large-scale developments, cut his teeth during the Second World War building single-family homes for rent in Norfolk, Virginia, using new construction technologies like prefabricated wall panels and a modified assembly line. After the war, Levitt purchased a potato farm on Long Island in New York, intending to use the techniques that his firm had perfected during the war to build a large number of single-family homes as rental units. However, federal loan guarantees for veterans made it far more profitable to build homes for owner occupancy. By the end of the war, federal policy was thus even more biased against rental housing than it had been before. Unsurprisingly, single-family, owner-occupied dwellings dominated the massive postwar building boom, continuing the trend established in the 1930s on a far greater scale.[65]

The Realtors' political and cultural work in the 1920s and 1930s created national housing policy that privileged suburban sprawl, middle-class privatization of social space, and racial segregation. In the process of shaping policy, the Realtors augmented their professional identity and authority, rooted in public, masculine spheres of public policy and expertise. Yet as numerous real estate men left their hometowns to join the war effort either on the front lines or as dollar-a-year men, a cadre of women brokers emerged to fill the vacuum. Ironically, the proliferating suburban domesticity that real estate men had brought to fruition in the 1940s and beyond created tremendous, unanticipated opportunities for women in real estate brokerage. The rise of "Rosie the Realtor" would pose implicit and explicit challenges both to the Realtors' masculine professionalism and to broader cultural and social definitions of middle-class identity.[66]

CHAPTER SIX

"Rosie the Realtor" and the
Re-Gendering of Real Estate
Brokerage, 1938–1950

The man customer likes to deal with a woman in real estate for several reasons. If he has a wife, or female relatives, he assumes that a woman will know better what they would like. Then, once he's made your acquaintance, he's amazed and delighted to find someone who can handle business like a man, and still make him feel like a superior being.

—Mary Amelia Warren, Realtor, 1941[1]

"Stay out of real estate," one of the town's leading citizens advised Laura Hale Gorton. "If there was a living in it, I'm quite certain that a man would have tried it years ago!" The world seemed pretty gloomy to Gorton in 1931, and this admonition undoubtedly provided no consolation. Recently widowed, supporting two young daughters and a large home with a mortgage, she possessed no special training yet had to earn a living for her family. Intrepidly ignoring the warning, Gorton acquired a real estate license and opened an office in Glastonbury, Connecticut. She figured: "[I would] sell that which I know best and believe in—my community" to people "seeking a home in the country and a pleasant neighborhood in which to bring up their children." In 1952 she handed over the business to her nephew, and in retirement she looked "with deep satisfaction" on "hundreds of homes, miles of streets winding through hills and a booming shopping center," a "monument to her vision and courage."[2] In her twenty-plus years in real estate, Gorton was not only financially successful but was also an institution builder. She was among the earliest members of the Women's Council of the National Association of Real Estate Boards, founded in 1938 by the leadership of the national association to help women brokers establish firm footing in the profession. Gorton became president of the Women's Council in 1948. She also served on the Realtors Washington Committee in 1949, playing a leading role in the effort of women Realtors to use their position as businesswomen to brand public housing as a "socialistic" affront to true American family values.

Like many women in her field, and in business in general, Laura Hale Gorton had entered the working world after losing her husband. While Gorton was typical of women entering the real estate field in the 1920s and 1930s, real estate women contrasted sharply with the mainstream of the female labor force. In 1930, 45 percent of the thirty thousand women in real estate were married, 39 percent were widowed or divorced, and 16 percent were single. In contrast, less than 26 percent of the overall white female workforce was married in 1930, nearly 60 percent was single, and 15 percent was widowed or divorced. In terms of age distribution, real estate women were also atypical: at forty-five, Gorton was fifteen years older than the average female worker. Nearly 70 percent of women in real estate in 1940 were forty-four years old or older, compared with less than 25 percent in the labor force as a whole.[3] In short, women in real estate in the 1930s and 1940s looked much like the female labor force as a whole in the 1960s and beyond. To explore the rise of "Rosie the Realtor" is therefore to investigate the history of middle-class femininity in the middle of the twentieth century.[4]

Gender Trouble on the Home Selling Front

The movement to professionalize real estate brokerage through the early 1920s was almost entirely a male affair, and not surprisingly, it drew upon traditionally masculine professional models. While the U.S. Census counted about three thousand women brokers in 1910, about 2 percent of the total, very few of them belonged to local real estate boards; the New York Real Estate Board, for example, counted about ten women members in 1920, about 1 percent of the total membership.[5] Until the early 1920s, women as brokers were virtually unmentioned in the archival or published records of the national association; interestingly, however, Sinclair Lewis presciently anticipated the first major wave of women entering the field in his novel *The Job*, which featured a woman real estate broker as its central character. As we have seen, the zenith of the Realtors' attempts to scientize the occupation occurred in the 1920s, at precisely the same moment as this first female wave was cresting. If the scientization efforts had something to do with protecting masculinity from the female incursion, male brokers rarely invoked technical language in defense of the masculine professional world they had created. The Realtors' attempt at scientization was part and parcel of a national trend in the 1920s.

In any case, there was a very prosaic gender tension at the heart of the field of real estate brokerage. Try as real estate men might to present their calling as manly and heroic, there was no denying that the primary commodity they sold, the family home, was considered "woman's place" in the early twentieth century. The home had emerged as an object of scientific knowledge at the end of the nineteenth century, underpinning claims for professionalization in a wide range of fields including social work, home economics, and housing reform, as well as real estate brokerage. But these professions, centered as they were on the home, were by and large marked feminine.[6] Thus from the outset, discourses of masculinity were a problematic source of cultural support for the professionalization of real estate brokerage.

As women streamed into the real estate field, first in the 1920s and then again in the 1940s, barely suppressed gender tensions bubbled to the surface. Women entered real estate sales and brokerage in the first decades of the century at rates of entry five to fifteen times higher than those of men; in 1930 women made up 14 percent of the field, up from a mere 2 percent in 1910.[7] As women entered the field in appreciable numbers, they also emerged as authors and subjects of articles in materials published by the national association, and appeared regularly on the program at national conventions.

In the 1920s real estate women were deemed suited to deal in residential property because of their "natural" roles as homemakers. Women brokers writing in the National Real Estate Journal rarely challenged this premise; in fact, they typically staked their claim for entry into the masculine world of sales on the basis of taken-for-granted, gendered knowledge—"women know homes better." But asserting the right to intervene in the "public," masculine world of commerce based on the cultural presupposition that women possessed special skills because of their traditional role in the "private" sphere turned out to be a subtly deconstructive maneuver. By the 1940s women brokers would appropriate this culturally prevalent belief to stretch, and finally to shatter, the boundaries expected to be observed by all women. Femininity worked in complex ways, as women real estate brokers attempted to enter the profession as colleagues equal to men, albeit on explicitly gendered terms in the 1940s. Unlike the typical story of sex-segmented markets, in which men abdicated the field of, say, secretarial work after a technological innovation made it possible to cheapen labor, in real estate women capitalized on structural weaknesses in the masculine professionalization project to capture the field.[8]

Like middle-class masculinity, middle-class femininity had at least two faces, and these complemented each other as often as they conflicted. Real estate women's efforts to join the profession were informed on the one hand by liberal individualism—the "privatized" form of feminism, the ideology of the sexually and economically independent New Woman that gathered strength in the 1920s, which asserted that women were capable of doing anything men could do, on their terms. On the other hand, what we might call "business maternalism" claimed that women could and should play a special role in the business world because of their innate moral qualities and particular experiences as women.[9]

In the 1920s and 1930s business maternalism prevailed, both within real estate brokerage and within larger narratives about business and gender. When *Fortune* magazine, for example, ran a three-part article on women in business in 1935, it focused almost entirely on women in helpmeet roles as secretaries and clerks to powerful men, and explicitly framed the "feminine invasion" of the office in terms of domesticity. Women were able to take over the functions in the office formerly held by men because, the writer argued, "what the [businessman] wanted in the office was something as much like the vanished wife of his father's generation as could be arranged—someone to balance his checkbook, buy his railroad tickets . . . take his daughter to the dentist, listen to his side of the story, give him a courageous look when things were blackest, and generally, know all, understand all."[10] Though women were quietly streaming into positions of responsibility in "masculine" fields like real estate brokerage, mainstream culture in the 1920s and 1930s, save for a few sociological novelists like Sinclair Lewis, was not ready to cede symbolic space.

In the early 1940s, women Realtors shifted their emphasis from taken-for-granted business maternalism toward liberal individualism with a twist, employing the ideology of domesticity to reestablish the ground lost during the Depression. In this second phase of women's incursion into the real estate field, a leading element among women Realtors openly derided the idea that they should fear posing a threat to men by encroaching upon their prerogatives. These women brokers charged through the gender barrier by self-consciously and ironically taking up the rhetoric of domesticity to create a female dominion in real estate. But with this "progressive" task of entering the field of real estate on more or less equal footing achieved, women Realtors again shifted the emphasis back toward maternalism to fervently—and effectively—oppose public housing and other "socialistic" ventures in the late 1940s and 1950s. By the 1950s women Realtors were on the cutting edge of the movement of women into business. The cold war provided the context in which they could augment their established role as guardians of the virtue of the republic through protection of the home, with strident advocacy of the "free enterprise system" as the sole means to achieve an abundance of "true homes," a powerful combination in American culture.

The New (Real Estate) Woman

Una Golden, the protagonist in Sinclair Lewis's novel, *The Job* (1917), was the first major fictional representation of a real estate woman. Una was a fairly typical character in the young genre of "New Woman fiction."[11] Thrust into the role of head of household upon her father's sudden death, she seized the opportunity to drag her mother out of Panama, Pennsylvania, to New York City in search of a new life. Lewis's novel traced Una's path to self-realization, her attempts at finding meaning in modern life through romance and work. Her life proceeded through a series of menial and tedious jobs, a not-quite-consummated romantic affair, and the death of her mother, the final symbolic break with her small-town past. After finding solidarity in the company of women in a church-run boarding house, she mustered the courage to assert herself at work. After a hasty marriage to a coarse traveling salesman nearly derailed Una's career aspirations, a female friend helped her find a job at a real estate office and a successful woman broker inspired her to get out of the feminine ghetto of stenography and into real estate sales. In real estate she was able to apply the expert knowledge of housing and community development that she had accrued by working with male brokers and to experience the autonomy and excitement promised by the business world. Una's stint as a real estate saleswoman emboldened her to take a great leap into the related field of hotel management.

As a mother and widow, Laura Hale Gorton had followed a traditional, almost archetypal path into the world of real estate; she had little choice but to enter the workforce to support her family. By contrast, Una Golden represented a "new woman" path, marked by a degree of free choice and personal aspiration. A young, childless woman, unhappily married to a marginal provider, she worked at numerous menial jobs before attaining a position at the real estate brokerage office of Truax and Fein, a firm to which she was finally "able to feel such loyalty as is supposed to distinguish all young aspirants." She began her career in real estate as a personal secretary to Daniel T. Truax, the senior partner in the firm. In contrast to the scorn that he would later heap on the real estate men in *Babbitt*, Lewis portrayed real estate men sympathetically in the earlier novel, treating as honest differences of style and substance the divergent approaches to the business represented by the principal members of the firm. Truax, the senior partner, who impressed the Real Estate Board with his "unsmiling insistence on the Dignity of the Profession," was a good judge of "what the people want," a member of the moderate wing of the profession. His junior partner Fein was a "Harvard Jew" and "perfectly the new type of business man," a strong professionalizer who fought for "real beauty in . . . suburban developments" modeled after those then being built by the Russell Sage Foundation in Forest Hills, New York. Representing a third, more classically entrepreneurial point of view, the sales manager, "Chaz" Salmond, held that real estate brokers "aren't in the business for our health—this idealistic game is O.K. for the guys that have the cash, but you can't expect my salesmen to sell this Simplicity and High-Thinking stuff to prospects that are interested in nothing but a sound investment with room for a garage and two kids."[12]

Una's loyalty to the firm, as well as her admiration for Fein and his progressivism, led her to devote her spare time to learning everything she could about real estate, studying "model houses, the lay of the land, the lines of sewers and walks," and even conjuring plans for garden suburbs. Through luck and pluck, Una got her break when Truax challenged her to win the business of a curmudgeonly old, rich couple. She succeeded in selling a lot in an expensive subdivision to the notoriously difficult customers, proving her mettle, and thereby "climb[ing] above the rank of assistant to the rank of people who do things." Una desired a permanent position as a salesperson because it was "obvious that, since women have at least half of the family decision regarding the purchase of suburban homes, women salesmen of suburban property should be at least as successful as men." Una persuaded Truax to put aside his conservative doubts about women salespeople and allow her to sell an entire subdivision that the firm had recently acquired on Long Island. She performed the task admirably. Backed by Fein, who had fallen in love with her, she demanded and obtained a position as the manager of the newly created women's sales department, at the substantial salary of $2,500 a year and with a staff of five women working under her. This advance into the world of real estate brokerage gave Una the fortitude to finally leave her slovenly and coarse husband. Completing the transformation to New Womanhood, she disavowed the need for "a man or man's love" and decided to adopt a child.[13]

While *The Job* was a fairly typical workplace romantic novel, that Lewis chose real estate brokerage as a potentially fulfilling and remunerative career for women was nearly clairvoyant, considering that the 1910 census had counted only about three thousand women brokers in the entire country, less than 3 percent of the total in real estate brokerage and a very minor occupation for women in the overall labor force. By the early 1920s real estate brokerage was an imaginable career option for women, and the figure of Una Golden provided at least a plausible model for a young woman to emulate— even though the majority of women actually practicing real estate brokerage were much older than the twenty-something Una.

In 1923 the *News Bulletin* of the Bureau of Vocational Information, a college women's employment service based in New York, published an article asking "What about real estate?" as a career for women. The article concluded that the "opportunities for the woman with vision and enthusiasm" were "unlimited." A follow-up survey by the Young Women's Christian Association of Brooklyn found that although there were few women engaged in real estate in New York City in 1923, the "advantages of the profession" that recommended it to women included the potential for financial success and the "intensely interesting" nature of the work "to the woman with initiative." Katharine Seaman, a broker who was one of ten female members of the huge New York Real Estate Board, denied that women were "handicapped" in the field but cautioned that "a woman has the same chance as a man but no better."[14]

For women brokers like Seaman, gender equity had two sides. It did mean that unlike in many fields of endeavor, especially those marked as feminine occupations, women in real estate tended to get equal pay for equal work, in large part because most if not all of a broker's compensation was in the form of commissions.[15] At the same time, women brokers often invoked a type of "separate spheres" argument to justify their place in the profession. A few women were engaged in commercial and industrial brokerage before the 1950s, yet it was only after women Realtors had exploited the ideology of domesticity to become firmly entrenched in residential brokerage in the 1940s and 1950s that they would have enough occupational authority to move into these more "masculine" fields in greater numbers.

Women as Realtors?

While women were rapidly entering the field of real estate brokerage in the 1920s, their acceptance into membership on real estate boards affiliated with the national association was another story. Through the 1920s and beyond, the charters of many prominent Eastern and Midwestern boards, including those of Chicago, Philadelphia, Kansas City, Columbus, and Pittsburgh, explicitly excluded women from membership. Since a real estate broker became a Realtor only through membership in a local board affiliated with the national association, a large and rapidly growing number of women held brokerage licenses but were excluded from the profession's leading organization. Exclusion from board membership not only was a matter of prestige but had economic and career ramifications, including lack of access to the increasingly important multiple-listing service, the crucial information-gathering function of local boards, and the educational programs and more general networking opportunities that board membership facilitated. Many women formed or joined lesser boards in the suburbs of major cities that excluded them. For example, the prominent broker Cora Ella Wright joined the board of Oak Park, Illinois, of which she was president in the late 1930s, because the Chicago Real Estate Board prohibited women from joining.

Women brokers persevered, pushing to form women's divisions within local boards. In California, they succeeded in forming a women's division at the state level in the early 1920s. In the mid-1930s, prominent women brokers organized themselves into a separate national organization, the Women's Council, and began a campaign to force recalcitrant boards to open their doors to women Realtors. During the Second World War, women Realtors, led by West Coast women who had played prominent roles in the profession since the 1920s, eloquently and adamantly asserted new claims for inclusion in the center of the profession. Their success, culminating in the opening of the boards in Philadelphia, Chicago, Pittsburgh, and eventually, Columbus in the period from 1935 to 1962 fundamentally altered the profession's identity. With the regendering of the profession, women were poised to dominate residential sales, giving women a solid and growing foothold in a very lucrative business field.

In the mid-1920s, male Realtors began to examine the place of women in real estate. The annual convention in 1925 featured a panel entitled "Women as Board Members." The three participants in the quasi-debate, all men, invoked three sorts of claims in affirming or rejecting the notion that boards should permit female membership. The chairman of the panel, Harvey Humphrey, secretary of the realty board in Fresno, California, set the tone, arguing that women Realtors on his board not only excelled at business, besting men in a recent home-selling contest in his city, but had a special role to play, particularly on the Pacific Coast, as guardians of "aesthetic beauty" in efforts to preserve and control ocean beaches. He called upon closed boards to "take cognizance" of women's achievements and admit them to full membership.

In Humphrey's mind, the field of real estate brokerage was already fairly equitable in terms of gender, and, he asserted, "there is no profession that has opened its doors to women as that of the Realtor." And this was partly true: There were few barriers to entry in the field—low or no start-up capital requirements, little or no formal training necessary, especially in comparison to traditionally male-dominated fields like law and medicine, or female-dominated professions like social work and teaching. The advent of real estate licensing laws in the 1920s and 1930s might have posed barriers to the entry of women. Licensing laws emphasized character over competence, and a woman new to the field of business might, in principle, have had trouble obtaining character references. Yet in practice this rarely seems to have been the case, and women got the necessary references from friends, clergy, fellow members of voluntary organizations, and former teachers.

Nevertheless, Humphrey felt compelled to reinforce the argument about competency with an invocation of women's innate advantages. In real estate, "woman is in her natural sphere; she has been making homes for ages, and so it is only natural that she should be interested in finding homes for other women," he asserted. "She exercises a spirit of fairness and unselfishness and gentleness that is often lacking in men." Thus women deserved board membership both because of their ability to achieve like men and because of their intrinsic natures, which facilitated achievement in real estate. Women naturally knew more about homes, and thus should be allowed to freely exercise their gendered expertise in business. Similarly, another participant in the panel, Clarence C. Lang of St. Louis, rested his affirmative case both on gender-neutral grounds—"character is a dominant factor in women as it is in men"—and on a subtly gendered claim of feminine moral superiority—"women [board] members honestly advise their clients." Women were entitled to membership in boards because, in Lang's words, they had been "tried and never found wanting."[16]

On the negative side of the debate, Pierce Jones of the venerable Chicago Real Estate Board—which refused membership to women until 1950—presented an exceptionally anemic case, and he knew it. Jones argued that since the board's headquarters was the "favorite club" of male Realtors, supplying members with such facilities as Turkish baths, barbershops, and smoking rooms, and since building equivalent facilities for women would be prohibitively expensive considering the small number of women who might join any given board, it would be unfair to women to allow them to join at this point. Nevertheless, Jones proceeded to cite a conversation he had with a "very brilliant and capable woman Realtor" who said that women would "be satisfied to come in and take what a board has to offer them," in other words the business contacts and prestige that membership brought with it. Jones conceded that "in the future women [may] come into the real estate business in such numbers that real estate boards can afford to take them in and give them what they should receive." On that day, Jones offered, he would "gladly join in welcoming them."[17] In sum, Jones completely ignored the views of the "very brilliant and capable" female Realtor, falling back on the very weak implicit claim of preserving a congenial, homosocial environment.

The flimsiness of his case notwithstanding, Pierce Jones represented the mainstream view among male brokers in the East and Midwest. With the exception of a few boards in Florida, in New Jersey, and on Long Island, female membership was disproportionately low east of the Rocky Mountains, and many of the larger and more prominent boards excluded women as a matter of policy. The story on the West Coast was quite different. Women held prominent positions in local boards as well as in the powerful California Real Estate Association in the early 1920s. For a variety of reasons having probably to do with a more fluid social structure and lack of rigid conventions due to continual inmigration, a succession of land booms from the 1880s onward, and an abundance of home-selling opportunities stemming from the preponderance of low-density, suburban development, the West Coast was in the vanguard for women in real estate very early on, producing many of the national leaders in the field. And the real estate men of the West Coast seemed not to mind the collegiality with women; they often expressed bemusement at the "squirmings of the effete East with regard to women Realtors," challenging East Coast members to come out to California, "where the women Realtors are recognized as among the best ethical brokers in the profession."[18] California women founded a women's division in 1924, held annual women's conventions, and produced a newsletter chronicling their activities. The West Coast women would lead a concerted and successful assault on the "men's club" point of view held by Jones, though not precisely along the lines suggested by his opponents.

Women's participation in real estate brokerage was distributed about evenly across the country, according to census data, but board membership was disproportionately male in many places, even where women were not explicitly barred. According to calculations derived from census data and rosters of Realtors and licensed brokers, about 8–9 percent of all real estate brokers were Realtors in the 1920s and 1930s. Many women held brokers' licenses or were listed in the census as brokers but did not belong to a local board. In Ohio in the mid-1940s, for example, there were only twenty-four women Realtors out of the several hundred Realtors licensed to practice in the state. Even in California, there was great variation: 21 percent of the members of the Real Estate Board in Berkeley were women in 1945, roughly at par with the national average for female participation in brokerage, yet the San Francisco board's membership was only 2.4 percent female.[19]

Part of this gender disparity existed because board membership was based on reputation and generally required a substantial initiation fee. These mechanisms of self-control, the central function of real estate boards (and all other professional organizations), were established to weed out less prosperous "curbstone brokers" and served, perhaps unintentionally, to raise barriers for women, who tended to enter the business on shakier financial ground than men, and with a less-developed network of business contacts. For men, real estate brokerage was often a second or even third career, whereas for women, at least until relatively recently, the choice to go into real estate was often dictated by family exigencies and was often a woman's first foray into the world of work outside the home.

Applications for membership in the Philadelphia Real Estate Board— which first admitted women in 1935—suggest that women applying for membership on boards, like the fictional Una Golden, often worked their way up at an established real estate firm, from stenographer or receptionist to saleswoman, and then finally to broker. Typically, a woman would work in a clerical position for a male broker for a few years, and then, desiring advancement, would ask her boss to provide a character reference so that she could obtain a sales license. Later, he would sponsor her for a brokerage license, and then for board membership. The Philadelphia board applications show that male brokers applied for board membership sooner after achieving a broker's license than women did, at a younger age on average, and were less likely to have been in clerical positions before making application. Many were also sons of brokers.[20] Madeline Spiess, the first female member of the Philadelphia Board and a founding member of the Women's Council, achieved membership when her husband, a past president of the board, passed away, leaving her in charge of a prominent brokerage. Spiess was the founder of the Philadelphia Real Estate Board's Women's Division, and a founding member and president, in 1942, of the Women's Council.[21]

Thus it seems that the relatively few women who joined boards did so after some time working within a real estate firm, while men who joined boards came from a wider range of business backgrounds, allowing them to join a board after only a short time in the real estate business. In the 1940s women brokers would note this paradox: that many women who had held a series of progressively responsible jobs in real estate firms and thus were familiar with professional norms were denied access to full membership in the field, while a man with far less experience in a real estate office could attain board membership.

Many older boards in the East and Midwest such as those in Chicago, Pittsburgh, Columbus, and Kansas City refused admission to women well into the 1940s and even into the 1950s and 1960s. Since membership in the national association was achieved through local board membership, most women in the 1920s through the 1940s were denied the prestige, business contacts, and organizational benefits enjoyed by male Realtors. However, since most boards did not formally exclude women in the 1920s, it seems plausible to conclude that the low rate of women's participation on local boards was more a function of history, cost, and occupational culture than deliberate institutional discrimination. High initiation and membership dues and a masculine business culture reinforced one another to keep women underrepresented on boards. The Women's Council was founded in part to ameliorate the "cultural" problem, as well as to put pressure on intractable boards.

Creating a Women's Space in Real Estate

By the 1920s women appeared with increasing frequency as the authors and the subjects of stories in the *National Real Estate Journal*, and by mid-decade they were playing high-profile roles at annual conventions. In recognition of women's increased participation in the field nationwide, the national association held a Conference of Women Realtors during its Twentieth Annual Convention in Seattle in 1927. The keynote speaker was an accomplished San Francisco broker, Grace Perego, who declared to the women assembled that "woman's place is not in the home when she wishes to embrace real estate as a career." Nor were women to be confined to the home-selling business. Perego had begun her career as a builder of apartments, and moved into selling country real estate before establishing a large brokerage firm.

She made an impassioned case for gender equality. "Which branch of real estate would women best be fitted for?" she asked rhetorically. Though many women made their "start in the real estate business selling homes because they *seem* naturally adapted to this line on account of their familiarity with home requirements," there was no necessary connection between gender and home sales. Women would sell homes only until they "found" themselves and developed a broader knowledge of real estate; then they would "invade any branch" they chose. Perego's career seemed to be a case in point. Attacking the notion of "women's place" in business, she noted that in her own business she employed exclusively men in some of her offices, exclusively women in others, and both men and women in still others. There was no intrinsic reason for women to deal exclusively with women, or to deal exclusively in their putatively natural sphere of residential property. Nevertheless, a gendered division of labor was indeed normal practice in real estate in the 1920s. Una Golden, a New Woman, was after all the manager of the women's sales department, assigned to selling suburban homes—and, in the end, she left the firm because of the senior partner's "unwillingness to accept women as independent workers."[22]

Perego's strong argument for gender equality was premature in 1927, a virtual voice in the wilderness, at least in the world of real estate at the national level. Much more prevalent was the belief that women possessed a particular "women's point of view" by nature. The vast majority of articles by women brokers in the *National Real Estate Journal* in the 1920s were written from this perspective, purporting to give "the Woman's Angle" on real estate. Louise Slocomb, "Realtoress" of Portland, Oregon, contended that women possessed "certain qualities" making them "peculiarly fit" for the profession. "Women's intuition" helped the woman Realtor to "enter into the prospect's psychology, to grasp the situation quickly and thoroughly," and once the situation was grasped, to use her "sharp wit" and "readiness to grasp detail" to "make the best of a given situation." Men had "courage, strength and foresight"; women, the "ability to handle details" and understand "fellow women." Slocomb suggested that these were complementary traits, implying that a firm with both male and female brokers would be most efficient. Homemakers by "nature," it was equally "natural" that women should be successful home brokers. "A woman has a definite idea of what a home should be; she appreciates its comforts and conveniences as no man can." Most important, to the woman, selling a house was "more than a mere business deal." The woman Realtor took "a personal interest in every home" that she sold. Her enthusiasm was "contagious" and was "transferred to the prospect."[23]

In the context of popular culture's discovery of the New Woman in the early 1920s, and the anxiety that it provoked, real estate women trod lightly, taking care not to appear too aggressively intrusive into the presumptive male world.[24] Perhaps worried that men reading the *National Real Estate Journal* in the 1920s might feel threatened by their entry into the real estate field, women Realtors were almost always quick to declare that they were "not seeking to deprive men of their laurels" nor "trying to take unto themselves masculine prerogatives." They were simply taking efficient advantage of the natural, sexual division of social labor that endowed men and women with different qualities. Since women possessed "alertness, sympathy, vision," and "that elusive intuitiveness," all invaluable aids in selling homes, and since it was assumed that homes must appeal first of all to women, women should no doubt be successful in selling them.[25]

Thus in the 1920s, women's claims for participation in the masculine world of real estate were almost invariably framed in terms of the inherent qualities that distinguished them from men. Women, it almost went without saying, were "extremely well fitted to sell homes." Undoubtedly, this essentialist argument helped women to create space in the profession in the 1920s, as rates of female participation doubled from 1920 to 1930.[26] The apparent compulsion on the part of both male and female brokers to reiterate the assertion, however, suggests that it performed some sort of boundary-maintenance function in the face of living proof—high-powered women brokers and developers like Grace Perego and Katherine Seaman—that women could succeed at any branch of real estate.

Unfortunately, the Great Depression almost drove women out of real estate altogether. About two-thirds of female brokers left the field between 1930 and 1940, and the economic crisis devastated the ranks of women Realtors. In search of new members, the leadership of the national association, its executive secretary Herbert U. Nelson and president Joseph Catherine in particular, turned toward women, actively encouraging the formation of the Women's Council of Realtors in 1938. The Women's Council was initially intended to make women feel more comfortable in the masculine environment of the annual conventions, by holding separate gatherings for female brokers and saleswomen. Nelson envisioned not a separate organization—such was not needed, he claimed, because most local boards did admit women—but an annual gathering that could enable "real estate women to get acquainted." Nelson told the forty or so women gathered at the initial meeting of the convention in Milwaukee in 1938 that an "informal" women's organization within the association would "aid the real estate calling by helping to raise the standards of practice and ethics and advancing the national association's educational program." Catherine similarly invoked business maternalism, asserting that women's "good intuition" made them "especially well qualified" to sell homes; thus he welcomed their participation in the affairs of the national association. The chairwoman of the meeting, Cora Ella Wright, suggested that one function of a women's council might be to conduct research with respect to laws affecting women's property rights. Echoing Nelson and Catherine, she asserted that women would "promote higher standards of business procedure and ethics," naturally.[27]

Participants in the first meeting revealed a wide range of experience and aspirations. Several women had founded their own real estate firms, others worked their way up through the ranks of established real estate companies, a few transferred skills learned in another business to real estate. Many had been active in real estate organizations on the local and state levels, and a handful had served as presidents of local boards. The women Realtors shared a sense of accomplishment through real estate. Strikingly, though, nearly every woman at the meeting referred to men. Some had drawn the men in their lives into the business with them, while others had been pulled into the business by their husbands or brothers, either in partnership or posthumously. Elva Cofer of Portland, Oregon, reported that she was "in charge of seventeen men" and believed that "women should cooperate more actively with men and seek their advice." Maude M. Butler of Tulsa told her colleagues that she had "been building houses ranging from $5,000 to $12,500," having become a member of the Tulsa Board "at the invitation of the men." Henrietta T. White of Los Angeles noted that in her city, where the board had long accepted women as members, separate women's meetings had allowed women to "open up" more than they would do in the board's regular, male-dominated meetings.[28]

The inaugural meeting of the Women's Council provided an important space in which women Realtors could come into their own. The laughter and camaraderie led one participant to claim, "My whole viewpoint with respect to real estate changed. Not only did I get more commissions. I got more pleasure out of my work," thanks to the Women's Council. Hazel M. Long of Cleveland, noted for her national advertising campaigns, regaled her sisters with a story about a "feminine house-hunter" who had been thoroughly pleased with one house until she noticed the bathroom's purple tiling, which she feared would clash with her underclothes.[29] Like a story recounted in Sinclair Lewis's *Babbitt* more than fifteen years earlier, Long's playful anecdote suggested simultaneous identification with and distancing from the butt of the joke: there was humor because the real estate women could imagine themselves in the same embarrassing position. The partial identification with "feminine house-hunters" provided a basis for women Realtors to advance their professional claims both as women, with special women's knowledge, and as aspirants to gender-neutral equality with men. Echoing the men's rhetoric about the "curbstone broker," women Realtors viewed "kitchen operators," the "many hundreds of untrained unaffiliated women . . . who hold real estate licenses," as the "big danger" to their legitimacy and professional aspirations.[30] In sum, it was incumbent upon women Realtors to use their expertise as women to both understand and overcome the concerns of "feminine house-hunters."

Though the national association's membership began to rebound after hitting rock-bottom in 1935, in the years leading up to the Second World War the organization was financially strapped, and the Women's Council was not a priority. Even the most supportive men, like Herb Nelson, saw the council as a mere "device for letting the women get together at conventions," not as any sort of incipient institution or formal division. Yet the annual gatherings attracted large groups of women because they provided a social space that had not existed in the past. Mary Avery, a Realtor from Miami, told Herb Nelson in late December 1940 that the demand for a formal Women's Division was growing. "A great many women are not at ease in the presence of men either in business or socially," she noted. "These same women will speak up very definitely in a women's setting and in a women's group do a lot of good work and get a lot of pleasure out of it."[31]

A woman Realtor's consciousness was stirring, but it was a divided consciousness. The founding members of the Women's Council were split over their long-range objectives: was it self-liquidation and assimilation into the "malestream," or was it creating a "women's world" within the profession?[32] Were women Realtors supposed to assimilate into the professional culture as established by the real estate men who had founded the national association, or was there to be a "women's way" of doing real estate?

At first, the latter, business maternalist view predominated, though with some subtle twists. Inviting women brokers to attend the Women's Council meeting at the NAREB convention in Los Angeles in 1939, Cora Wright stressed the opportunity to "cash in on the women's angle" in real estate practice. During the meeting in Philadelphia in 1940, the Women's Council pledged itself to increase the membership of the national association and to support fully the new Urban Land Institute in its advocacy of private enterprise solutions to the problem of urban blight. At the same meeting, they discussed "why women naturally specialized" in residential real estate. Yet President Newton C. Farr, whose hometown Chicago Real Estate Board remained closed to women, found himself in hostile territory when he insinuated that women tended to dabble in the business rather than take it on full time. He was met, one source noted, by jeers and heckling from the all-woman audience, who asked him why an unethical and part-time male broker should be eligible to apply for membership in the esteemed Chicago board while a full-time, ethical female broker was not.[33] The meritocratic, egalitarian argument made by Grace Perego thirteen years earlier was beginning to bubble to the surface in the space provided by the Women's Council. The Second World War would provide a new context in which women Realtors could advance claims for inclusion on more equalitarian grounds.

Rosie the Realtor®

On the eve of American entry into the Second World War, nearly twelve million American women were in the paid labor force, accounting for one-fourth of all workers. At the zenith of the war mobilization in 1944, for the first time in history married women outnumbered single women in the work force. As in many other sectors of the economy, the mobilization for war had drawn women into the real estate field to fill the gaps left by men drafted into military service. Local women's councils of Realtors proliferated during the war, and real estate boards that accepted women garnered many new female members.

In sharp contrast to other sectors of the economy, women remained in the real estate business after the war. While men's participation in the field increased by about 20 percent between 1940 and 1950, women's participation increased by 97 percent. This change reflected the major shift in the postwar decade of women into what government statisticians called the Financial, Insurance, and Real Estate (FIRE) sector: While women constituted 33.6 percent of FIRE workers in 1940, they were 44.3 percent in 1950—the largest structural shift by gender of the decade. Other industries returned to their pre-war gender distributions, but the distribution in the FIRE sector shifted permanently. Women who entered the world of paid labor for the first time during the Second World War flocked to the manufacturing sector in the greatest numbers, and for the duration of the war they dramatically changed the gender distribution in that sector. But by 1950 the occupational structure had returned to the pre-war norm of segregation on the basis of sex—women who remained in the labor force after the war reverted to occupations that were feminized before the war. But in real estate, as well as in sales and clerical work, there was not only a "significant increase in females within the category" but also "a trend for women to enter formerly male" occupations such as real estate brokerage. In short, while Rosie the Riveter is well known, she was short-lived. Rosie the Realtor was one of the permanent legacies of the war.[34]

As it would turn out, Rosie the Realtor was a bellwether of sorts for labor market trends in the postwar years, particularly the entrance of married women permanently into the labor force. Before the war, the real estate labor force differed markedly from the aggregate labor force in its composition and in the character of the work performed, particularly for women. Merely 15 percent of real estate women in 1930 were single, versus 54 percent in the overall female labor force. Over 60 percent of real estate women were forty-five years old or older in 1940, as opposed to about 21 percent in the overall labor force. So in many respects, from the perspective of 1930 or 1940 real estate women were anomalous. Yet from the perspective of 1960 or 1970, real estate women of the 1930s and 1940s look quite typical. In 1960, 23.6 percent of the female labor force was single, 55.1 percent married, and 21.3 divorced, quite close to the figures for real estate women in 1930. In 1960 more than 60 percent of the female labor force was over the age of thirty-five. In 1970 more than 75 percent of women in real estate were over thirty-five.

Further, exploring the history of Rosie the Realtor also helps to bridge the tension in the scholarship on women's work in the 1940s and 1950s, between those who interpret the war as a watershed during which a nascent feminist consciousness emerged, a precursor of the social changes of the 1960s and 1970s, and those who see it as an aberrant moment in which women's war work was largely a "temporary extension of domesticity."[35] The history of real estate women is also the history of the divided consciousness of twentieth-century middle-class womanhood: independent women grounded their claims to economic participation both in liberal notions of equality and maternalistic ideas of women's special role in society.

The Second World War provided an opportunity for women to rethink their place in the labor force in general, and in the real estate profession in particular. Early in the war years, women Realtors began to assert vigorous claims for full and equal membership in the profession. Women Realtors shifted their own strategy for entering the profession toward a more liberal individualist orientation and self-consciousness about gender assumptions as tactically useful. The transcript of the Women's Council meeting in Detroit in 1941 provides an extraordinary record of the shift from business maternalism to a vigorous liberal individualism, in the context of the war mobilization. The first of two keynote speakers, Herbert U. Nelson, executive secretary of the national association, opened the breakfast meeting with a notable, un-abashedly confessional address, "Visual Nuisances and Their Effects on Real Estate." Expressing implicit gratitude to the Women's Council for the opportunity to escape the hardheaded, masculine world of the larger convention and discuss important issues that only its members would understand, he prefaced his talk with a somewhat awkward disclaimer. "This subject," billboard regulation, "is a hobby of mine toward which men in the organization express themselves with a certain amount of tolerance but concerning which I think they are rather indifferent." He proceeded to make a case for a campaign against ugliness by drawing analogies with other nuisances: "We recognize that you can't put a boiler factory where people have to sleep and eat, but we go on year after year tolerating billboards and outdoor advertising which is just as destructive of amenity values." Assigning the blame for the proliferation of unattractiveness explicitly to excessive "commercialism"— that is, on the unfettered entrepreneurial activities of the men in the general convention beyond the walls of the Women's Council meeting—he implored the women to join his crusade. "I don't know where a job like this belongs," he admitted sheepishly. "I doubt if I could get a committee of men in the organization to take an interest in this matter, which is so important to real estate, but I feel very strongly that somebody in our group should take a hand in it." If the women Realtors were to make any particular special contribution to the real estate field, it would have to be "a matter of this kind, in which I assume women have perhaps a better understanding and a more sensible mind and spirit than the men." Speaking in women's space, Nelson was obligated to lay bare his premises. And his speech served its purpose. The Women's Council voted unanimously to adopt "visual nuisances" as their annual project.[36]

As if in ironic, almost mocking, response to Nelson's earnest, sensitive-male petition, Mary Amelia Warren, a young and ambitious Realtor from California, used the women's space to deliver a rousing, sometimes sarcastic, though never nasty address decrying male superiority and sketching a plan for a female invasion of residential real estate. She began with a brief gloss on the Darwinian struggle for women brokers to survive the Depression by working harder than men, by conducting themselves in real estate on the basis of knowledge gained from the imperative for household economizing in the 1930s. When brokerage firms were collapsing and incomes and real estate values plummeting, "real estate WOMEN stepped in and began to make order out of chaos." The rules of the domestic economy shifted. "People were shopping for bargains as they'd never shopped before. Commissions were HARD TO MAKE. But women were accustomed to making that extra effort to please people . . . to making dollars go as far as they could." Women, experienced in economizing during hard times, "attacked" the Depression-era real estate crisis with the "same methods by which they ran their households."[37]

The process of natural selection during the 1930s left women brokers well adapted to succeed in the post-Depression period. Warren noted that the real estate ads in California in the late 1930s and early 1940s were abounding with instructions to "call Jane Doe" or "Consult Mrs. So and So." Why, she asked? "If ANY of you think that the use of those feminine names is a mark of sentimental appreciation for the lifesaving services we real estate women rendered to our [male] brokers during the depression," she declared sarcastically, "then you've either got your psychology and economics mixed, or you DON'T know California brokers!" Women were so active and successful in California real estate precisely because "Mrs. John Q. Public" had grown to appreciate the "EXTRA services the woman Realtor performs," as well as her subtly different approach to home selling. "All through the beautifully dead past," Warren mischievously avowed, as if speaking directly to Felix Isman, the misogynous Philadelphia Realtor we encountered in chapter 3, "when MEN were doing the house choosing, the majority of houses changed hands because one man convinced another that 'this is a real buy.'" But in the new world of the 1940s, things were very different. Of course women were interested in construction, "they *demand* that a house be adequately built"; but reflecting the new sensibilities of the age of consumption, Warren asserted, "the majority of them are more interested in LIKING the house for twenty years than watching it *endure* for a hundred."[38] The message was clear: women's values—consumer values—had become the engine of the economy.

Thus, Warren continued, reaching the climax of her speech, "for reasons that we actively engaged in the profession readily understand, in BUYING a home more and more people are saying, I'D RATHER DEAL WITH A WOMAN . . . *Those six words* have endowed you and me with a profession."[39] This new slogan for women Realtors was tantamount to a new strategy for women real estate brokers: to capitalize on society's gender *assumptions*, to employ hitherto taken-for-granted notions about innate female differences *instrumentally*. She explicated the basis for her contention that women were poised to dominate real estate brokerage:

> Throughout history womankind has been credited with the virtues of gentleness, honesty, sincerity, and unselfishness. Whether we actually possess these attributes in undue measure would be a subject of academic interest. But tradition has endowed us, and being human, we've striven to merit the reputation . . .
>
> The man customer likes to deal with a woman in real estate for

several reasons. If he has a wife, or female relatives, he assumes that a woman will know better what *they* would like. Then, once he's made your acquaintance, he's amazed and delighted to find someone who can *handle* business like a man, and *still* make him feel like a superior being. And, on the average, he endows you unquestionably with a noble character (seeing that you're in such a difficult and competitive field) and likes to feel HE's helping you carry your burden by dealing with you.[40]

If this new breed of women Realtors claimed the territory of home sales as their own sphere, that claim was no longer a declaration of innate moral prerogative, but only an attenuated Victorian domesticity tagged onto a self-interestedly gendered "expertise" in manipulating home buyers—"that element that presupposes you'll act as an interested human being," a woman, instead of a "commission minded salesman." The new slogan for woman Realtors in the 1940s and beyond—"I'd rather deal with a woman"—was a perfect collapse of the commercial motives and gendered morality that separate spheres were intended precisely to avoid. Victorian women did not "deal," at least not so obviously, or in those terms. Women Realtors, at least some of them, appropriated the vestiges of Victorian ideology for their own purposes, playing ironically with the language to cash in on stereotypes.[41] They had taken the ideology of domesticity to its logical extreme: societal *assumptions* about women's "natural" inclinations were refashioned as cultural capital, readily convertible to the cold, hard cash of commissions.[42] It should come as no surprise, Warren declared, that "more and more of the FEMALE OF THE SPECIES are selling more and more houses," getting more involved in real estate organizations, taking advantage of the growing opportunities for real estate education, and so forth.[43]

But alas, there was a dark side to the story of feminine progress in real estate, Warren concluded. "The MALE ANIMAL FEARS women in business," Warren seethed, beginning the second half of her talk. Perhaps because they are "doing pretty well" in their new roles, in many offices male brokers "permit" women to "draw in the business, initiate sales, and work out most of the details," and then have men step in at the last minute to close the transaction. Warren related an anecdote about a female rental agent who had taken some prospective renters out to see an apartment when she discovered that they were actually interested in buying the entire building. She rushed the people back to the office to meet a salesman, only to find him missing.

"No doubt he'd just run out for a haircut," Warren quipped irreverently. The agent took them back out to thoroughly inspect the property, and piqued their interest enough that by the time they returned to the office, they were ready to place a deposit. By this time, the salesman was back, "so he graciously stepped in, gave the customers the usual receipt to bind the deal, and 'earned' his commission. Wasn't it wonderful?" she asked, her voice dripping with contempt.[44] Worse still, there were still real estate boards that failed to admit women, and women Realtors needed to apply pressure to open them up.

What was to be done? "Why are we attending a meeting of the WOMEN's Council? For sociability? To be sure!! There is no greater pleasure than the meeting of kindred spirits." But "besides just the pleasure" of women's solidarity, "WE MUST COUNCIL!" That was the true task of the Women's Council, to Warren and her allies: for them to use the women's space to inspire each other, to convince each other "we 'belong,'" to construct a female business identity. She envisioned women Realtors developing the self-confidence to demand, like Una Golden, positions of greater responsibility within their firms, demanding that closed boards open themselves to women members, demanding to be treated as equals rather than inferiors. She implored her fellow women Realtors to take advantage of their historically conditioned talents for accommodation and compromise and to "believe in the essential soundness of the scheme of things," to remain the moral foundation of American society. "The *effective* way to *inspire* other women is to be, yourself, an outstanding success! I'D RATHER DEAL WITH A WOMAN!" she closed, to an ovation by over one hundred astonished and inspired women brokers. The transcript made no note as to whether Herb Nelson remained in the room during this speech, but it was reprinted in the *National Real Estate Journal*, to be read by the entire membership of the national association.[45]

Madeline Spiess of Philadelphia, chairwoman of the Women's Council in 1942–43, aimed to heed Warren's call to demand that closed boards open themselves to women. Spiess had become a real estate broker almost by default, when her husband, the prominent Philadelphia broker Richard T. Spiess, passed away fairly suddenly in the mid-1930s. She oversaw the formation of the Women's Division of the Philadelphia Real Estate Board in 1939–40, which grew steadily throughout the war years, and she was the first woman member of that eminent board. She pledged to help "organize the real estate women" in Pennsylvania and throughout the country "to such degree that wide pressure can be brought to bear upon the boards to give full recognition to the women as Realtors, without any group separation as to sex." She instructed state chairwomen to canvass the boards in their states to discover which had "definite rulings" against women members. Their report revealed that in the West and Southwest virtually all boards were open to women, while in the East and Midwest boards were more likely to be closed to women, either by statute or by custom. In those cities, such as Columbus, Ohio, in which boards did not permit women to become members, Spiess urged the formation of local Women's Council chapters.

However, there was some opposition to the formation of local councils from both women and men Realtors. Particularly in California and other places where they enjoyed free access to the privileges of board membership, some women feared that "separatism," as they called it, would lead to erosion of the equal status they enjoyed. The men worried that separate women's organizations might detract from the strength of the local board itself, might divide the loyalties of women brokers. Perhaps there was also a fear that women might develop autonomy in their own space, might conspire against men, but this fear remained unvoiced. Spiess argued that the opportunity for a separate organization would ultimately allow for the development of a "non-separation point of view" in the industry.[46] She wanted local councils to serve as semi-autonomous spaces, like the Women's Division she had founded in Philadelphia, in which women Realtors could gain the requisite confidence to join the "malestream" of the profession. Spiess and others viewed local council chapters as something more than a ladies' auxiliary to the local board, but less than a fully autonomous group of women brokers plotting their own course. Nonetheless, tension over "separateness" hung over the Women's Council throughout the 1940s.

Toward the end of her tenure in office, Spiess urged the transformation of the Women's Council from a sort of women's club into a professional women's business association. A list of objectives prepared by Spiess's vice-chairwoman, Belle Knowles, enumerated ten specific goals for the council, a mixture of liberal and maternalist ideas. Women Realtors should "demand the same recognition for ability that is accorded the men of the profession," and should work to "secure general recognition of the importance of women in the real estate profession," goals premised on liberal ideas about equality. At the same time, Spiess and her officers wanted the Women's Council to help carve a special niche for women. The council aimed, therefore, to "keep women aware of the significance and responsibilities of women in a profession dealing in American homes," implicitly invoking a taken-for-granted premise that as women, female Realtors had special authority with respect to matters domestic. Further, this objective implied that as businesswomen, they had a special *political* duty. Finally, the council intended to extend Herbert Nelson's plea for help with billboard control into a broader objective of "enlarg[ing] the concept of esthetic values among Realtors, as important and significant factors in rebuilding our cities, reorganizing our industries and reconstructing a world for a new era of peace." The Women's Council, as a professional society, "should aim to make some contribution of its own toward the scientific understanding of real estate," Knowles argued, and who better than women to study the impact of "beauty and ugliness" on real estate values? "Is it too much to hope that women Realtors may find aesthetics a fifth [factor of production], and so add something to the science of real estate?"[47] Thus, echoing the men's efforts of the 1920s, women Realtors sought to appropriate the cultural authority of science to justify their claim to professional status. But as we have seen, the men's attempt was not entirely successful, and the Women's Council tended to ignore the suggestion in practice. There would be far more important women's work vying for the council's attention.

From 1938 until 1945, the Women's Council existed at the behest of the board of directors of the national association. For the first half-decade of the council's existence, the men who ran NAREB allowed the organization a great deal of autonomy, largely because it was perceived as a sort of ladies' auxiliary, a social club that made women feel more comfortable at national meetings. As women began to take a greater role in the industry during the wartime mobilization, as leading women Realtors were attempting to transform the council into a professional businesswoman's organization, in tacit response the NAREB leadership began to dictate the terms of membership and to exercise greater authority. Late in 1943, the national association decreed that only women Realtors could belong to the Women's Council, and that the organization had no authority to collect dues. Carol Laux of St. Louis, Spiess's successor to the leadership of the council, seemed to concur with the men's implicit concerns when in her first letter to the membership in March 1943 she voiced doubts about women's business sensibilities and maturity. Speaking to the anxieties attendant upon the large number of married women flocking into war work in 1942–43, Laux, who ran a brokerage in partnership with her husband, challenged the council membership to prove (to men, of course) "that women can share the business world on a competitive basis, and not be petty." She implored women Realtors to demonstrate that women "are progressive and not aggressive, workers and not 'queen bees.'" For Laux, male approval was the ultimate arbiter of women's achievement: she urged each woman Realtor to "do a job that a man would be proud of."[48]

Thus, within the Women's Council, there was a divide between those West Coast women like Mary A. Warren, who had complete confidence in women's acumen and their place in the business world, and others, mainly Midwesterners like Carol Laux, who seemed to harbor doubts. On the one hand, feisty liberal rhetoric found broad support. For example, the council's *Bulletin* approvingly published the words of the prominent San Francisco Realtor Geneve Schaffer, who in response to criticism that women were not doing their part in war activities retorted, "When women have equal rights, perhaps they will do more."[49] On the other hand, the *Bulletin* also published Elsie Smith Parker's poem "For the Woman Realtor," which represented the woman Realtor in a kind, diminutive, desexualized, nonthreatening idiom, as an older and demure woman who would make a home buyer, ostensibly male, feel completely at ease.

Perhaps Parker was responding, unconsciously or not, to the abject terror at the core of the indictment leveled by Philip Wylie at what he perceived as the rising manipulative and emasculating power of women in American society. "Momism" and "momworship" burst into the American lexicon in 1942 when Wylie published *Generation of Vipers*, a vituperative attack on American gender relations inspired in part by *Life* magazine's publication, on Mother's Day 1941, of a photo of a division of U.S. troops spelling out the word "mom" on a drill field. Surely the woman Realtor was not part of Wylie's "huge class of idle, middle-aged women" who satanically manipulated men into believing that "the dowry went the other way," then "handing her the checkbook and going to work in the service of her caprices."[50] Yet Parker's verse suggests an attempt to temper the militant self-confidence of Mary Amelia Warren and Geneve Schaffer with a bit of kindly maternalism of the non-momist sort. The woman Realtor could be a successful and independent businesswoman, yet at the same time maintain a nonthreatening, soothing demeanor—a safe haven in the heartless world of commerce.

She's a quiet little woman,
Has a patient, friendly air,
Knows the costs of lots and taxes,
Has gentle voice and graying hair,
And SHE sells homes . . .
Shows you to this place and that one,
Picks out one for you to see,
Never urges, never argues—
"Here you have an apple tree—"
For SHE loves homes . . .[51]

The Women's Council saw great success in 1944. It began the year with seven local chapters and 733 members, and ended with thirty-two chapters and 1,146 members. By the end of 1944 women Realtors made up about 6.1 percent of NAREB's membership, definitely lagging behind the proportion of women in real estate nationally, yet at the same time showing great growth potential. The male leadership of the national association noted that 413 new Realtors had been drawn into the organization by the Women's Council, and it became clear to some that the rapidly growing number of women brokers represented a tremendous pool of future members. Hazel Long, who returned from war work in Washington to lead the Women's Council in 1944, finally persuaded the national association in 1945 to grant the council status as a division, thus allowing it to establish its own bylaws and collect dues of its own, set at $3 per annum. This turned out to be a mixed blessing. Until 1945 membership in the Women's Council was underwritten entirely by the national association, was cost-free, and entailed little commitment on the part of women. After 1945 the Women's Council measured its own achievements in part by the number of women Realtors it was able to persuade to pay dues. Many women expressed ambivalence about formalizing the Women's Council, concerned that such a move would permanently institutionalize the separation between men and women in the field. Again, this was of particular concern in areas such as California and Florida, where women had long been accepted as equals.

Nevertheless, and especially in those states, local chapters of the Women's Council continued to form, and the organization grew. By May 1945 there were thirty-two chapters and over 1,200 members. Grace Perego and Geneve Schaffer, both equality-minded brokers, formed a chapter in San Francisco to increase women's participation in the San Francisco Real Estate Board, which admitted women but suffered from very low female membership. A Women's Council was established in Berkeley, even though the Berkeley Real Estate Board enjoyed strong female participation. In the East, the president of the national association, Van Holt Garrett, pressured the venerable Pittsburgh Real Estate Board, still closed to women in 1945, to invite Maybelle Alkire, secretary of the neighboring Bradsford Real Estate Board, to attend its annual banquet. Three years later, the Pittsburgh board opened its doors to women members. As a further sign of the changing times, Simmons College, a business-oriented women's college in Boston, introduced a real estate major in 1945.

At the end of the war, women Realtors broadened the scope of their activities and began explicitly discussing their political responsibilities as women in real estate, figuring themselves as defenders of "private enterprise." As Ruth F. Ulrich, chairwoman of the Florida Women's Council, put it, women had "discovered" during the war that it was "to their own interest to be more adequately informed on the legislation of their state and nation," laws that "might improve or detract from their right to private enterprise," and as a result they became interested in joining the organization. In 1945 the Women's Council involved itself in the public policy arena, first lobbying for an enhanced real estate licensing law in Florida, and then, at the national level, informing President Truman of their opposition, as real estate women, to the continuance of wartime price and rent controls. Women had traditionally let men "do the work" of monitoring legislation and expressing preferences with regard to such masculine issues as tax and fiscal policy, but no longer. "It is not morally right," Ulrich informed her fellow women Realtors, "that women in the real estate field should enjoy the fruit" of men's lobbying efforts without playing an active role. The Women's Council could and should augment the political and social influence of the National Association of Real Estate Boards, should become a "good pressure group . . . working for the continuance of private enterprise."[52]

Women Realtors soon discussed ways in which they could be of particular service in protecting the nation from "the extreme leftists in our social planning" who aimed at "taking over our business lock, stock, and barrel." Maude Butler of Tulsa suggested that women Realtors use customary women's networks, such as Parent-Teacher Associations and civic and religious groups, to disseminate information on the most important piece of wartime legislation to affect the real estate industry, the Servicemen's Readjustment Act, known colloquially as the G.I. Bill. In their "advisory capacity as Realtors," the women had a responsibility to make sure that veterans received the full benefit of the act, which augmented the Federal Housing Administration's mortgage insurance program by covering down-payments for veterans. Through the G.I. Bill, Margery Dunham of Seattle noted, "the government is attempting to help the veteran become established in life, and it is our duty to put safeguards around that little stake upon which the veteran is basing dreams of future security." Women Realtors felt a particular obligation to make sure that veterans were not deceived into entering loan agreements for homes that appraisers for the Veteran's Administration would not approve or sold homes that they would not be able to afford over time. Interpreting the law for veterans and safeguarding their interests "may mean a lot of work for us and it may not be very remunerative, but the question [is]," Dunham asked, "What do we owe our veterans? For those of us who have stayed at home and wished we could do something to help, this may be the opportunity to do our patriotic bit." Hazel P. Foster, a Realtor from Portland, suggested that the Women's Council take advantage of women's organizational acumen and establish a "system throughout the local chapters" that would aid the many "wandering home seekers" to sell a home in one city and find a home in another. As businesswomen, they were not altruists. Foster suggested that a system be worked out "so that we may both profit and render real assistance."[53]

By the end of the war, women Realtors had institutionalized their place within the profession's leading organization, just in time to help the National Association of Real Estate Boards tap into the swelling ranks of female brokers. Women Realtors began to articulate their place in the field in terms of patriotic service to promote and defend homeownership. They were divided in their loyalty within the profession, and about whether to support the Women's Council and its aim of providing a separate women's space for developing women's business confidence and applying organized pressure on those boards that still refused admission to women. Women Realtors perceived a special role for themselves as women in real estate, at the same time as they wanted to become part of the "malestream" in the National Association of Real Estate Boards. The immediate postwar years would give women Realtors a cause around which maternalist and liberal individualist impulses could converge: public housing.

CHAPTER SEVEN

Domesticity, Gender,
and Real Estate in the 1950s
and Beyond

I believe in my America, the Land of Freedom and the Home of peoples from all the earth, who have and seek the comforts derived from the pursuit of free enterprise . . . I will encourage every mother to instill in the minds of her children the joys and privileges of living in their own home.

—Creed for Women Realtors, 1950[1]

By the late 1940s women had made significant inroads into residential broker-age and into positions of leadership within the organized real estate profession. As the cold war intensified, the leadership of the National Association of Real Estate Boards increasingly turned to women Realtors to mobilize support for policies favorable to the industry and against those seen as detrimental to it. Women Realtors adroitly deployed both liberal-individualist rhetoric about freedom of enterprise and maternalist rhetoric about the bedrock centrality of the owner-occupied home to American civilization to lend feminine moral support to the crusade against public housing. At the same time as women real estate brokers and sales agents were carving out new public space as businesswomen, American culture was, yet again, examining the impact of white-collar work and domesticity on middle-class manhood. Ironically, in the 1960s and 1970s some women began to attempt to liberate themselves from the confinement of the same homes that other women Realtors had sold to them and their husbands; residential real estate brokerage was often a path away from domesticity for some women, a means for achieving independent middle-class status, at the same time as it promoted domesticity as an unequivocal social good.

The second-wave feminism of the late 1960s and 1970s contained within it both a radical critique of patriarchal capitalism and a liberal desire to facilitate entry for women into traditionally male fields of endeavor. Echoing discussions from the 1930s and 1940s, businesswomen in the 1960s and 1970s were torn about whether to operate within their own sphere or join the "male-stream." Local women's councils of Realtors proliferated at the same time as feminist consciousness-raising circles, and the influx of women into the business and into the ranks of Realtors accelerated. Real estate brokerage seemed to offer women a potentially remunerative and high-powered career in business coupled with the flexibility to allow them still to perform their duties as mothers and wives. This promise, combined with the economic malaise of the 1970s, inspired tens of thousands of women to pursue careers in real estate that resembled neither Laura Hale Gorton's desperate struggle to survive nor Una Golden's quest for feminine autonomy. By the 1970s a new representation of the woman Realtor had emerged in the guise of "Suzy Soldsine," an autobiographical character created by the Realtor and author Mary Shern. A self-described apolitical and conservative woman, Susy Soldsine got into real estate to increase her personal spending power and add some fulfillment to her boring personal life. Through the Soldsine character, Shern asserted married women's right to balance home life and career—at the same time as she disavowed feminism's role in making a career possible and ignored the stagflationary economy's role in making a second income necessary.[2]

Maternalism and the Struggle against Public Housing

In 1949 Herbert U. Nelson wrote to the president of the Women's Council, Maude Butler, and formally requested the women Realtors' help in "the defense against socialism in housing." He attended the Women's Council board meeting in January 1949, and as he had done in his address to the Council eight years earlier, he proposed a special mission for women Realtors at mid-century. However, unlike in his previous, somewhat trivial request for women's help in combating ugliness, Nelson now placed women Realtors at the center of a national struggle against government-built housing, calling upon them to help lead a campaign to protect the nation's private property from "inconsistent taxation and the evil of confusing public housing with slum clearance." It was incumbent upon women Realtors to appeal to American women, "especially to the American mother and the American woman with property investments," to pay careful attention to legislation aimed at using the "slum-clearance slogan to get entry for public housing."[3] Nelson's plea assumed a new moral and political role for women Realtors, one in which their authority not only as women but also as *business*women could serve a vital purpose. Nelson's battle cry drew women Realtors into the heart of the domestic cold war.

The fight was joined around the Omnibus Housing Act of 1949. The proposed legislation provided for massive federal aid for slum clearance, something the national association had long favored because it would provide new urban frontiers for construction and would foist the costs of clearance onto the government. But the bill, cosponsored by Senators Robert Taft of Ohio, Allen Ellender of Louisiana, and Robert F. Wagner of New York, also committed the federal government to building over 800,000 units of public housing—thereby, in the national association's view, overstepping the bounds of proper government intervention in the housing market. Women Realtors went on a veritable crusade against the proposal and against similar local and state laws, appearing on television and radio and on newspaper op-ed pages.

Mobilizing their collective authority as women, mothers, and middle-class businesswomen, they argued that public housing projects lacked true home spirit, undermined the American family, and threatened the central institution of American society, the private home. Women Realtors hoped to pre-empt or deflect some of the criticism leveled at the profession for appearing to operate solely in the economic self-interest of the real estate industry.

Nevertheless, the act passed in 1949, and the Realtors faced a tide of criticism, not only from traditional political opponents but from many civic groups as well. The women's campaign to depict the profession as concerned solely with the public welfare was a failure. Yet the male leadership of the national association retained faith in women Realtors' capacity to at least improve the industry's public image. In early 1950 the national association's president, Robert P. Gerholtz, appeared before the Women's Council to ask them to do some damage control. "Let them understand we are not just selfish," he besought the women Realtors.[4]

A sexual division of political labor was emerging in the real estate profession. The men largely waged the war on the front lines in Washington through the Realtors Washington Committee. The women Realtors were responsible for community education on the home front about the "right of every man and woman to own a home built by and sold by private industry and institutions," in the words of the Realtor Anne L. Brown. As the cold war heated up in Korea in 1950, Gerholtz again addressed the women Realtors. "Our industry is confidently counting on you, as we enter a period in which your patriotic work in behalf of our American heritage, and your closely related professional purpose of strengthening home ownership in America will be needed as never before."[5] The women Realtors accepted the challenge, responding with a "Creed for Women Realtors," which they published in the first issue of their revamped journal, the *Woman Realtor*:

> I believe in my America, the Land of Freedom and the Home of peoples from all the earth, who have and seek the comforts derived from the pursuit of free enterprise, worship of God in their own way and self-expression of their own individual talents . . . I promise to defend, with all my strength of conviction, every movement which will help to maintain the right of individual home ownership, and to support a fair program of taxation based on economic thrift. I rededicate myself to serve the cause of my fellow man, to wisely use and preserve American soil, whether it be used for home-ownership, industrial or commercial expansion, or, for the pursuit of happiness. And, I will encourage every mother to instill in the minds of her children the joys and privileges of living in their own home.[6]

The creed, published two months after the surprise North Korean attack on South Korea in June 1950, and a few weeks before Douglas MacArthur's landing at Inchon to begin direct American involvement in the Korean War, committed women Realtors to providing a link between the domestic and public policy spheres. They accepted their new moral and political role with enthusiasm, premised as it was on an assertion of women brokers' professional, middle-class status, and their efforts quickly produced results. In 1952 women Realtors in Los Angeles mobilized the women's vote against a $205 million public housing project, offering space in their offices to register voters, and using their cars to transport women, "housewives, especially," to the polls. The referendum was defeated by a vote of three to two.[7]

If the cold war was, as Elaine Tyler May and others have argued, at least in part about the "domestic containment" of women in the home, and if women's roles in activities like civil defense were part of a cultural tendency toward infusing the "traditional role of women with new meaning and importance" and helping "fortify the home as a place of security amid the cold war," then women Realtors and businesswomen more generally deserve an important place in that story. The cold war may have been about taming female sexuality and independence, and large numbers of American women may have "donned their domestic harnesses" as May asserts, but women Realtors played a large part in perpetuating the ideal and purveying the yoke.[8] Women Realtors counseled each other to focus their sales pitch to women not on "bricks and mortar or clapboards," but always on "the family scene before an open fire in the living room." As a prominent woman Realtor put it in 1952, "Sell her a kitchen with ideas galore, the smell of pies baking and roasts searing . . . Sell her happiness in a setting where she plays the leading role with very little fear of being replaced. Sell her security for herself and those she loves."[9]

Thus, women Realtors' increasing public role and prominence in real estate helped to reproduce an ideology and the material conditions that kept many women "contained" in the home. Drawing upon culturally prominent ideas about women's proper place in society, women Realtors carved a large and growing niche for themselves in the world of residential real estate, selling homes at the same time as they participated in broadening the career options for American women. As women flocked to white-collar jobs along with millions of men, and as the mass of American families increasingly came to live privatized, domestic lives in nondescript suburban tract homes, many scholars and pundits began, once again, to question the impact of these trends on middle-class American masculinity.

Work and Middle-Class Masculinity in the 1950s

The end of the Second World War and the subsequent creation of a permanent standing military by the National Security Act of 1947 inadvertently created a new problem: What to do, economically, with the constant stream of demobilized soldiers? The federal government and business embarked on a concerted effort to glamorize middle-class, white-collar work and its attendant "way of life." *White-Collar Worker*, a training film produced in 1950 by RKO Pathé for the Department of the Army, depicted "career opportunities in office work" through the fictional character Ed Holt, a white man in his mid-thirties. Holt moved from the shop floor, where he had long been a machinist, to a position in the back office—an unquestionable move "up" in the film's narrative. By exchanging his well-paid but "dirty" blue-collar job for clean hands and an office replete with new tools like a fountain pen, an ink blotter, and filing cabinets, Holt donned the white collar that signified true middle-class respectability in postwar America.

The shift from manual to mental labor, though, presented both opportunities and challenges. The film, ostensibly aimed at soldiers making the transition from active duty to civilian life, focused on the benefits of moving off the shop floor—but hints about the costs of giving up the blue-collar world persistently emerged. Strikingly, aside from noting that Holt's new work was "clean," the film ignored the nature of the occupation itself entirely. We see Holt attending a company-sponsored job-training program, where he and other upwardly mobile blue-collar tradesmen learn the necessary skills for white-collar advancement. However, other than vague references to drafting and mathematics, the film divulged nothing about the sort of work Holt was supposed to perform in his new position. Instead, it concentrated almost entirely on his social and home life. We observe Holt and his fellow workers engaged in animated conversation in the company cafeteria. The narrator asked the audience to imagine the topic of discussion among these responsible, white-collar professionals: Might they be chatting about the weighty subjects of the day, for example politics or art? No, they were discussing that great American pastime, baseball. Though now wearing white collars rather than blue, they were still the same happy-go-lucky Americans they had been on the shop floor, not bound by class interest or status consciousness. Finally, we are transported into Ed Holt's domestic sphere, his "typical middle class neighborhood and the relationships which develop among neighbors." The camera follows Holt and his carpool back to their suburban subdivision, where the paterfamilias plays baseball with his son and the neighborhood boys, chats with a neighbor, tinkers with his car, and inspects a loose front step on his tract home.[10]

In the end, the film associated the white collar not with the particularities or opportunities of work but with a lifestyle. A white-collar job was a means to a middle-class end, figured in terms of what the historian Margaret Marsh has called "masculine domesticity."[11] A man's dominion over his home compensated, the film implied, for his lack of authority, autonomy, and opportunity to exercise his creativity at work. The film subtly poked fun at white-collar work, showing Holt sullying his clean hands—but not his white collar—when the fountain pen that his wife gave him as a gift for graduating from the training program sprang a leak. The job was a mere means to an end—the true rewards of a happy home and family life. Ed Holt, one archetype of a new twentieth-century middle-class man, worked to live.

There were, of course, competing representations of middle-class masculinity and work in popular culture. Henry David Epstein, a thirty-two-year-old Realtor profiled in the *Saturday Evening Post*, was Ed Holt's contemporary white-collar compatriot. For Epstein work itself was at life's center and conferred great satisfaction. He "started his climb toward affluence" from a position "quite a few rungs below the bottom of the ladder," the story in the *Post* quipped. Family financial problems and the death of his father forced Epstein to drop out of the University of Pennsylvania in 1941, and he quickly took over his father's business. From the start, he was a broker on a mission, "going in for [big] deals and fast money instead of just plugging along on commissions," never passing up any "reasonable risk." By the time he was drafted into the military in 1943, he had managed to pay off his family's debts, and to buy a car and a row house. In the army he achieved five awards, but his independent personality bristled under the military's stifling rules. His propensity to "judge a situation on its own merits, reach his own conclusion, and act accordingly" did not ingratiate him to his superior officers. When he returned from his tour of duty, he borrowed $2,000 from his mother, formed a partnership with another Realtor, and began to buy and sell houses. His big break came late in 1947 when he acquired and converted a three-hundred-unit rental housing project in Chester, Pennsylvania, and sold the homes to individual families, netting a profit of $200,000. He never again had trouble obtaining financial backing for his projects.[12]

Epstein calmly and quietly dedicated himself to the "national ambition of making a few million dollars," according to the *Post*. His family had lost its home in Philadelphia during the Great Depression, an experience that had affected the young man greatly, and so Epstein was "hot on homeownership." In 1953 Epstein, "the most remarkable thing" to "happen to real estate since the Louisiana Purchase," acquired 5,400 homes in Levittown, New York, in a much publicized $42 million deal, and converted the rental units into a "community" of "individually owned homes" at a multimillion-dollar profit. Big projects such as the Levittown conversion allowed him to combine his two great passions in real estate: facilitating homeownership and solving intricate financial puzzles. "Never happier" than when "poring over sheets of complicated figures, sprinkled with tricky clauses and whereases," Epstein had an "ability to see through complex problems" that was his greatest business strength.[13]

In this narrative of middle-class manhood, Epstein's identity derived primarily from his work, from his entrepreneurial skill and derring-do. Yet he was simultaneously a benevolent social engineer, choosing a career in real estate to spread the gospel of homeownership and prevent others from suffering the tragic loss of home that had befallen his family. Epstein, who was unmarried, was also a "patriarch" at heart, intent on keeping his family together in the Philadelphia area. He had "nothing against women personally," and he planned to get married as soon as he met "some girl" who could "stand" him. In the meantime, he bought a home big enough that his sister, her husband and children, and his widowed mother could live together nearby.[14] Thus his professional success, inspired by his personal experience with loss in the 1930s, allowed him to provide for others and his own family. Henry Epstein lived to work, and it was through work that Epstein realized himself as a middle-class man.

While both Henry Epstein and Ed Holt were men in the business world, they represented very different models of middle-class masculinity at mid-century. Holt, a team player aiming to work his way up step by step within a hierarchical corporate structure, expressed his manhood primarily through the performance of manual labor around his own home and participation in family and civic life. The freewheeling and autonomous Epstein, by contrast, exuded manly confidence in his ability to consummate the next big deal and in his penchant for risk. The home was central to the construction of both men's manhood: for Holt the home's gender-enhancing properties inhered in its symbolic exchange value as a commodity and as a site for performing masculine domesticity. For Epstein, the home both symbolized his masculine familial authority and was the material basis for his professional identity and the source of his power as an entrepreneur. Holt likely went into debt to purchase his modicum of patriarchy, while Epstein amassed great wealth in purveying homes. "If I can't find a town to buy," Epstein—"the man who buys whole towns"—concluded, "I may build one."[15] Holt was the classic organization man, while Epstein represented an alternative path: that of a relatively autonomous business professional.

Like the classic texts of the immediate postwar period—notably C. Wright Mills's *White Collar*, David Riesman's *The Lonely Crowd*, William Whyte's *The Organization Man*, and Sloan Wilson's *The Man in the Gray Flannel Suit*—the film *White-Collar Worker* and the profile of Henry Epstein in the *Saturday Evening Post* put forth representations of masculinity that testified to the problematic relationship between masculinity and white-collar work in the United States in the twentieth century. Henry Epstein shared Mills's romanticism about the "true" middle-class American man as an autonomous actor and virtuous citizen, grounded by his work and his relationship to property. Real estate brokerage as a career met men's needs to feel vital to the social fabric of the republic, to play the creative role of the *homo faber*. At the same time, as professionals, real estate brokers were drawn toward modern, technocratic ideas about efficiency and standardized knowledge. Yet their occupational identities were bound tightly to the promotion of precisely the sort of domesticity that was Ed Holt's touchstone. The tensions between the entrepreneur and the organization man, the "man of the family" and the partner in a nuclear family centered on a home of its own, the risk taker and the planner, the "doer" and the "knower"—these were the two souls in the breast of the middle-class American man in the middle of twentieth-century America. The burgeoning suburban domesticity that *White-Collar Worker* championed for Ed Holt—and which Henry Epstein helped to create in Levittown—constituted both the conditions under which second-wave feminism would emerge in the 1960s and a major opportunity for women Realtors.

Women in Real Estate in the 1950s and Beyond

By 1960 women Realtors and the rest of the female labor force converged demographically in terms of marital status, but diverged in terms of age distribution. The marital status of women Realtors in 1960 differed only slightly from that of the female working population as a whole, a dramatic shift from the 1930s. According to a survey conducted in 1959 of the membership of the Women's Council, 58 percent of women Realtors were married, while 18 percent were single and 24 percent widowed or divorced. The aggregate female labor force had just about caught up to women Realtors: in 1960, about 56 percent of the white female labor force was married, while nearly 24 percent was single and 19 percent widowed or divorced. In terms of age distribution, nearly 57 percent of women Realtors were fifty years of age or older in 1959. A study in California in 1954 corroborated this for a population of brokers that included both Realtors and non-Realtors: it found the median age of all residential brokers to be fifty, with 68 percent of brokers forty-six years of age or older. The median age at entry for California brokers was forty-one, and well over half stayed in the business for eight years or more. In the overall labor force, barely 40 percent of female workers were forty-five or older.[16] These data lead inevitably to the conclusion that women in particular tended to enter real estate later in life, after childbearing years, and very often remained in the business until retirement age. Laura Hale Gorton, for example, stayed in the business for twenty years, retiring at sixty-five.

Women Realtors were, on the whole, considerably better educated than the female population as a whole in the late 1950s. The survey by the Women's Council found that 25 percent of women Realtors had college degrees in 1959, and 47 percent had attended some college. In the total population over the age of twenty-five, only 6 percent of white women had completed four or more years of college, and another 9.5 percent had attended for one to three years. It should be noted that women Realtors were also somewhat better educated on average than female brokers. A study of real estate brokers and salespersons in California in 1954 found that 15 percent of female brokers were college graduates, and 34 percent had attended some college.[17]

Women Realtors were well ahead of the female labor force in terms of income as well. One-half of Women's Council members reported that their entire income came from their real estate earnings, and about one-quarter reported that they supported their families entirely on that income; 93 percent of women Realtors classified themselves as self-employed, and of these, 46 percent employed at least two salespersons. The emphasis continued to be on residential property, with 93 percent of women respondents claiming residential brokerage as their primary activity in the field. Women Realtors also tended to do very well for themselves financially, as long as they had been in the business for three years or more. More than half the respondents claimed average annual earnings over the period 1956–59 of $8,000 or more, with 34 percent reporting incomes of greater than $10,000, more than five times the income per capita for women in 1960 of $1,861.[18]

The survey also canvassed several hundred firms employing women brokers and saleswomen about "women's qualifications for real estate selling," tacitly assuming some sort of essential difference. Predictably, only about 5 percent of the 464 executives responding claimed that gender was irrelevant. About 60 percent of the firms surveyed enumerated qualifications "associated with their sex" in response to an open-ended question about desirable qualities possessed by women. Of these, by far the most often cited were "women's point of view" and that "women clients like women salespeople," followed by women's intuitive "understanding [of] the home's importance" and "special knowledge" of the home. The other major category of response was women's "desirable character and personality traits." Of these, most often noted were persistence and determination, followed distantly by patience, loyalty, and enthusiasm—a reversal of the rank-ordering of qualities embedded in the stereotypical portrait of women in the 1950s. On the whole, 60 percent of the real estate executives polled noted sex-specific traits. As the survey's lead author, Beryl McClaskey, observed, "the woman as traditional figure associated with the home appears to have an advantage," corroborating a point made by Mary Amelia Warren in 1941.

While the positive traits revolved largely around women's putative natural advantages, the most prevalent "undesirable traits" of women in real estate were related to "personality" and "attitude." Women's biggest problems in real estate were lack of sufficient motivation and emotional immaturity— their feelings got hurt too easily, they had personality conflicts with co-workers and prospects, and they were unwilling to "take criticism." This set of beliefs reflected quite closely the skeptical admonition about women's business maturity sent to women Realtors by the president of the Women's Council, Carol Laux, in 1943. Interestingly, conflicts between domestic concerns and work were mentioned by barely 20 percent of the respondents, about as many as mentioned lack of technical knowledge.[19]

Women Realtors escaped stereotypes of femininity as they marketed the very product—the family home—and mobilized the very ideologies that depended on and reinforced those stereotypes. They often did this self-consciously; that is, they deployed stereotypical femininity in ways that helped them succeed at a "man's game," all the while realizing that calling brokerage a "man's game" itself gave them an advantage, made them seem more "human" and thus less like "pushy salesmen," and that they could more easily sell houses. At the same time, male Realtors, once they realized that women had done this successfully, beat a retreat into the manly hustle and bustle of commercial realty, dramatically slowing women's entry into that subfield. Women thus came to predominate in residential real estate brokerage. The challenge of "women's ways of selling" was rather fundamentally a challenge to deeply held notions about middle-class manliness, and about women's "proper role" in the business world. The story of Rosie the Realtor problematizes the ways in which business practices come to be normalized as belonging to either the "woman's sphere" or the "man's sphere," how certain practices, like sales, become marked as either masculine or feminine—and how these codings are challenged and change with time.

According to the available evidence, residential real estate had become a "woman's world," in California and elsewhere, by the 1950s. In 1954 nearly 70 percent of the women brokers in the state reported devoting more than 70 percent of their total real estate activity to single-family houses, versus 53 percent of the male brokers. As a result, at least in California in 1953, the median income of female brokers was $3,200, considerably lower than male earnings of $4,300.[20] By 1960 over 25 percent of real estate brokers were women, a huge proportion for sales careers, and a far higher proportion than in any of the traditional learned professions. By the mid-1960s, real estate "portraits of success" featured women brokers prominently. One noted business writer found that seven of the ten top-earning brokers in the 1970s were women.[21]

The Solipsistic Saga of Suzy Soldsine

The liberal feminist impulse that had provided at least part of the energy fueling women brokers' assault on the field in the 1920s and 1940s had largely dissipated by the 1950s. Women Realtors in particular became important figures in a political culture that exalted "free enterprise" and vilified public solutions to housing and other social problems, helping to set the stage for the conservatism of Barry Goldwater and Ronald Reagan from the 1960s to the 1980s. Perhaps it is not accidental that the so-called neoconservative revolution or the "right turn" beginning in the 1960s began in southern California, long a bastion for women Realtors.

Suzy Soldsine, a fictional character created by the author and Realtor Mary Shern, offers an illuminating narrative of the ways in which conservative businesswomen came to deny liberal feminism's role in creating the conditions of possibility for their achievements. For these women, participation in the real estate business became a means of achieving personal fulfillment, an escape from the boredom of their daily lives, rather than a political statement about the equality of women. In the mid-1970s Suzy sent her third and last child off to school and found herself "alone in the house—and lonely." She and her neighbor, Marjorie, commiserated over the "problem of how to fill their newfound free time." After discussing the scintillating possibilities of shopping "without the kids underfoot," going to "luncheons and movies," forming a bridge club, and taking up a hobby, Suzy mused that "there's got to be more to life" than being a homemaker. She contemplated finding a job, asking herself whether she could handle both it and her "primary responsibility," running the household—"or would life become a schizophrenic nightmare?" She wondered what her friends, relatives, mother, and especially her husband would think. Would she be less respected as a mother if she went to work? "Herein lies one of life's mysteries: when junior falls off the monkey bars and breaks a bone, and mother can't be reached because she's at a matinee, that's OK; but if mother can't be reached because she's out making an honest dollar, it's definitely not OK." In her comfortable social world, with a loving husband who supported his family with ease, she ruminated, "a job would make [me] a maverick."[22]

Determined nevertheless, the bored housewives put their heads together, and after Marjorie remarked that Suzy could sell "a curling iron to Kojak," they stumbled upon the idea of opening a boutique, an "anything shop" to sell "whatever strikes our fancy." Fortified with a well-chilled martini, they presented their scheme to their husbands for approval, but the men were "merciless," bombarding them with all manner of detail concerning the start-up costs, operating expenses, and tax obligations of a small business—about which they were totally ignorant. Suzy, who had graduated from high school "with a major in sock hops, cheerleading, and recess," started to have "the uncomfortable feeling that this was a quiz and she was flunking." But then her husband John pushed the wrong button. "If you have so much free time," he asked, "then why don't you try volunteer work?" Incensed, Suzy enumerated the litany of church and civic organizations that constituted the totality of her life outside the home. She was a "class mother, a den mother, and a playground mother." She was a mother to three children, and a wife. "What she hadn't been for too many years" was her own person. "It isn't a question of whiling away idle hours," she exclaimed. "I want an identity, my own pocket money, and my own victories."[23]

While Marjorie demurred, losing enthusiasm and energy in the face of the men's censure and derision, Suzy was steeled in her conviction, her private feminist consciousness awakened. "I'm not prepared to get all my kicks for the rest of my life beaming over John's promotions or Mike's merit badges!" With that, the scheme of collaborating with Marjorie dissolved, and the "stage was now set for some well-meaning friend to suggest" that Suzy try real estate. She was told it would be an "ideal career for a homemaker." She'd "be her own boss, work only when it was convenient, meet lots of interesting people, and make a scandalous amount of money"—which, of course, she'd already begun to spend in her mind. John did not object to "a working wife," as she had thought he might; her fears that he would take the suggestion as an affront to his masculine ability to provide for the family proved unfounded. She stealthily dropped the idea of going into real estate "over the morning coffee" while John was "deeply engrossed in the morning paper," and "since no significant opposition was mounted, the die was cast." Suzy Soldsine had chosen real estate—or it had chosen her.[24]

Thus our story of women in real estate has come full circle. We began with Laura Hale Gorton, a woman driven by the death of her husband to support her family during the Great Depression. She carefully weighed her career options against her family needs and responsibilities, choosing real estate consciously because it enabled her, without special training, to use her intimate knowledge of home and community to fulfill both her own need for a large income and her desire to have a career that would serve a social purpose, helping people find "a home in the country and a pleasant neighborhood in which to bring up their children." Along the way, her hard work earned not only riches but the "deep satisfaction" of having created a "monument to her vision and courage," materialized in "hundreds of homes, miles of streets winding through hills and a booming shopping center." Helping to build her profession by leading the Women's Council and "advancing the security, peace, and happiness which make up an American home" through her political work on the Realtors Washington Committee capped a full life for Gorton, who died accidentally in 1953.[25] For Gorton's generation of women Realtors, the single-family owner-occupied home was not only, or even primarily, a site of personal struggle but one laden with civic and geopolitical significance, a true bulwark against rapidly encroaching anti-American values that required vigilance on the part of women, and especially real estate women, in the public arena.

Suzy Soldsine, by contrast, entered real estate for reasons almost entirely self-centered. "To be in real estate," Shern wrote in her own voice in the preface to her "lighthearted story," "is to experience total immersion. If one stays, it must be something more than a career and closer to a flaming love affair." Real estate helped Suzy to achieve goals "ranging from the frivolous to the sublime," supported her "latent passion for sinful luxuries," and "sustained" her "through such whims as collecting crystal, cars, and condominiums." Gently yet deliberately deriding what she perceived to be the project of the women's movement, then in full swing, Suzy declared that she was neither a " 'militant feminist' " nor a "militant anything." She explicitly denied interest in all political "causes," viewing them with "about the same attitude" that she felt "toward kidney stones—abject terror." As for the feminist goal of equal pay for equal work, although it seemed "fair," it did not really concern her, since she never aspired to be a "front-line soldier, to join a men's club, to use the men's washroom, to wear men's clothes, or even to don Bella Abzug's hats." Her "bras were never for burning," she continued, whimsically, as if women's liberation were a quaint anachronism, and the idea of gender-neutral equality a bit absurd. She harbored "no rancor for men," declaring proudly, "like so many thousands of other Americans, I am woman, wife, mother, and Realtor." Anticipating the so-called postfeminists of the 1990s, she echoed Mary Amelia Warren's words from 1941, though this time in explicit opposition to the liberal feminist agenda that informed Warren's wartime speech before the Women's Council: "I fail to become upset over the shifting sands of sexual roles in society. I choose my role and let others do the same. In real estate, we can pursue our course *because* we're women, not in spite of it, and do our task without losing an ounce of femininity. Therefore, I more or less oppose equal rights. Why should women give up the edge we've so richly deserved and so long enjoyed?"[26]

A grueling few weeks showing the difficult Mr. and Mrs. Green around dozens of houses reaffirmed Suzy's conviction that "residential selling is women's work." For men, the house was a "major asset," while to women it was "an environment . . . the setting within which they perform the infinitely varied tasks of homemaking. The layout of the house and the quality of the equipment have everything to do with making the homemaker's job manageable or miserable." Once a means to the end of achieving equality within a man's world of brokerage, in the "woman's world" of real estate in which Suzy Soldsine came of age, femininity had again become a taken-for-granted attribute of women brokers. Suzy worked primarily to fulfill her own personal needs, her consumer desires. "Like most women she knew," Suzy "decided what she wanted to spend first," then she "worked out ways of making it possible." A woman has an "innately positive attitude about her chances of wheedling money out of dear old dad, darling husband, or kind fate," Suzy asserted. Consequently, "the feminine approach is ideally suited to the flexibility of commission earnings," another reason, Suzy reflected with satisfaction, "why women go so well with real estate."[27] One wonders what Grace Perego, Mary Amelia Warren, or even Laura Hale Gorton would have made of this sentiment. The productive tension between liberal feminist impulses toward equality in the business world and maternal concern for civic welfare that had driven the movement for full female inclusion in real estate seemed to have dissipated. A career in real estate became for at least some women a means to achieve self-fulfillment and consumerist goals within the privatized world of the nuclear family.

By 1980 the gender composition of the aggregate real estate labor force was evenly split, though there remained significant internal differences among Realtors. In 1978 men made up over three-quarters of real estate brokers and of the managers and owners of real estate firms; parity with women was reached only in the late 1990s. Additionally, women's participation lagged far behind men's in the lucrative commercial and industrial sector well into the 1990s; in 1996 women accounted for 54 percent of residential Realtors but only 15 percent of commercial realtors. Yet certain trends were unmistakable: women were quickly catching up with men in most of the field. By 2000 the typical Realtor was a fifty-two-year-old, married, white woman with at least some college education and a gross personal income of $47,700, well above the national median.[28] Real estate women had achieved the material and social substrates of an independent, feminine, middle-class identity: financial self-sufficiency, stable careers, and majority membership in a powerful professional association.

CONCLUSION

Status plays a decisive role in the formation of personality at the various stages of development, for if young people are to learn to live adaptively as mature people in our society they must be trained by the informal controls of our society to fit into their places.

— W. Lloyd Warner, 1949[1]

Cultural History: One Big Middle Class?

The professionalization of a particular occupation, real estate brokerage, provides a window into broader processes of middle class formation and identification in twentieth-century America. While it might be an exaggeration to assert that America had literally become a "nation of realtors," as the historian Robert Binkeley did in 1929, the metaphor was nonetheless apt.[2] The Realtor, Binkeley argued, "makes that characteristic [American] combination of definitely known practical fact with vaguely felt and distant ideal . . . He is both prophet and business man." The rise of the Realtors was a paradigmatic case in the history of the new twentieth-century American middle class. The Realtors drew on a wide range of discourses—gender ideals, notions about property and propriety, social science concepts, racial ideologies—to construct a new middle-class identity that irrevocably blurred the boundaries between professional and entrepreneur.

By 1940 the boundaries of the category "middle class" had become so capacious that virtually every American thought he—or she—belonged to it. From the mid-1930s onward, American identity itself was largely cast in terms of membership in one big "middle class." In 1939 the Gallup Poll found that more than three-quarters of the American public saw themselves as members of the middle class, even in the midst of the Great Depression; moreover, a significant number of Americans identified themselves as middle class even when they considered themselves poor. In 1940 a poll by *Fortune* magazine obtained similar results.[3]

By the time the sociologist Lloyd Warner published his landmark study *Social Class in America: The Evaluation of Status* in 1949, the "informal controls" of "our society" that he held to be so important seemed firmly in place. Yet Warner was concerned. "The lives of many," he wrote, "are destroyed because they do not understand the workings of social class." His purpose in publishing *Social Class in America* was essentially therapeutic: "to provide a corrective instrument" that would "permit men and women better to evaluate their social situations and thereby better adapt themselves to social reality and fit their dreams and aspirations to what is possible." The sociologist's urgent tone and his insistence that young people "must be trained" suggested anxiety about the efficacy of the mechanisms of socialization that he found so necessary. In the decade following publication of the book, of course, these mechanisms of social control would be frontally attacked, first by young African Americans and then by an increasingly broad cross-section of American society—primarily the same "young people" who Warner hoped would learn to "live adaptively."[4]

But in 1949 most Americans seemed to believe that they were members of the middle class. "Middle class" had come to mean something to almost every American by the 1940s. The cluster of associations evoked by the term was in large measure anchored by two key terms. The first, "homeowner," became a virtual metonym for "middle class." To be middle class meant, at least, to own—or to aspire to own—a home of one's own. As this book has demonstrated, government, business, and civic groups cooperated closely from the 1920s onward to promote this ideal. In the 1930s and 1940s they crafted policies that allowed many Americans to realize what came to be called "the American dream" of homeownership.

When the historian James Truslow Adams first introduced the phrase "the American dream" in his book *The Epic of America* (1931), it had no association with homeownership. Adams, a scholar and critic, believed that America was in danger of becoming a land of "yes men" because of the spread of big business, and that the precious promise of American life he termed the American dream envisioned "a land in which life should be richer and fuller for every man, with opportunity for each according to his ability or achievement." Adams wrote with both the hedonistic materialism of the 1920s and the not-yet-recognized-as-great depression of the 1930s in mind, and he defined the American dream in explicitly nonmaterialistic terms. "[T]he American dream that has lured tens of millions of all nations to our shores has not been a dream of merely material plenty, though that has doubtless counted heavily. It has been much more than that. It has been a dream of being able to grow to fullest development as man and woman, unhampered by the barriers which had slowly been erected in older civilizations, unrepressed by social orders which had been developed for classes rather than for the simple human being of any and every class."[5]

The cultural and political work of the Realtors and their allies in Washington and elsewhere definitively associated the American dream with homeownership. Today it is virtually redundant to speak of "the American dream of homeownership." Thus, Adams's notion of the dream "of being able to grow to fullest development" has been conflated to possession of a home of one's own "for the simple human being of any and every class," whom Franklin Roosevelt referred to as "the common man." The owned home became a stand-in for and a symbol of this broader goal of human fulfillment. Critics of homeownership, such as John C. Keats in his book *Crack in the Picture Window* (1956), disparaged the suburban tract home as a "little box on a concrete slab," the suburban development as a "fresh-air slum," an assemblage of "identical boxes" that spread "like gangrene" across the country. To critics, the real estate industry's political machinations that succeeded in eliminating rent control essentially coerced young families into buying cheaply built and unaesthetic houses in stultifying and ersatz communities. Nevertheless, even the critics had to admit that the ticky-tacky boxes were "selling like hotcakes."[6] Further, as the historian of the suburbs Barbara Kelly has demonstrated, many Americans "expanded the dream," creatively reconfiguring even the most mundane tract houses into family homes with style and character.[7]

The second keyword that anchored the cultural hegemony of the middle class, "professional," was a bit more diffuse. Certainly not all Americans were, or aspired to be, professionals. Yet most, if not all, did aspire to attain the respect for their work concomitant with the designation, and professionalism became a crucial marker of middle-class status. Thus throughout the twentieth century, Americans referred to an increasing number of occupations as "professions," including many that entailed primarily manual labor or had no rigorous, formal educational requirements. By the 1950s Americans listened to professional journalists on the radio, as they drove cars maintained by professional mechanics, on the way to a professional dry-cleaner, to retrieve clothing to pack for a vacation planned by a professional travel agent. The permeation of the discourse of professionalism into ever-widening occupational spheres represented at once a democratization of the category "profession" and a dilution of its social power. In some ways this tendency was reminiscent of the attack on privilege during the Jacksonian era. However, the crucial difference is that twentieth-century American society was absolutely dependent upon technical expertise for even the most prosaic operations in daily life.[8] The expansive discourse of professionalism signified a new set of resources through which Americans without heroic roles to play in political or economic life, without diplomas from élite institutions, and without celebrity status could conceive of themselves as part of a great and vital national class. The imagined American community comprised one huge middle class well before mid-century.

Bounded by these two axes—"homeowner" and "professional"—"middle class" became an extraordinarily amorphous position in American social space. Politically, however, alignment with the "middle class" was unbeatable from the New Deal onward, as Franklin Roosevelt first discovered with the Home Owners Loan Corporation in 1932.[9] A group representing by definition the common interest rather than any special interest, the middle class is so influential that it is virtually impossible for a modern American politician to lose support by pandering to it. And it is almost equally unimaginable for an American politician to gain broad support by invoking the interests of any other class, since these are presumed not to exist. The capacious formlessness of the category "middle class" has been the essence of its cultural durability and political utility.

Fear of the Other America

Paradoxically, scholars and critics have often called for clarity in studies of the middle class. In 1979 the social historian Peter Stearns called for a "more precise" definition. In *The Emergence of the Middle Class* (1989), Stuart Blumin argued that the lack of clearly defined criteria and boundaries for middle-class membership constituted a "failed" emergence in the late nineteenth century. In a further attempt to clarify, in her book *Fear of Falling* (1989), Barbara Ehrenreich isolated a fragment of the middle class she called the "professional middle class" (PMC) and analyzed its turn away from the Democratic Party and towards Reaganite Republicanism. The PMC turned to the right largely, she argued, because of its increasing class-consciousness—that is, the increasing self-awareness among professionals and managers that they are a class among others, and not a universal class.

Until the "discovery" of poverty and the working class in the 1960s the middle class was characterized by its lack of self-consciousness, facilitated by the tendency in American culture to everywhere represent it as representing everyone. The working class's conspicuous absence in mainstream American culture—produced, for the most part, by the prolific professional middle class itself—after the 1930s exemplified, in Ehrenreich's words, a "naïve mid-century idea that the middle class was America." This book has suggested that perhaps this was not such a "naïve" idea in the strict sense of the term—this "middle class unconsciousness" was the result of a variety of social, cultural, and economic forces that came together in historically specific ways during the 1920s through the 1950s.[10] The middle class's amorphousness was integral to its unconsciousness.

As Ehrenreich tells the story, the "discovery" of the poor and working class—symbolized by the publication of Michael Harrington's tract *The Other America* (1962)—demonstrated to members of the PMC that they were not in fact a universal class. There was an "other America," the discovery of which produced a rupture in the dialectics of middle-class identity. The middle class's hegemony was shattered, and in an attempt to deal with the anxiety attendant upon its newfound self-consciousness, the PMC invented such notions as the "underclass" and the "culture of poverty," styled itself as an élite, and largely turned toward neoconservatism. Ironically, the outcome of this work on the "other America" by Harrington, an avowed socialist, helped to set in motion a rightward shift among the very liberals he had hoped to push leftward.[11]

The implications of Ehrenreich's argument are profound: American "middle class" culture depended upon the successful suppression, in the public mind, of the existence of class "others." Furthermore, I would argue, the deviantization and racialization of these others as the "underclass," "welfare queens," "crack-addicts," and so forth were thus a mechanism for attempting to restore the middle class's lack of awareness of their own social position. But once the genie of class consciousness is out of the bottle, can it be compelled to return?

Of course, poverty in America had been discovered at least once before. In

1890 Jacob Riis published *How the Other Half Lives*, sparking one of the major movements of the Progressive era, housing reform.[12] In this book I have contended that the various tendencies collapsed under the rubric of progressivism helped forge the "middle class unconsciousness" of which Ehrenreich analyzed the unraveling. For the middle decades of the twentieth century, the new class managed to nearly forget about its own existence. The rise of the Realtor was a paradigmatic case in the formation of a middle class increasingly unaware of itself as a class, of the development of its tendency to everywhere represent itself and its interests as representing and representative of everyone.

Real Estate Redux

Real estate brokers developed and deployed strategies to sell houses that helped to reify a particular notion of home and neighborhood as the "normal" desideratum for a "middle-class" American family. The home became the single most significant commodity in the American economy, and ideas about property ownership and debt were transformed from producerist, republican notions into consumerist ideals. As Realtors—dealers in both domestic and metropolitan spaces as well as the ideology of homeownership—attempted to fashion themselves as professional entrepreneurs, they helped to transform received notions of professionalism, stretching it to the point of near-synonymy with "middle class." In turn, middle class became a meaningfully meaningless category of identity. It was meaningful because by 1940 almost nine-tenths of Americans considered themselves members of the middle class and responded to its invocation by politicians, pundits, and scholars as if their membership in it were self-evident. Yet the category was meaningless because it was virtually impossible for the same politicians, pundits, and scholars to demarcate the concept with any precision. The middle class continues to elude, and elide, precise definition, despite its centrality to twentieth-century American political culture. Imprecision and amorphousness are precisely what gave—and give—this category its political and cultural power.

APPENDIX

Characteristics of Brokers

Table 1: Real Estate Agents by Sex, 1910–1980

Year	MALE			FEMALE			TOTAL	
	Number	%	% Change	Number	%	% Change	Number	% Change
1910	122,935	97.7		2,927	2.3		125,862	
1920	139,927	93.8	13.8	9,208	6.2	214.6	149,135	18.5
1930	203,119	86.6	45.2	31,308	13.4	240.0	234,427	57.2
1940	100,856	90.8	−50.3	10,254	9.2	−67.2	111,110	−52.6
1950	120,235	85.6	19.2	20,277	14.4	97.7	140,512	26.5
1960	148,957	76.1	23.9	46,785	23.9	130.7	195,742	39.3
1970	180,801	68.0	21.4	85,140	32.0	82.0	265,941	35.9
1980	354,160	55.0	95.9	289,972	45.0	240.6	644,132	142.2

Derived from *17th Census of the United States: 1950, Population, United States Summary*, table 125, 1-267; *Statistical Abstract of the United States: 1995*, section 13: Labor Force, Employment, and Earnings, table 649, 412.

Table 2: Female Occupations, including Real Estate Agents, by Marital Status, 1930

	SINGLE		MARRIED		WIDOWED, DIVORCED		
	Number	%	Number	%	Number	%	Total
Real Estate Agents	4,782	15.0	14,391	45.3	12,614	39.7	31,787
Trade	460,226	47.9	339,428	35.3	161,447	16.8	961,101
Professionals	1,115,307	73.1	294,297	19.3	116,356	7.6	1,525,960
Total	5,734,825	53.9	3,071,302	28.9	1,826,100	17.2	10,632,227

Derived from *15th Census of the United States: 1930, Population*, vol. v: *General Report on Occupations*, table 5.

Table 3: Structure of the Female Labor Force by Age, 1945–1970 (in Percent)

	16–19	20–24	25–44	45–64	65+
1945	14.09	17.15	43.36	22.85	2.54
1950	9.31	14.56	44.90	28.06	3.17
1960	8.86	11.13	40.60	35.52	3.90
1970	10.30	15.50	36.99	33.86	3.35

Derived from U.S. Bureau of the Census, *Historical Statistics of the United States*, series D 29-41, 131.

NOTES

Introduction

1 Charles Franklin Palm, *The Middle Classes: Then and Now* (New York: Macmillan, 1936), 3.

2 Robert C. Binkeley, "A Nation of Realtors," *New Republic*, 9 October 1929.

3 Joseph P. Day, "Unification of Thought and Purpose," *National Real Estate Journal* 1, no. 3 (15 May 1910), 116.

4 The term "professional project" is borrowed from the sociologist Magali S. Larson, *The Rise of Professionalism: A Sociological Analysis* (Berkeley: University of California Press, 1977).

5 Robert Wiebe, *Search for Order, 1877–1920* (New York: Hill and Wang, 1967), esp. chap. 5.

6 Daniel Rodgers, "In Search of Progressivism," *Reviews in American History* 10, no. 4 (December 1982): 123.

7 Quotes are from Jan Cohn, *Creating America: George Horace Lorimer and the Saturday Evening Post* (Pittsburgh: University of Pittsburgh Press, 1989), 6.

8 Edward Mott Woolley, "Inner Secrets of a Real Estate Broker's Rise," *Saturday Evening Post*, 4 May 1912.

9 Woolley, "Inner Secrets"; Tom P. Morgan, "The Talented Bilfinger," *Harper's New Monthly Magazine* 84, no. 502 (March 1892): 649.

10 Woolley, "Inner Secrets."

11 Ibid.

12 Margo A. Conk, *History of Occupational Statistics* (Ann Arbor, Mich.: UMI Research Press, 1983).

13 Michael Kimmel, *Manhood in America: A Cultural History* (New York: Free Press, 1996).

14 Works dealing with the "demand side" of American housing include Gwendolyn Wright, *Building the Dream: A Social History of Housing in America* (New York: Pantheon, 1981); Clifford E. Clark, *The American Family Home, 1800–1960* (Chapel Hill: University of North Carolina Press, 1986); and Margaret S. Marsh, *Suburban Lives* (New Brunswick, N.J.: Rutgers University Press, 1990).

15 See Catherine Beecher and Harriet Beecher Stowe, *The American Woman's Home, or*

The Principles of Domestic Science, Being a Guide to the Formation and Maintenance of Economical, Healthful, Beautiful, and Christian Homes (Hartford: Stowe-Day Foundation, 1975 [1869]); Kathryn Kish Sklar, *Catherine Beecher: A Study in American Domesticity* (New York: W. W. Norton, 1976). On the home as a symbol, see Clark, *The American Family Home*; Jan Cohn, *The Palace or the Poorhouse: The American House as a Cultural Symbol* (Lansing: Michigan State University Press, 1979); Dolores Hayden, *The Grand Domestic Revolution: A History of Feminist Designs for American Homes, Neighborhoods, and Cities* (Cambridge: MIT Press, 1981); Gwendolyn Wright, *Moralism and the Model Home* (Chicago: University of Chicago Press, 1980). On urban planning, see Robert Fishman, "The American Planning Tradition: An Introduction and Interpretation," in Robert Fishman, ed., *The American Planning Tradition: Culture and Policy* (Washington: Woodrow Wilson Center, 2000), 1–29; Mary Sies and Christopher Silver, "The History of Planning History," in Mary Sies and Christopher Silver, eds., *Planning the Twentieth-Century American City* (Baltimore: Johns Hopkins University Press, 1996), 1–24; M. Christine Boyer, *Dreaming the Rational City: The Myth of American City Planning* (Cambridge: MIT Press, 1983). On housing reformers, see Roy Lubove, *The Progressives and the Slums: Tenement House Reform in New York City, 1890–1917* (Westport, Conn.: Greenwood, 1974). On home economists, see Nancy K. Berlage, "The Establishment of an Applied Social Science: Home Economists, Science, and Reform at Cornell University, 1870–1930," in Helene Silverberg, ed., *Gender and American Social Science: The Formative Years* (Princeton: Princeton University Press, 1998), 185–212. On social work, see John Ehrenreich, *The Altruistic Imagination: A History of Social Work and Social Policy in the United States* (Ithaca: Cornell University Press, 1985); Daniel Walkowitz, "The Making of a Feminine Professional Identity: Social Workers in the 1920s," *American Historical Review* 95, no. 4 (October 1990): 1051–75; Walkowitz, *Working with Class: Social Workers and the Politics of Middle-Class Identity* (Chapel Hill: University of North Carolina Press, 1999).

16 For a genealogy of the term "American dream," see Merle Curti, "The American Exploration of Dreams and Dreamers," *Journal of the History of Ideas* 27, no. 3 (July–September 1966): 391–416.

17 Gail Radford, *Modern Housing for America: Policy Struggles in the New Deal Era* (Chicago: University of Chicago Press, 1996).

18 While I believe that the cultural pressure to own homes affects African Americans and other Americans of color as much as it does white Americans, and that the formation of the black middle class is bound to the same social and cultural matrix of homeownership and professionalization as that of the white middle class, much more research is needed on this topic.

19 Constance Perin, *Everything in Its Place: Social Order and Land Use in America* (Princeton: Princeton University Press, 1977), 32–34.

20 Walkowitz, *Working with Class*, 207–8.

21 Harold Wilensky, "The Professionalization of Everyone?" *American Journal of Sociol-*

ogy 70, no. 2 (September 1964): 137–58; Amitai Etzioni, *The Semi-professions and Their Organization: Teachers, Nurses, Social Workers* (New York: Free Press, 1969); JoAnne Brown, "Profession," in Richard Wightman Fox and James T. Kloppenberg, eds., *A Companion to American Thought* (Oxford: Basil Blackwell, 1995), 543–46; Walkowitz, "The Making of a Feminine Professional Identity"; Anne Witz, *Professions and Patriarchy* (London: Verso, 1992).

22 Jackson Lears has made similar arguments about advertisers' attempts to straddle the line between "premodern" notions of labor as creative and "modern" ideas about efficiency and standardized knowledge. See T. J. Jackson Lears, *Fables of Abundance: A Cultural History of Advertising in America* (New York: Basic Books, 1994).

23 The notion of "bricolage" is poached from the anthropologist Claude Lévi-Strauss. While Lévi-Strauss employs the term *bricoleur* to distinguish the engineer, who operates according to concepts, from the "scientist of the concrete," who operates "by means of signs," I use it in a somewhat ironic mode to suggest a sort of "post-professionalism" inaugurated, in part, by the real estate men. Like Lévi-Strauss's *bricoleur*, the real estate men built "ideological castles out of the debris of what was once a social discourse," namely the discourse of "true professionalism." Lévi-Strauss, *The Savage Mind* (Chicago: University of Chicago Press, 1966), 16–32. On "true professionalism," see Bruce Kimball, *The "True Professional Ideal" in America: A History* (Cambridge, Mass.: Basil Blackwell, 1992).

24 Ernesto Laclau and Chantal Mouffe, *Hegemony and Socialist Strategy: Towards a Radical Democratic Politics* (New York: Verso, 1985), 67.

Chapter 1 *"Doing Something Definite"*

1 Tom P. Morgan, "Bilfinger," *Harper's New Monthly Magazine* 79, no. 471 (August 1889): 484.

2 The conjunction of "real estate" and "agent" or "broker" first appeared in 1854, according to the *Oxford English Dictionary* (2d edition, 1989). For the purposes of this book, "broker" and "agent" will be used interchangeably, as they are in both modern everyday practice and contemporary sources. After the spread of licensing laws in the 1920s, the term "broker" generally came to refer to a person licensed to deal in the sale and transfer of real property, while "agent" more typically refers to a salesperson working for a licensed broker.

3 "The Durand Property," *Harper's New Monthly Magazine* 9, no. 50 (July 1854): 238–43.

4 Tom P. Morgan, "The Talented Bilfinger," *Harper's New Monthly Magazine* 84, no. 502 (March 1892): 649–50.

5 Morgan, "The Talented Bilfinger," 649.

6 William V. Ebersole, "The Interchange and Call System," *National Real Estate Journal* 10, no. 6 (December 1914): 430.

7 Chronology of board formation from *Who's Who in the Executive Council of the National Association of Real Estate Boards* (Chicago: NAREB, 1959).

8   This figure is comparable to other national professional associations. For example, in 1920, 9.2 percent of lawyers belonged to the American Bar Association. Figures from Corinne Lathrop Gilb, *Hidden Hierarchies: The Professions and Government* (New York: Harper and Row, 1966), 121.

9   Figures on founding dates of NAREB-affiliated boards from *Who's Who in the Executive Council of the National Association of Real Estate Boards*. On membership in 1917, see "First Roster of Realtors," *National Real Estate Journal*, June 1917. Evidence supporting the claim that prominent brokers generally belonged to NAREB-affiliated boards can be found in various *Who's Who* guides, such as *Who's Who in Philadelphia in Wartime* (Philadelphia: Stafford's News Service, 1920).

10 Kenneth T. Jackson, *Crabgrass Frontier: The Suburbanization of the United States* (New York: Oxford University Press, 1985), 135.

11 John H. Tigchon, "The Detroit Real Estate Board," *National Real Estate Journal* 1, no. 3 (15 May 1910): 87; "Organizing a Real Estate Exchange," *National Real Estate Journal* 1, no. 4 (15 June 1910): 170.

12 W. D. Juday to Richard T. Ely, 3 April 1918, Richard T. Ely Papers (State Historical Society of Wisconsin Microfilm Publication 924, reel 60), Library of Congress, Washington.

13 Morgan, "Bilfinger" and "The Talented Bilfinger"; Ring Lardner, "Own Your Home," *Redbook Magazine*, April 1915, 488–500; Sinclair Lewis, *Babbitt* (New York: NAL Penguin, 1961 [1922]).

14 Pearl Janet Davies, *Real Estate Achievement in the United States: A History of the Efforts within the Business of Real Estate to Set Up Standards of Practice, Analyze the Factors That Affect Real Estate Use, Bring about a Satisfying Environment for Family Life, Business, and Industry, and Help Create Conditions for a Wide and Secure Real Estate Ownership* (unpublished MS, n.d.[1960?], 2 vols.), chap. III, 5, Archives of the National Association of Realtors, Chicago.

15 Fred E. Case, *Real Estate Market Behavior in Los Angeles: A Study of Multiple Listing System Data* (Los Angeles, 1963), 48–49.

16 L. M. Krepleever, "Merit of Efficiency Brings Success to a Local Organization," *National Real Estate Journal* 4, no. 1 (15 September 1911): 45.

17 Herbert U. Nelson, *Administration of Real Estate Boards* (New York: Macmillan, 1925), chap. 10.

18 Case, *Real Estate Market Behavior in Los Angeles*, 52.

19 Leo Grebler, David Blank, and Louis Winnick, *Capital Formation in Residential Real Estate: Trends and Prospects* (Princeton: Princeton University Press, 1956).

20 Betsy Pegg, *Dreams, Money, and Ambition: A History of Real Estate in Chicago* (Chicago: Chicago Real Estate Board, 1983).

21 Everett C. Hughes, *The Growth of an Institution: The Chicago Real Estate Board* (New York: Arno, 1979 [1931]), 18.

22 "Why the Chicago Real Estate Board Is a Success," *National Real Estate Journal* 2, no. 1 (15 September 1910): 26.

23 By-Laws, Chicago Real Estate Board (1910), quoted in Hughes, *The Growth of an Institution*, 19.

24 "New Brass-Bound and Iron-Clad Lease," *Chicago Tribune*, 18 March 1883, as cited in Hughes, *The Growth of an Institution*, 19.

25 Ernest M. Fisher, *Principles of Real Estate Practice* (New York: Macmillan, 1925), 37, 286–91.

26 Pegg, *Dreams, Money, and Ambition*, 23.

27 Hughes, *The Growth of an Institution*, 20–21.

28 Sinclair Lewis satirized unscrupulous tactics like these in *Babbitt*, 41–44.

29 "Why the Chicago Real Estate Board Is a Success," 26.

30 For a detailed discussion of the impact of a local board in Los Angeles, see Marc A. Weiss, *The Rise of the Community Builders: The American Real Estate Industry and Urban Land Planning* (New York: Columbia University Press, 1987).

31 "Work of Local Exchanges," *National Real Estate Journal* 2, no. 2 (15 October 1910): 94.

32 Folder 150, box 59, series VIII, Membership Applications, Records of the Philadelphia Board of Realtors, Urban Archives, Philadelphia; folder 102, box 59, series VIII, Records of the Philadelphia Board of Realtors, Urban Archives, Philadelphia.

33 The use of the masculine pronoun is deliberate; until 1943, there were no female applicants to the Philadelphia Real Estate Board.

34 Folder 072, box 59, series VIII, Records of the Philadelphia Board of Realtors, Urban Archives, Philadelphia.

35 "Philadelphia Board Builds Home," *National Real Estate Journal*, June 1922, 27.

36 "Initiating a Realtor," *National Real Estate Journal* 22, no. 4 (14 February 1921): 30.

37 Michael S. Kimmel, "Masculinity as Homophobia: Fear, Shame, and Silence in the Construction of Gender Identity," in Joseph A. Kuypers, ed., *Men and Power* (Amherst, N.Y.: Prometheus, 1999), 108.

38 Charles A. Robbins, "Realtor Talks on Salesmanship: The Successful Salesman Must Be Sincere, Courageous, and Industrious," *Pittsburgh Realtor* 10, no. 21 (4 March 1924): 3.

39 Robbins, "Realtor Talks on Salesmanship."

40 Hughes, *The Growth of an Institution*, 1.

Chapter 2 A (National) Middle-Class Consciousness

1 "The Song of the Real Estate Dealer," *National Real Estate Journal* 11, no. 6 (June 1915): 329.

2 W. W. Hannan, "The National Association of Real Estate Exchanges," *National Real Estate Journal* 1, no. 1 (15 March 1910): 2.

3 "Realty Men Band to 'Kill' Sharks," *Chicago Tribune*, 10 May 1908, 14.

4 Everett C. Hughes, *The Growth of an Institution: The Chicago Real Estate Board* (New York: Arno, 1979 [1931]), 19.

5   "Realty Men Band to 'Kill' Sharks," 14.

6   "Advantages of Local Organization," *National Real Estate Journal* 2, no. 3 (15 November 1910): 150–51.

7   "Third Annual Convention of the National Association of Real Estate Exchanges," *National Real Estate Journal* 1, no. 3 (15 July 1910): 221.

8   *National Real Estate Journal* 1, no. 4 (15 June 1910): 169.

9   "City in Hands of Real Estate Men," *Minneapolis Journal*, 15 June 1910, 1–2.

10   " 'Get Together,' Hannan Urges," *Detroit Free Press*, 24 June 1909, § A, p. 7; "Good Finish to Meeting," *Detroit Free Press*, 26 June 1909, § A, p. 1.

11   "The Real Estate Convention," *Minneapolis Journal*, 17 June 1910, 5.

12   Ibid., 3.

13   "Real Estate!," *Rocky Mountain News*, 18 July 1911, 6.

14   *National Real Estate Journal* 10, no. 3 (September 1914): 206.

15   "Third Annual Convention of the National Association of Real Estate Exchanges," 232–33.

16   Ibid., 230.

17   "Denver Convention a Record Breaker," *National Real Estate Journal*, 15 August 1911, 400–401.

18   David R. Summers, "The Story of the Convention," *National Real Estate Journal* 12, no. 1 (15 July 1915): 10.

19   Summers, "When Good Fellows Get Together," *National Real Estate Journal*, 15 August 1911, 405.

20   "Denver Convention a Record Breaker," 401.

21   Proceedings of Annual Convention, *National Real Estate Journal*, July 1915, 122.

22   "Realty Men Romp in the Snow," *Rocky Mountain News*, 22 July 1911, 2.

23   "Behave Like College Boys," *Louisville Courier-Journal*, 20 June 1912, 1.

24   Verna M. Belcher, "Our Convention and Our Ladies," *National Real Estate Journal* 10, no. 3 (September 1914): 206–7.

25   "Five Minutes of Oratory," *National Real Estate Journal*, September 1914, 148–50.

26   "Realty Men's 'Smoker' Hotter Than Its Name," *Los Angeles Times*, 22 June 1915, § 2, pp. 1, 3.

27   Sigmund Freud, *Jokes and Their Relation to the Unconscious* (New York: W. W. Norton, 1989 [1909]).

28   "Seattle Real Estate Man Honored," *National Real Estate Journal* 3, no. 2 (15 April 1911): 102.

29   "A Story of Success," *National Real Estate Journal* 2, no. 2 (15 October 1910): 23–24.

30   Ibid., 24.

31   W. W. Hannan, "The Successful Real Estate Operator," *National Real Estate Journal*, 6 12 February 1912, 510–11.

32   Ibid., 510.

33   Ibid., 511.

34   Ibid.

35 "Real Estate and the Young Man," *National Real Estate Journal* 9, no. 1 (January 1913): 291–92.

36 Andrew Abbott, *The System of Professions: An Essay on the Division of Expert Labor* (Chicago: University of Chicago Press, 1988), 3.

Chapter 3 Character, Competency, Professionalism

1 Alexander S. Taylor, "Benefits of the National Association," 24 June 1915 (address to Los Angeles Convention), *National Real Estate Journal* 11, no. 6 (June 1915): 79 (emphasis in original).

2 James B. Gilbert, *Work without Salvation: America's Intellectuals and Industrial Aliena-tion, 1880–1910* (Baltimore: Johns Hopkins University Press, 1977), chaps. 4–5; John Higham, "The Reorientation of American Culture in the 1890s," in John Higham and Paul K. Conkin, eds., *New Directions in American Intellectual History* (Baltimore: Johns Hopkins University Press, 1977).

3 Abraham Flexner, *Is Social Work a Profession?* (New York: New York School of Philanthropy, 1915), 10, 15.

4 E. Orris Hart, "Ethics," *National Real Estate Journal*, 20 October 1915, 331.

5 Joseph E. Sterrett, "Accountancy," *Every-Day Ethics: Addresses Delivered in the Page Lecture Series, 1909, before the Senior Class of the Sheffield Scientific School, Yale University* (New Haven: Yale University Press, 1910), 16–40.

6 *Annals of the American Academy of Political and Social Science* 101 (May 1922).

7 Louis D. Brandeis, *Business: A Profession* (Boston: Maynard, 1914); Edgar L. Heermance, *The Ethics of Business: A Study of Current Standards* (New York: Harper and Brothers, 1926); Heermance, *Codes of Ethics: A Handbook* (Burlington, Vt.: Free Press Printing, 1924); Arthur J. Eddy, *The New Competition: An Examination of the Conditions Underlying the Radical Change That Is Taking Place in the Commercial and Industrial World—The Change from a Competitive to a Coöperative Basis* (Chicago: A. C. McClurg, 1915). Quotes are from Heermance, *The Ethics of Business*, 3, and Heermance, *Codes of Ethics*, 1–2.

8 Frank S. Craven, "The Real Estate Profession and Ethics," *National Real Estate Journal* 4, no. 4 (15 October 1911): 166.

9 Herbert Croly, *The Promise of American Life* (Boston: Northeastern University Press, 1989 [1909]).

10 Robyn Muncy, "Trustbusting and White Manhood in America, 1898–1914," *American Studies* 38, no. 3 (fall 1997); Henry A. Stimson, "The Small Business as a School of Manhood," *Scribners Magazine* 93, no. 557 (May 1904): 337–40.

11 Craven, "The Real Estate Profession and Ethics," 166.

12 Gilbert, *Work without Salvation*, chap. 3.

13 Walter Lippmann, *Drift and Mastery* (New York: M. Kennerley, 1914).

14 "Denver Convention a Record Breaker," *National Real Estate Journal* 3, no. 6 (15 August 1911): 398.

15 Frontspiece, *National Real Estate Journal* 4, no. 1 (15 September 1911).

16 L. D. Woodworth, "Brokerage Methods That Win," *National Real Estate Journal* 11, no. 4 (15 April 1915): 214.

17 Edward B. Boynton, "A Plea for Higher Ideals," *National Real Estate Journal* 1, no. 4 (15 June 1910): 172.

18 Craven, "The Real Estate Profession and Ethics," 166.

19 Ring Lardner, "Own Your Own Home," *Redbook Magazine*, April 1915, 488–500.

20 Craven, "The Real Estate Profession and Ethics," 166.

21 Richard B. Watrous, "The Relation of Real Estate Men to City Planning," *National Real Estate Journal* 11, no. 1 (15 January 1915): 9.

22 Marc A. Weiss, *The Rise of the Community Builders: The American Real Estate Industry and Urban Land Planning* (New York: Columbia University Press, 1987); William S. Worley, *J. C. Nichols and the Shaping of Kansas City* (Columbia: University of Missouri Press, 1993).

23 Hannan, "Why Should Local Real Estate Exchanges Join the National Association?," *National Real Estate Journal* 4, no. 4 (15 December 1911): 336–37.

24 "Code of Ethics, National Association of Real Estate Exchanges," adopted at the National Association convention at Los Angeles, 24 June 1915.

25 "Denver Convention a Record Breaker," 414, 422.

26 Clifford Siskin, "Wordsworth's Prescriptions: Romanticism and Professional Power," in Gene W. Ruoff, ed., *The Romantics and Us: Essays on Literature and Culture* (New Brunswick: Rutgers University Press, 1990), 308–11.

27 James Truslow Adams, "The Crisis in Character," *Harper's Magazine*, July 1933; Stuart Chase, "The Luxury of Integrity," *Harper's*, August 1930.

28 John T. Kenney, "Legal Recognition of Real Estate Brokers," *National Real Estate Journal* 5, no. 2 (15 April 1912): 124.

29 Victor C. Alderson, "Artist or Artisan—Which?," *Quarterly of the Colorado School of Mines* 4, no. 1 (July 1909): 4.

30 Kenney, "Legal Recognition of Real Estate Brokers," 124.

31 Ibid., 125.

32 J. J. Kenna, "Opposes Licenses for Brokers," *National Real Estate Journal* 11, no. 1 (January 1915): 50.

33 Ibid.

34 "Comprehensive Review of License Laws," *National Real Estate Journal* 24, no. 3 (29 January 1923): 32–37; Xueguang Zhou, "Occupational Power, State Capacities, and the Diffusion of Licensing in the American States, 1890–1950," *American Sociological Review* 58 (August 1993): 543.

35 Minutes, 1919–79, vol. 1: 1919–25, pp. 17–39, 41–61, Records of the Wisconsin Real Estate Examining Board, series 1799, State Historical Society of Wisconsin, Archives Division, Madison.

36 Minutes, 1919–79, vol. 2: 1925–28, pp. 725–27, Records of the Wisconsin Real Estate

Examining Board, series 1799, State Historical Society of Wisconsin, Archives Division, Madison.

37 Minutes, 1919–79, vol. 1, "Report of Annual Meeting," 4 August 1920, p. 84, Records of the Wisconsin Real Estate Examining Board, series 1799, State Historical Society of Wisconsin, Archives Division, Madison.

38 "Comprehensive Review of License Laws," 35.

39 "Real Estate Books," advertisement, *National Real Estate Journal* 10, no. 5 (November 1914): 349.

40 Minneapolis Real Estate Board, "The REALTOR Tradition in Minneapolis, 1887–1987," September 1985, mimeographed document, Archives of the National Association of Realtors, Chicago (hereafter NAR Archives).

41 Pearl Janet Davies, *Real Estate Achievement in the United States: A History of the Efforts within the Business of Real Estate to Set Up Standards of Practice, Analyze the Factors That Affect Real Estate Use, Bring about a Satisfying Environment for Family Life, Business, and Industry, and Help Create Conditions for a Wide and Secure Real Estate Ownership* (unpublished MS, n.d.[1960?]), IV, 1, 84, NAR Archives.

42 Minutes of the Board of Directors, Washington, 27–28 January 1916, Minute Books, 1914–20, NAR Archives.

43 *Webster's International Dictionary* (1917), addendum, 88.

44 *Minneapolis Real Estate Board v. Northwestern Telephone Exchange Co.*, 13 September 1920, District Court of Hennepin County, Minnesota, cited in Davies, *Real Estate Achievement in the United States*, vol. 2, chap. 5, part 6, pp. 41–42.

45 Frank Ward O'Malley, "Thence by Seagoing Hack," *Saturday Evening Post*, 27 November 1920, 8–9, 89–98.

46 "Apology to Realtors," *Saturday Evening Post*, 13 February 1921, 14.

47 Davies, *Real Estate Achievement in the United States*, vol. 2, chap. 5, part 6, p. 43.

48 Ibid., p. 42.

49 "Girard's Talk of the Day," *Philadelphia Inquirer*, 2 November 1927, 7 November 1927.

50 Henry Louis Mencken, *The American Language: An Inquiry into the Development of English in the United States*, supplement 1 (New York: Alfred A. Knopf, 1975 [1945]): 565–66.

51 "The Detroit Real Estate Board Course in Real Estate," *National Real Estate Journal*, April 1916, 248–49.

52 "Detroit Real Estate Board Course," 250.

53 "Report on Educational Course," *National Real Estate Journal*, August 1917, 234–35.

54 Ibid., 236.

55 Ibid., 237.

56 "Report on Real Estate Text Books," *National Real Estate Journal*, August 1917, 237.

Chapter 4   Applied Realology

1   J. C. Nichols, "Responsibilities and Opportunities of a Real Estate Board," *Proceedings of the General Sessions of the National Association of Real Estate Boards at the Seventeenth Annual Convention, Washington, D.C., June 3–6, 1924* (Chicago, 1924), 21.

2   Richard T. Ely, "Research in Land and Public Utility Economics," *Journal of Land and Public Utility Economics* 1, no. 1 (January 1925): 3.

3   Ely to Dr. Don Lescohier, 2 April 1918, reel 60, Richard T. Ely Papers (microfilm), State Historical Society of Wisconsin, Madison (hereafter Ely MSS).

4   Benjamin J. Rader, *The Academic Mind and Reform: The Influence of Richard T. Ely in American Life* (Lexington: University of Kentucky Press, 1966), chap. 6; Mary O. Furner, *Advocacy and Objectivity: A Crisis in the Professionalization of American Social Science, 1865–1905* (Lexington: University Press of Kentucky, 1975), chap. 7.

5   Ely to H. Trustran Eve, 5 April 1918, reel 60, Ely MSS; Ernest M. Fisher, *Principles of Real Estate Practice* (New York: Macmillan, 1923), 13.

6   Ely to Dr. Don Lescohier, 2 April 1918, reel 60, Ely MSS; Ely to Albion Small, 13 April 1918, reel 60, Ely MSS; Ely to W. D. Juday, 5 April 1918, reel 60, Ely MSS.

7   Richard T. Ely, *Property and Contract in Their Relations to the Distribution of Wealth* (Port Washington, N.Y.: Kennikat, 1971 [1914]), 96, 2, 541, 107; Gregory S. Alexander, *Commodity and Propriety: Competing Visions of Property in American Legal Thought, 1776–1970* (Chicago: University of Chicago Press, 1997), 1–7.

8   Ely to Herbert U. Nelson, 5 April 1918, reel 60, Ely MSS; Ely to Nelson, 21 May 1918, reel 60, Ely MSS.

9   E. D. Chassell to Frederick E. Taylor, 29 September 1920, reel 72, Ely MSS.

10   Irving E. Macomber to Ely, 19 February 1921, reel 73, Ely MSS.

11   J. B. Mansfield to Ely, 6 October 1920, reel 72, Ely MSS.

12   Ely to Taylor, 25 October 1920, reel 72, Ely MSS.

13   Richard T. Ely, Prospectus of the Institute for Research in Land Economics and Public Utilities, 1924, Ely MSS (n.d., 1924), 7.

14   Ely to Mansfield, 29 October 1920, reel 72, Ely MSS.

15   Ely to Frank Fetter, 12 November 1921, reel 76, Ely MSS.

16   Ibid.

17   Henry S. Pritchett to Ely, 24 November 1922, reel 81, Ely MSS.

18   Irving B. Hiett to Paul E. Stark, 19 November 1921, reel 76, Ely MSS.

19   Ely to Hiett, 21 November 1921, reel 76, Ely MSS.

20   Ely to G. Arner, 2 October 1922, reel 80, Ely MSS.

21   C. M. Nichols to Ely, 15 August 1923, reel 83, Ely MSS.

22   Ely to A. H. Nelson, 18 November 1921, reel 76, Ely MSS; Ely to A. H. Nelson, 25 November 1921, reel 76, Ely MSS.

23   Pritchett to Ely, 24 November 1922, reel 81, Ely MSS; William E. Shannon to Ely, 26 December 1922, reel 82, Ely MSS.

24   Stark to Ely, 10 July 1922, reel 79, Ely MSS.

25 Ely to H. U. Nelson, 10 November 1922, reel 81, Ely MSS.

26 Ely to H. U. Nelson, 26 February 1923, reel 82, Ely MSS.

27 T. H. Nelson to H. U. Nelson, 13 February 1923, reel 82, Ely MSS; H. U. Nelson to T. H. Nelson, 15 February 1923, reel 82, Ely MSS; Ely to T. H. Nelson, 23 February 1923, reel 82, Ely MSS.

28 T. H. Nelson to Platt Lawton, 2 April 1923, reel 83, Ely MSS; Ely to H. C. Taylor, 23 April 1923, reel 83, Ely MSS; Ely to A. H. Nelson, 30 April 1923, reel 83, Ely MSS.

29 Ely to W. S. Learned, 5 May 1923, reel 83, Ely MSS.

30 Ralph E. Heilman, "Education for the Realtor of Today and Tomorrow," *Proceedings of the General Sessions of the National Association of Real Estate Boards at the Seventeenth Annual Convention, Washington, D.C., June 3–6, 1924* (Chicago, 1924), 34.

31 Heilman, "Education for the Realtor of Today and Tomorrow," 35–36. See also John S. Brubacher, "The Evolution of Professional Education," T. R. McConnell, G. Lester Anderson, and Pauline Hunter, "The University and Professional Education," B. Richard Teare Jr., "Engineering," and Richard L. Kozelka, "Business: The Emerging Profession," in Nelson B. Henry, ed., *Education for the Professions: The Sixty-first Yearbook of the National Society for the Study of Education* (Chicago: University of Chicago Press, 1962); Louis D. Brandeis, *Business: A Profession* (Boston: Maynard, 1914).

32 Richard T. Ely, "Real Estate Education in the Future," 235–36.

33 John B. Spilker and Paul Gregory Cloud, *Real Estate Business as a Profession* (Cincinnati: Bachmeyer-Lutmer, 1921); new editions were produced in 1926, 1940, and 1949.

34 Richard T. Ely, "Landed Property as an Economic Concept and as a Field of Research," *American Economic Review* 7, no. 1 (March 1917).

35 Richard T. Ely, *Ground under Our Feet: An Autobiography* (New York: Macmillan, 1938), 187.

36 Ernest M. Fisher, *Principles of Real Estate Practice* (New York: Macmillan, 1923), 3–5, 76.

37 Herbert U. Nelson, "The Objectives and Content of Real Estate Courses," *Annals of Real Estate Practice*, vol. 1: *General Real Estate Topics* (Chicago: NAREB, 1925), 203–10.

38 Fisher, *Principles of Real Estate Practice*, 3. See Abraham Flexner, *Is Social Work a Profession?* (New York: New York School of Philanthropy, 1915); Abraham Flexner, *Medical Education in Europe: A Report to the Carnegie Foundation for the Advancement of Teaching* (New York, 1912).

39 Martin Kaufman, *Homeopathy in America: The Rise and Fall of a Medical Heresy* (Baltimore: Johns Hopkins University Press, 1971); Susan Smith-Cunnien, *A Profession of One's Own: Organized Medicine's Opposition to Chiropractic* (Lanham, Md.: University Press of America, 1998).

40 Frederick M. Babcock, *The Appraisal of Real Estate* (New York: Macmillan, 1924), 12–14.

41 Ibid., 2.

42 Ibid., 2–11.

43 Ibid., 15–17.

44 Ibid., 50–56.

45 Rose Helper, *Racial Policies and Practices of Real Estate Brokers* (Minneapolis: University of Minnesota Press, 1969), 201 and chaps. 7–8; Kenneth T. Jackson, "Race, Ethnicity, and Real Estate Appraisal: The Home Owners Loan Corporation and the Federal Housing Administration," *Journal of Urban History* 6 (August 1980): 419–52; W. Edward Orser, *Blockbusting in Baltimore: The Edmondson Village Story* (Lexington: University Press of Kentucky, 1994).

46 Marc A. Weiss, "Richard T. Ely and the Contribution of Economic Research to National Housing Policy, 1920–1940," *Urban Studies* 26 (1989); Jackson, "Race, Ethnicity, and Real Estate Appraisal"; Kenneth T. Jackson, *Crabgrass Frontier: The Suburbanization of the United States* (New York: Oxford University Press, 1985), 198; Helper, *Racial Policies and Practices of Real Estate Brokers*.

47 A. S. Adams, "Report of the Committee on Code of Ethics," *Proceedings of the General Sessions of the National Association of Real Estate Boards at the Seventeenth Annual Convention, Washington, D.C., June 3–6, 1924* (Chicago, 1924), 76.

48 Richard T. Ely and Charles J. Galpin, "Tenancy in an Ideal System of Land Ownership," *American Economic Review* 9, no. 1 (March 1919): 180–212.

49 Helper, *Racial Policies and Practices of Real Estate Brokers*, 201.

50 See Jeffrey M. Hornstein, "A Nation of Realtors®: The Professionalization of Real Estate Brokerage and the Construction of a New American Middle Class" (PhD diss., University of Maryland, 2001), chap 4.

51 Pierre Bourdieu and Jean-Claude Passeron, *Reproduction in Education, Society and Culture* (London: Sage, 1977); Randall Collins, *The Credential Society: An Historical Sociology of Education and Stratification* (New York: Academic, 1979).

52 Adams, "Report of the Committee on Code of Ethics," 73.

53 J. C. Nichols, "Responsibilities and Opportunities of a Real Estate Board," 21.

54 Ibid.

55 Nichols, "Responsibilities and Opportunities of a Real Estate Board," 23.

56 Thomas Shallcross Jr., "A Realtor's Viewpoint of Zoning and Its Effect on Values and Development," *Real Estate Magazine* (Philadelphia), March 1927, 7, 30.

57 Ibid., 30.

58 Andrew Harrison, "Mr. Philadelphia: Albert M. Greenfield, 1887–1967" (PhD diss., Temple University, 1997), 11, 25.

59 Albert M. Greenfield to N. B. Kelly, 14 April 1927, folder 15: Zoning, Correspondence, 1927, Albert M. Greenfield Papers, Historical Society of Pennsylvania, Philadelphia (hereafter Greenfield MSS). Marc Weiss discusses briefly the conflict between Realtors who were mainly brokers and investors in short- and medium-term ventures, like Greenfield, and community-builders, like Nichols. See Weiss, *The Rise of the Community Builders*, 48–52.

60 Horace Groskin, "Zoning Restriction Will Reduce Present and Future Real Estate Values," pamphlet, n.d. (1925?), box 013, folder 10: Zoning; Greenfield MSS.

61 Ibid.

62 Nichols, "Responsibilities and Opportunities of a Real Estate Board," 22; Greenfield to N. B. Kelly, 14 April 1927, Greenfield MSS; Harrison, "Mr. Philadelphia," 25; Robert Pearson and Brad Pearson, *The J. C. Nichols Chronicle: The Authorized Story of the Man, His Company, and His Legacy, 1880–1994* (Kansas City, Kan.: Country Club Plaza, 1994).

63 "What Qualities Made For Business Success? An Address by Albert M. Greenfield before the Young Men's Hebrew Association, Sunday April 2nd [1922]," box 013, folder 7: Young Men's Hebrew Association, Correspondence, 1922, Greenfield MSS.

64 Glenn Frank, "The Realtor as the New Pioneer," *Annals of Real Estate Practice* (Chicago: National Association of Real Estate Boards, 1928), 1–11.

65 Aaron Sakolski, *The Great American Land Bubble: The Amazing Story of Land-Grabbing, Speculations, and Booms from Colonial Days to the Present Time* (New York: Harper and Brothers, 1932), chap. 16; Leo Grebler, David Blank, and Louis Winnick, *Capital Formation in Residential Real Estate: Trends and Prospects* (Princeton: Princeton University Press, 1956), 39.

66 Richard T. Ely, *Hard Times: The Way In and the Way Out* (New York: Macmillan, 1931), esp. chaps. 2–3; Richard T. Ely, "Real Estate in the Business Cycle," *AER* 22, no. 1 (March 1932): 137–43; Richard T. Ely et al., "Round Table Discussions: Land Economics," *AER* 21, no. 1 (March 1931): 132.

Chapter 5   The Realtors Go to Washington

1 Leonard Reaume, "Proposed for 1930," *National Real Estate Journal*, 3 February 1930, 15.

2 See appendix, table 1, for details. In 1920–40 the census data show a 25.5 percent drop in the number of brokers, while NAREB membership actually increased 13.3 percent in the same period. The proportion of brokers joining NAREB rose steadily in the postwar period, an increase in large part due to the influx of women.

3 Gail Radford, *Modern Housing for America: Policy Struggles in the New Deal Era* (Chicago: University of Chicago Press, 1996), 177.

4 Southern Pine Service Association promotional poster, box 455, Records of the Real Estate Division, Records of the U.S. Housing Corporation [USHC], 1917–52, Record Group 3, National Archives II, College Park, Maryland (hereafter Records of the Real Estate Division).

5 U.S. Department of Labor, Information and Education Service, *Suggestions for Own-Your-Own-Home Campaigns* (Washington: Government Printing Office, 1919), 6–8, box 453, Records of the Real Estate Division.

6 For a discussion of American exceptionalism in these terms, see Dorothy Ross, *Origins of American Social Science* (New York: Cambridge University Press, 1991), chap. 2. On the notion of development "in space rather than in time," see Henry Nash Smith, *Virgin Land* (Cambridge: Harvard University Press, 1955); and Andrew Martin Kirby, "The Great Desert of the American Mind: Concepts of Space and

Time and Their Historiographic Implications," in JoAnne Brown and David Van Keuren, eds., *The Estate of Social Knowledge* (Baltimore: Johns Hopkins University Press, 1993).

7   Ross, *Origins of American Social Science*, 25, 390.

8   U.S. Department of Labor, *Suggestions for Own-Your-Own-Home Campaigns*, 4.

9   Bartholomew O'Toole to Douglas Fairbanks, 4 December 1917, box 462, Records of the Real Estate Division.

10 U.S. Bureau of the Census, *Mortgages on Homes* (Washington: Government Printing Office, 1923).

11 Ibid., 41–45; on the structural changes in home financing, see Marc A. Weiss, *The Rise of the Community Builders: The American Real Estate Industry and Urban Land Planning* (New York: Columbia University Press, 1987), 31–36.

12 Weiss, *The Rise of the Community Builders*, 32–35; Miles Colean, *The Impact of Government on Real Estate Finance in the United States* (New York: National Bureau of Economic Research, 1950), 44–47.

13 Mary Corbin Sies and Christopher Silver, "The History of Planning History," in Mary Corbin Sies and Christopher Silver, eds., *Planning the Twentieth-Century American City* (Baltimore: Johns Hopkins University Press, 1996), 3–4.

14 "Own Your Home" campaign handbook, Retail Service Bureau, National Lumber Manufacturers' Association, May 1919 (emphasis in original), box 455, Records of the Real Estate Division.

15 "Own Your Home" campaign handbook, box 455, Records of the Real Estate Division.

16 "Who Gets Your Pay?" (pay stub insert, St. Paul, Minn., Real Estate Board, Southern Pine Association), "Additional Suggestions" (pamphlet, n.d.), "Call a Meeting Today" (pamphlet, n.d.), all in box 455, Records of the Real Estate Division.

17 *History of "Own Your Home" Campaign in Philadelphia* (Philadelphia: Ware Brothers, 1919), 21, 27.

18 Ibid., 21, 27, 32, 39; Janet Hutchison, "Building for Babbitt: The State and the Suburban Home Ideal," *Journal of Policy History* 9, no. 2 (1997): 188.

19 Better Homes in America, *Guidebook of Better Homes in America: How to Organize the 1924 Campaign*, publication no. 1 (Washington, 1924), 5–7.

20 Caroline Bartlett Crane, *Everyman's House* (Garden City, N.Y.: Doubleday, 1925), 1–2; Marie Meloney, "Better Homes," *Delineator*, October 1922, 9; Report of Executive Director, Better Homes in America, February 1927, Commerce Papers, box 65: Better Homes in America, Herbert C. Hoover Presidential Library, West Branch, Iowa (hereafter HHPL).

21 Crane, *Everyman's House*, 43; italics in original.

22 Ibid., 45–48.

23 Ibid., 125.

24 Herbert Hoover, "The Home and the Nation," *Child Welfare Magazine*, April 1926, 450.

25 Lamont, Foreword, *President's Conference on Home Building* (Washington, 1932), vii.

26   Minutes of the Meeting of the Board of Directors, Savannah, Georgia, 19–20 February 1917, Minute Books, 1914–20, Archives of the National Association of Realtors, Chicago (hereafter NAR Archives), 236.

27   "Thomas Shallcross," "William M. Garland," "John L. Weaver," and "Frederick E. Taylor," *Presidents of the National Association of Realtors: A History* (Chicago: NAR, 1980); Editorial, *Boston Transcript*, 13 August 1918, cited in Pearl Janet Davies, *Real Estate Achievement in the United States: A History of the Efforts within the Business of Real Estate to Set Up Standards of Practice, Analyze the Factors that Affect Real Estate Use, Bring About a Satisfying Environment for Family Life, Business, and Industry, and Help Create Conditions for a Wide and Secure Real Estate Ownership* (unpublished MS, n.d.[1960?], 2 vols.), chap. IV, part 2, 39, NAR Archives.

28   Minutes of the Board of Directors of the National Association of Real Estate Boards, Chicago, 9–10 January 1920, Minute Books, 1914–20, 235, NAR Archives; Weiss, *The Rise of the Community Builders*, 28; Radford, *Modern Housing for America*, 16–17; Kenneth T. Jackson, *Crabgrass Frontier: The Suburbanization of the United States* (New York: Oxford University Press, 1985), 192–93.

29   Ann E. Rae, "Long Term Financing By B&L Associations," *Proceedings of the Mortgage and Finance Division of the National Real Estate Association at the Seventeenth Annual Convention* (Chicago: NAREB, 1924), 30.

30   Oldfield and Smith cited in Radford, *Modern Housing for America*, 48; "Encourage Private Initiative in Building," *National Real Estate Journal*, 18 July 1921, 16.

31   "Minutes, Board of Directors, New Haven, Conn., April 27–28, 1921," *Board of Directors Minutes: 1921*, bound logbook, NAR Archives, 366, 399.

32   Kendrick G. Clements, *Hoover, Conservation, and Consumerism: Engineering the Good Life* (Lawrence: University Press of Kansas, 2000), 37–38.

33   "Minutes, Board of Directors Meeting, New Haven, Conn., April 27–28, 1921," NAR Archives, 501.

34   Ibid.

35   William R. Tanner, "Herbert Hoover's War on Waste 1921–28," in Carl E. Krog and William R. Tanner, eds., *Herbert Hoover and the Republican Era: A Reconsideration* (Lanham, Md.: University Press of America, 1984), 1–35.

36   Tanner, "Herbert Hoover's War on Waste," 27–28.

37   "Hoover Declares Time Ripe to Push Home Building Revival," *Building Supply News*, 26 September 1922, Commerce Papers, box 64: Building and Housing, 1922, May–December, HHPL.

38   Herbert Hoover, "Home Ownership Will Develop Citizenry," *National Real Estate Journal*, 18 July 1921, 18–20.

39   John M. Gries, "The Home Buyer and His Problems," *National Real Estate Journal*, 6 November 1922, 41–43; John M. Gries to Herbert Hoover, 29 December 1924, Commerce Papers, box 64: Building and Housing, 1924, HHPL.

40   Herbert Hoover to President Harding, 9 February 1922, Commerce Papers, box 63: Building and Housing, 1922, January–April, HHPL.

41 Weiss, *The Rise of the Community Builders*, 64–68; M. Christine Boyer, *Dreaming the Rational City: The Myth of American City Planning* (Cambridge: MIT Press, 1983), chap. 7.

42 Hoover to Irving Hiett, 1 May 1922, and Don Goss to secretaries of all NAREB Boards, 8 May 1922, Commerce Papers, box 64: Building and Housing, 1922, May–December, HHPL.

43 Minutes, Board of Directors, Philadelphia Real Estate Board, 3 March 1925, box 1, series 1, administrative subseries 1A, Minutes, 1924–29, Folder 1-001: Papers of the Philadelphia Board of Realtors, Urban Archives, Temple University, Philadelphia; Thomas Shallcross Jr., "A Realtor's Viewpoint of Zoning and Its Effect on Values and Development," *Real Estate Magazine* (Philadelphia), March 1927, 7, 30; Horace Groskin, "Zoning Restriction Will Reduce Present and Future Real Estate Values," pamphlet, n.d. (1925?), box 013, folder 10: Zoning; Albert M. Greenfield Papers, Historical Society of Pennsylvania, Philadelphia.

44 "Standardize Practice for Title Closing," *National Real Estate Journal*, 23 March 1925, 24–25; "California Has Standard Forms," *National Real Estate Journal*, 10 August 1925, 38–39; Charles G. Edwards, "A Great Sifting Process," *National Real Estate Journal*, 20 April 1925, 29–30; "Stop Watches Double Income on Business Property," *National Real Estate Journal*, 27 July 1925, 21–22; Harry G. Atkinson, "Standard Test for Real Estate," *National Real Estate Journal*, 10 August 1925, 23–24; Fred M. Clark, "How Salesmen May Develop Their Whole Power," *National Real Estate Journal*, 21 September 1925, 34–36; Edwards, "What Is It All About? What Has It Accomplished?," *National Real Estate Journal*, 7 September 1925, 19–20.

45 Weiss, *The Rise of the Community Builders*, 73–76.

46 Marc A. Weiss, "Richard T. Ely and the Contribution of Economic Research to National Housing Policy, 1920–1940," *Urban Studies* 26 (1989): 123.

47 Weiss, *The Rise of the Community Builders*, 141–52; Weiss, "Richard T. Ely and the Contribution of Economic Research"; on HOLC / FHA and racism, see Rose Helper, *Racial Policies and Practices of Real Estate Brokers* (Minneapolis: University of Minnesota Press, 1969), 201 and chaps. 7–8; Kenneth T. Jackson, "Race, Ethnicity, and Real Estate Appraisal: The Home Owners Loan Corporation and the Federal Housing Administration," *Journal of Urban History* 6 (August 1980); Jackson, *Crabgrass Frontier*, chap. 11.

48 Radford, *Modern Housing for America*, 194–95.

49 Leonard Reaume, "Proposed for 1930," *National Real Estate Journal*, 3 February 1930, 15–17; Davies, *Real Estate in American History*, 156.

50 Herbert U. Nelson to Walter Newton, 12 March 1930, Presidential Papers, box 73, Building and Housing Correspondence, 1930 January–May; HHPL.

51 Data from Jackson, *Crabgrass Frontier*, 193–94; Grebler, Blank, and Winnick, *Capital Formation in Residential Real Estate*, 332.

52 *Address of President Hoover at the Opening Meeting of the President's Conference on Home Building and Home Ownership* (Washington: Government Printing Office, 1931), 1, 2.

53 President's Conference on Home Building and Home Ownership, *Housing Objectives and Programs*, xiv, 1, 6–15; Radford, *Modern Housing for America*, 178.

54 President's Conference on Home Building and Home Ownership, *Housing Objectives and Programs*, 7; Weiss, *The Rise of the Community Builders*, 143.

55 President's Conference on Home Building and Home Ownership, *Housing Objectives and Programs*, xiv, 1, 6–15; Weiss, *The Rise of the Community Builders*, 143; Edward A. MacDougall, "Report on President's Conference on Home Building and Home Ownership," Presidential Papers, box 74: Building and Housing—White House Conference on Home Building and Home Ownership 1932, HHPL.

56 "The President's Page," *National Real Estate Journal*, May 1933, 13; "House Passes Relief Bill for Small Home Owners," *National Real Estate Journal*, May 1933, 17.

57 Weiss, *The Rise of the Community Builders*, 145–49.

58 Grebler, Blank, and Winnick, *Capital Formation in Residential Real Estate*, 332.

59 Figures derived from ibid., 333–34.

60 Joseph Arnold, *The New Deal in the Suburbs: A History of the Greenbelt Town Program* (Columbus: Ohio State University Press, 1971).

61 Radford, *Modern Housing for America*, 184–98.

62 Thomas J. Sugrue, *The Origins of the Urban Crisis: Race and Inequality in Postwar Detroit* (Princeton: Princeton University Press: 1996), 29, 73–75.

63 Philip J. Funigiello, *The Challenge to Urban Liberalism: Federal-City Relations during World War II* (Knoxville: University of Tennessee Press, 1978), 100. On the FHA and redlining, Jackson, "Race, Ethnicity, and Real Estate Appraisal."

64 Funigiello, *The Challenge to Urban Liberalism*, 80–83.

65 Ibid., 105–7; on housing starts see Grebler, Blank, and Winnick, *Capital Formation in Residential Real Estate*, 332.

66 "Rosie the Realtor" is borrowed from Pearl Janet Davies, official historian of the Women's Council of Realtors. See Pearl Janet Davies, *Women in Real Estate: A History of the Women's Council of the National Association of Real Estate Boards* (Chicago: Women's Council of the National Association of Real Estate Boards, 1963), 38. See also Sally Ross Chapralis, *Progress of Women in Real Estate: 50th Anniversary, Women's Council of Realtors* (Chicago: Women's Council of Realtors, 1988), 13.

Chapter 6 *"Rosie the Realtor"*

1 Mary Amelia Warren, "Home Selling for Women," Minutes of Breakfast Meeting, Women's Council, NAREB, Detroit, 5 November 1941, 4, typescript, archives of the Women's Council of Realtors, Chicago (hereafter WCR Archives).

2 Edwin Stoll, "Women Make Good Realtors," *Lifetime Living*, December 1952, 32.

3 Claudia Goldin, *Understanding the Gender Gap: An Economic History of American Women* (New York: Oxford University Press, 1990), 26; U.S. Bureau of the Census, *15th Census of the U.S.: 1930, Population*, vol. 5: *General Report on Occupations*, table 5; U.S. Bureau of the Census, *16th Census of the U.S.: 1940, Population*, vol. 3, part 1, table 65.

4 For relevant sources see note 66 to chapter 5, above.

5 Interview with Katharine Seaman, microfilm reel F104, Records of the Bureau of Vocational Information.

6 See Catherine Beecher and Harriet Beecher Stowe, *The American Woman's Home, or The Principles of Domestic Science, Being a Guide to the Formation and Maintenance of Economical, Healthful, Beautiful, and Christian Homes* (Hartford: Stowe-Day Foundation, 1975 [1869]); Kathryn Kish Sklar, *Catherine Beecher: A Study in American Domesticity* (New York: W. W. Norton, 1976); Dolores Hayden, *The Grand Domestic Revolution: A History of Feminist Designs for American Homes, Neighborhoods, and Cities* (Cambridge: MIT Press, 1981); Gwendolyn Wright, *Moralism and the Model Home* (Chicago: University of Chicago Press, 1980); Roy Lubove, *The Progressives and the Slums: Tenement House Reform in New York City, 1890–1917* (Westport, Conn.: Greenwood, 1974); Nancy K. Berlage, "The Establishment of an Applied Social Science: Home Economists, Science, and Reform at Cornell University, 1870–1930," in Helene Silverberg, ed., *Gender and American Social Science: The Formative Years* (Princeton: Princeton University Press, 1998), 185–212; Daniel Walkowitz, "The Making of a Feminine Professional Identity: Social Workers in the 1920s," *American Historical Review* 95, no. 4 (October 1990): 1051–75.

7 Derived from *15th Census of the U.S.: 1930, Population,* vol. 5, table 5; *16th Census of the U.S.,* table 65.

8 On secretarial work, see Sharon Hartman Strom, *Beyond the Typewriter: Gender, Class, and the Origins of Modern American Office Work, 1900–1930* (Urbana: University of Illinois Press, 1992).

9 "Business maternalism" bears the traces of other scholars' attempts to capture in neologisms the irony of the "doubled quality and consciousness of women's participation in civic life," in the words of Nancy F. Cott. I am indebted in particular to Linda Kerber's notion of "republican womanhood" and to Seth Koven's notion of "civic maternalism." Cott, "What's in a Name? The Limits of 'Social Feminism'; or, Expanding the Vocabulary of Women's History," *Journal of American History* 76, no. 3 (December 1989): 829; Kerber, "The Republican Mother: Women and the Enlightenment—An American Perspective," *American Quarterly* 28, no. 2 (summer 1976): 187–205; Kerber, *Women of the Republic: Intellect and Ideology in Revolutionary America* (Chapel Hill: University of North Carolina Press, 1980), 185–231. On gender and welfare, see Linda Gordon, "Single Mothers and Child Neglect, 1880–1920," *American Quarterly* 37, no. 2 (summer 1985): 173–192; Seth Koven and Sonya Michel, "Womanly Duties: Maternalist Politics and the Origins of Welfare States in France, Germany, Great Britain, and the United States, 1880–1920," *American Historical Review* 95, no. 4 (October 1990): 1076–1108; Robyn Muncy, *Creating a Female Dominion in American Reform, 1910–1935* (New York: Oxford University Press, 1991); Linda Gordon, "Social Insurance and Public Assistance: The Influence of Gender in Welfare Thought in the United States, 1890–1935," *American Historical Review* 97, no. 1 (February 1992): 19–54.

10 "Women in Business: II," *Fortune* 12, no. 2 (August 1935): 50–57; quote on 55.

11 Maureen Honey, *Breaking the Ties That Bind: Popular Stories of the New Woman, 1915–1930* (Norman: University of Oklahoma Press, 1992).

12 Sinclair Lewis, *The Job: An American Novel* (Lincoln: University of Nebraska Press, 1994 [1917]), 283–84.

13 Ibid., 279, 282–83, 287, 310–12.

14 Helen Duey Hoffman, "What about Real Estate?," *News Bulletin of the Bureau of Vocational Information* 1, no. 12 (15 March 1923): 1–2, 6–7; interview with Katharine Seaman, microfilm reel F104, Records of the Bureau of Vocational Information.

15 A survey of real estate firms conducted by the Women's Council of Realtors in the late 1950s corroborates this claim of pay equity: the majority of firms responding stated that their saleswomen earned the same as or more than their salesmen. See Beryl Rogers McClaskey, *The Status of Women in Real Estate* (Chicago: Women's Council of NAREB, 1962).

16 Harvey Humphrey, "Women as Board Members," *Annals of Real Estate Practice: Administrative Problems of Real Estate Boards: Proceedings and Reports of the Realtor Secretaries Division*, vol. 9 (Chicago, 1925): 41–43; Lang, "Women as Board Members," *Annals of Real Estate Practice*, vol. 9 (Chicago, 1925): 45–47.

17 Pierce Jones, "Women as Board Members," *Annals of Real Estate Practice*, vol. 9 (Chicago, 1925): 49–51.

18 "Miscellaneous Listings," *National Real Estate Journal* 26, no. 9 (4 May 1925): 72.

19 Kathy Peiss, " 'Vital Industry' and Women's Ventures: Conceptualizing Gender in Twentieth Century Business History," *Business History Review* 72 (summer 1998): 219–41. For complete membership data on Realtors, see tables in the appendix.

20 Box 59, series VIII, Membership Applications, Records of the Philadelphia Board of Realtors, Urban Archives, Philadelphia.

21 Sally Ross Chapralis, *Progress of Women in Real Estate: 50th Anniversary, Women's Council of Realtors* (Chicago: Women's Council of Realtors), 11.

22 "In What Type of Real Estate Activity Are Women Succeeding Best?," Conference of Women Realtors, National Association of Real Estate Boards, Twentieth Annual Convention, Seattle, 10–13 August 1927, typescript, WCR Archives; Lewis, *The Job*, 315.

23 Louise Slocomb, "Women in the Real Estate Profession," *National Real Estate Journal* 22, no. 11 (21 November 1921): 34–35; Slocomb, "The Realty Woman as Broker," *National Real Estate Journal* 22, no. 12 (5 December 1921): 26–27.

24 For a useful overview of the image of women in the 1920s, see Leila Rupp, *Mobilizing Women for War: German and American Propaganda, 1939–1945* (Princeton: Princeton University Press, 1978), 51–73; William H. Chafe, *The American Woman: Her Changing Social, Economic, and Political Roles, 1920–1970* (New York: Oxford University Press, 1972), esp. chap. 2.

25 Slocomb, "Women in the Real Estate Profession," 34–35.

26 Slocomb, "The Realty Woman as Broker," *National Real Estate Journal* 22, no. 12 (5 December 1921): 26–27. The business historian Angel Kwolek-Folland has shown

that women also entered the field of personnel management on these gendered grounds. See Kwolek-Folland, *Incorporating Women: A History of Women and Business in the United States* (New York: Twayne, 1998), 111.

27 Minutes of the Organization Meeting of the Women's Council, 11 November 1938, WCR Archives.

28 Ibid.; Pearl Janet Davies, *Women in Real Estate: A History of the Women's Council of the National Association of Real Estate Boards* (Chicago: Women's Council of the National Association of Real Estate Boards, 1963), 11.

29 Women's Council Minutes, 11 November 1938; Davies, *Women in Real Estate*, 11.

30 Davies, *Women in Real Estate*, 26.

31 Mary Avery quoted in ibid., 19.

32 Chapralis, *Progress of Women in Real Estate*, 28; Mary Shern, *Real Estate, a Woman's World: The Saga of Suzy Soldsine, Super Salesperson* (Chicago: Real Estate Education, 1977).

33 Davies, *Women in Real Estate*, 12, 16, 17.

34 Lynda de la Viña, "An Assessment of World War II's Impact on Female Employment: A Study of the Decade 1940–1950" (PhD diss., Rice Unversity, 1982), 76, 105. For full data on real estate brokers over time by sex, see appendix, table 1; on sectoral distribution of women before and after the Second World War, see de la Viña, 57–59. De la Viña notes that 70 percent of women who entered the paid labor force during the war had previously been either housewives (43.5 percent) or students (26.5 percent); these aggregate proportions are mirrored in the FIRE sector.

35 Ruth Milkman, "Gender, Consciousness, and Social Change: Rethinking Women's World War II Experience," *Contemporary Sociology* 16, no. 1 (January 1987): 21–25. For the "change" argument, see Andrea S. Walsh, *Women's Film and Female Experience, 1940–1950* (New York: Praeger, 1984); Sherna Berger Gluck, *Rosie the Riveter Revisited: Women, the War, and Social Change,* (Boston: Twayne, 1987). For the "continuity" argument, see D'Ann Campbell, *Women at War with America: Private Lives in a Patriotic Era* (Cambridge: Harvard University Press, 1984); Maureen Honey, *Creating Rosie the Riveter: Class, Gender, and Propaganda during World War II* (Amherst: University of Massachusetts Press, 1984); Karen Anderson, *Wartime Women: Sex Roles, Family Relations, and the Status of Women During World War II* (Westport, Conn.: Greenwood, 1981).

36 Minutes of Breakfast Meeting, Women's Council, 5 November 1941, Detroit, WCR Archives.

37 Mary Amelia Warren, "Home Selling for Women," Minutes of Breakfast Meeting, Women's Council, NAREB, Detroit, 5 November 1941, 2, WCR Archives; emphasis in original.

38 Warren, "Home Selling for Women," 3; emphasis in original.

39 Ibid.; emphasis in original.

40 Ibid., 4.

41 For lively anecdotal accounts of enormously successful women realtors, see Robert L. Shook, *The Real Estate People: Top Salespersons, Brokers, and Realtors Share the*

Secrets of Their Success (New York: Harper and Row, 1980), and Chapralis, *Women's Progress in Real Estate*. Additionally, interviews with several local real estate board secretaries, as well as with officials of the Women's Council, have repeatedly emphasized the prominence of women in the field today.

42 As Kathryn Kish Sklar argued in *Catherine Beecher: A Study in American Domesticity*, "far from instilling obedience, the ideology of domesticity could, for example, lead women to repudiate both heterosexuality and their familial responsibilities . . . Women have always been praised for their readiness to put the needs of others before their own, but not until Catharine Beecher's lifetime were they led to accept self-sacrifice as a positive good and as the female equivalent to self-fulfillment" (xiv). The women Realtors clearly played with this notion in the 1940s, though not always consciously.

43 Warren, "Home Selling for Women," 4.

44 Ibid., 6

45 Ibid.

46 Spiess cited in Davies, *Women in Real Estate*, 28–29.

47 Ibid., 27.

48 Ibid., 31.

49 *Bulletin of the Women's Council of the National Association of Real Estate Boards* 2 no. 2 (July 1944): 19.

50 Philip Wylie, *Generation of Vipers* (New York: Rinehart, 1942), chap. 11; quotes from 184, 186. A less vituperative version of the same basic thesis, that "masculinized" women had emasculated their husbands and trapped their sons in perpetual adolescence, appeared in Ferdinand Lundberg and Marynia Farnham, *Modern Woman: The Lost Sex* (New York: Harper and Brothers, 1947).

51 Elsie Smith Parker, "For the Woman Realtor," *Bulletin of the Women's Council of the National Association of Real Estate Boards* 1, no. 3 (September 1943): 1.

52 Ruth F. Ulrich, "The Woman Realtor's Responsibility," *Bulletin of the Women's Council of the National Association of Real Estate Boards* 2, no. 6 (June 1945): 7–8.

53 Margery Dunham, "The G.I. Bill," *Bulletin of the Women's Council of the National Association of Real Estate Boards* 2, no. 6 (June 1945): 9–11.

Chapter 7 Domesticity, Gender, and Real Estate

1 "Creed for Women Realtors," *Woman Realtor*, August 1950, 32.

2 Mary Shern, *Real Estate, A Woman's World: The Saga of Suzy Soldsine, Super Salesperson* (Chicago: Real Estate Education, 1977).

3 Nelson cited in Pearl Janet Davies, *Women in Real Estate: A History of the Women's Council of the National Association of Real Estate Boards* (Chicago: Women's Council of the National Association of Real Estate Boards, 1963), 67.

4 Gerholtz cited in ibid., 72–73.

5 "A Message to Realtors," *Woman Realtor*, August 1950, 14; "To the Women Realtors of America," *Woman Realtor*, August 1950, 3

6   "Creed for Women Realtors," 32.

7   Davies, *Women in Real Estate*, 83.

8   Elaine Tyler May, *Homeward Bound: American Families in the Cold War Era* (New York: Basic Books, 1988), esp. chap. 4; quotes from 105, 113.

9   Edwin Stoll, "Women Make Good Realtors," *Lifetime Living*, December 1952, 68.

10 *White-Collar Worker*; Motion Picture 306.238, Records of the United States Information Agency, Record Group 306, National Archives, College Park, Maryland.

11 Margaret S. Marsh, *Suburban Lives* (New Brunswick: Rutgers University Press, 1990), 74–83.

12 Hugh Scott, "The Man Who Buys Whole Towns," *Saturday Evening Post*, 23 January 1954, 125.

13 Ibid., 30, 124.

14 Ibid., 128.

15 Ibid.

16 Beryl Rogers McClaskey, *The Status of Women in Real Estate* (Chicago: Women's Council of NAREB, 1962), 7; Claudia Goldin, *Understanding the Gender Gap: An Economic History of American Women* (New York: Oxford University Press, 1990), 26; Sherman J. Maisel and Albert H. Schaaf, "Characteristics and Performance of Real Estate Brokers and Salesmen in California," Real Estate Research Program, University of California, Berkeley, October 1956, 54–55; U.S. Bureau of the Census, *Statistical Abstract of the United States, 1982–83* (Washington: Government Printing Office, 1982), table 627, p. 377.

17 McClaskey, *Status of Women in Real Estate*, 7; Maisel and Schaaf, "Characteristics and Performance of Real Estate Brokers," 50.

18 McClaskey, *Status of Women in Real Estate*, 11, 13; U.S. Bureau of the Census, *Statistical Abstract of the United States, 1991* (Washington: Government Printing Office, 1991), 172, 431; U.S. Bureau of the Census, *Statistical Abstract of the United States, 1982–83* (Washington: Government Printing Office, 1982), 143, 438.

19 McClaskey, *Status of Women in Real Estate*, 14–17.

20 Maisel and Schaaf, "Characteristics and Performance of Real Estate Brokers," 53, 55.

21 Robert L. Shook, *The Real Estate People: Top Salespersons, Brokers, and Realtors Share the Secrets of Their Success* (New York: Harper and Row, 1980).

22 Shern, *Real Estate, a Woman's World*, 2–3.

23 Ibid., 6–7.

24 Ibid.

25 Stoll, "Women Make Good Realtors," 32; Davies, *Women in Real Estate*, 90.

26 Shern, *Real Estate, a Woman's World*, viii–ix.

27 Ibid., 42–43.

28 "Women Still Rare in Business Realty," *Minneapolis–St. Paul Business Journal*, 25 September 1998; NAR Economic Research Group, 2001 National Association of Realtors Member Profile: Demographic, Economic, and Professional Characteristics of REALTORS (Washington, 2001), 6–7.

Conclusion

1 W. Lloyd Warner, *Social Class in America: A Manual of Procedure for the Measurement of Social Status* (New York: Harper and Row, 1960 [1949]), 24.

2 Robert C. Binkeley, "A Nation of Realtors," *New Republic*, 9 October 1929.

3 *The Gallup Poll: Public Opinion, 1935–1971* (New York: Random House, 1972), 1:148; "The American Middle Class," *Fortune*, April 1940.

4 Warner, *Social Class in America*, 24.

5 James Truslow Adams, *The Epic of America* (Boston: Little, Brown, 1931), 405.

6 John C. Keats, *The Crack in the Picture Window* (Boston: Houghton Mifflin, 1957), xi–xii.

7 Barbara M. Kelly, *Expanding the American Dream: Building and Rebuilding Levittown* (Albany: State University of New York Press, 1993).

8 Burton Bledstein, *The Culture of Professionalism: Higher Education and the American Middle Classes* (New York: W. W. Norton, 1976), chap. 1.

9 Gail Radford, *Modern Housing for America: Policy Struggles in the New Deal Era* (Chicago: University of Chicago Press, 1996), 179–80.

10 Barbara Ehrenreich, *Fear of Falling: The Inner Life of the Middle Class* (New York: Pantheon, 1989); Peter Stearns, "The Middle Class: Toward a Precise Definition," *Journal of Comparative Studies in Society and History* 12 (1979); Stuart Blumin, *The Emergence of the Middle Class: Social Experience in The American City, 1760–1900* (New York: Cambridge University Press, 1989).

11 Ehrenreich, *Fear of Falling*, 13.

12 Jacob Riis, *How the Other Half Lives: Studies among the Tenements of New York* (New York: Scribner's, 1890).

BIBLIOGRAPHY

Manuscript Collections

Richard T. Ely Papers, State Historical Society of Wisconsin, Madison.
Albert M. Greenfield Papers, Historical Society of Pennsylvania, Philadelphia.
Records of the Philadelphia Board of Realtors, Urban Archives, Philadelphia.
Archives of the National Association of Realtors, Chicago.
Archives of the Women's Council of Realtors, Chicago.
John Ihlder Papers, Franklin D. Roosevelt Presidential Library, Hyde Park, New York.
Commerce Papers, Herbert C. Hoover Presidential Library, West Branch, Iowa.

Periodicals

National Real Estate Journal
The Philadelphia Realtor
The Woman Realtor

Books and Articles

Abbott, Andrew. *The System of Professions: An Essay on the Division of Expert Labor* (Chicago: University of Chicago Press, 1988).
Adams, James Truslow. "A Business Man's Civilization," *Harper's Magazine*, July 1929.
———. "The Crisis in Character," *Harper's Magazine*, August 1933.
Alexander, Gregory T. *Commodity and Propriety: Competing Visions of Property in American Legal Thought, 1776–1970* (Chicago: University of Chicago Press, 1997).
Anderson, Karen. *Wartime Women: Sex Roles, Family Relations, and the Status of Women during World War II* (Westport, Conn.: Greenwood, 1981).
Arnold, Joseph. *The New Deal in the Suburbs: A History of the Greenbelt Town Program* (Columbus: Ohio State University Press, 1971).
Babcock, Frederick. *The Appraisal of Real Estate* (New York: Macmillan, 1924).
Beard, Charles A. "Review of *Property and Contract in their Relation to the Distribution of Wealth*," *Political Science Quarterly* 30, no. 3 (September 1915): 510–11.
Beecher, Catherine, and Harriet Beecher Stowe. *The American Woman's Home, or The*

Principles of Domestic Science, Being a Guide to the Formation and Maintenance of Economical, Healthful, Beautiful, and Christian Homes (Hartford: Stowe-Day Foundation, 1975 [1869]).

Bell, Daniel. *The Coming of Post-industrial Society: A Venture in Social Forecasting* (New York: Basic Books, 1973).

———. *The Cultural Contradictions of Capitalism* (New York: Basic Books, 1976).

Berlage, Nancy K. "The Establishment of an Applied Social Science: Home Economists, Science, and Reform at Cornell University, 1870–1930," in Helene Silverberg, ed., *Gender and American Social Science: The Formative Years* (Princeton: Princeton University Press, 1998), 185–212.

Berle, Adolf A. *Power without Property: A New Development in American Political Economy* (New York: Harcourt Brace, 1959).

Berle, Adolf A., and Gardiner C. Means. *The Modern Corporation and Private Property* (New York: Macmillan, 1932).

Bernstein, Michael A. *The Great Depression: Delayed Recovery and Economic Change in America, 1929–1939* (New York: Cambridge University Press, 1987).

Berthoff, Rowland. "Independence and Enterprise: Small Business in the American Dream," in Stuart W. Bruchey, ed., *Small Business in American Life* (New York: Columbia University Press, 1980), 28–48.

Binkeley, Robert C. "A Nation of Realtors," *New Republic*, 9 October 1929.

Blackford, Mansel G. *A History of Small Business in America* (New York: Twayne, 1991).

Bledstein, Burton. *The Culture of Professionalism: Higher Education and the American Middle Classes* (New York: W. W. Norton, 1976).

Blumin, Stuart. *The Emergence of the Middle Class: Social Experience in the American City, 1760–1900* (Cambridge: Cambridge University Press, 1989).

Bott, Elizabeth. "Psychoanalysis and Ceremony," in J. S. La Fontaine, ed., *The Interpretation of Ritual: Essays in Honour of A. I. Richards* (London: Tavistock, 1972), 205–37.

Boyer, M. Christine. *Dreaming the Rational City: The Myth of American City Planning* (Cambridge: MIT Press, 1983).

Bradley, Joseph F. *The Role of Trade Associations and Professional Business Societies in America* (State College: Pennsylvania State University Press, 1965).

Brandeis, Louis D. *Business: A Profession* (Boston: Maynard, 1914).

Brown, JoAnne. "Profession," in Richard Wightman Fox and James T. Kloppenberg, eds., *A Companion to American Thought* (Oxford: Basil Blackwell, 1995), 543–46.

———. "Professional Language: Words That Succeed," *Radical History Review* 34 (1986).

Bruchey, Stuart W. *Enterprise: The Dynamic Economy of a Free People* (Cambridge: Harvard University Press, 1990).

Butler, Judith. *Gender Trouble: Feminism and the Subversion of Identity* (New York: Routledge, 1990).

Campbell, D'Ann. *Women at War with America: Private Lives in a Patriotic Era* (Cambridge: Harvard University Press, 1984).

Carnes, Mark, and Clyde Griffen, eds. *Meanings for Manhood: Constructions of Masculinity in Victorian America* (Chicago: University of Chicago Press, 1990).

Case, Fred E. *Real Estate Market Behavior in Los Angeles: A Study of Multiple Listing System Data* (Los Angeles: Real Estate Research Program, University of California, 1963).

Cassedy, James T. *Medicine in America: A Short History* (Baltimore: Johns Hopkins University Press, 1991).

Chafe, William. *The American Woman: Her Changing Social, Economic, and Political Roles, 1920–1970* (New York: Oxford University Press, 1972).

Chandler, Alfred P. *The Visible Hand: The Managerial Revolution in American Business* (Cambridge: Harvard University Press, 1977).

Chapralis, Sally Ross. *Progress of Women in Real Estate: 50th Anniversary, Women's Council of Realtors* (Chicago: Women's Council of Realtors, 1988).

Chase, Stuart. "The Luxury of Integrity," *Harper's*, July 1930.

Clark, Edward C. *The American Family Home, 1800–1960* (Chapel Hill: University of North Carolina Press, 1986).

Clements, Kendrick G. *Hoover, Conservation, and Consumerism: Engineering the Good Life* (Lawrence: University Press of Kansas, 2000).

Cohn, Jan. *Creating America: George Horace Lorimer and the Saturday Evening Post* (Pittsburgh: University of Pittsburgh Press, 1989).

———. *The Palace or the Poorhouse: The American House as a Cultural Symbol* (Lansing: Michigan State University Press, 1979).

Colean, Miles. *The Impact of Government on Real Estate Finance in the United States* (New York: National Bureau of Economic Research, 1950).

Comaroff, Jean, and John Comaroff. *Of Revelation and Revolution: Christianity, Colonialism, and Consciousness in South Africa* (Chicago: University of Chicago Press, 1991).

Conk, Margo. *History of Occupational Statistics* (Ann Arbor: UMI Research Press, 1983).

Cott, Nancy F. *The Grounding of Modern Feminism* (New Haven: Yale University Press, 1987).

———. "What's in a Name? The Limits of 'Social Feminism'; or, Expanding the Vocabulary of Women's History," *Journal of American History* 76, no. 3 (December 1989).

Crane, Caroline Bartlett. *Everyman's House* (Garden City, N.Y.: Doubleday, 1925).

Croly, Herbert. *The Promise of American Life* (Boston: Northeastern University Press, 1989 [1909]).

Curti, Merle. "The American Exploration of Dreams and Dreamers," *Journal of the History of Ideas* 27, no. 3 (July–September 1966): 391–416.

Davies, Pearl Janet. *Real Estate in American History* (Washington: Public Affairs, 1958).

———. *Women in Real Estate: A History of the Women's Council of the National Association of Real Estate Boards* (Chicago: Women's Council of the National Association of Real Estate Boards, 1963).

Davis, Clark. *Company Men: White-Collar Life and Corporate Cultures in Los Angeles, 1892–1941* (Baltimore: Johns Hopkins University Press, 2000).

Dorfman, Joseph P. *The Economic Mind in American Civilization*, vols. 4–5, *1918–1933* (New York: Viking, 1959).

DuBoff, Richard B., and Edward S. Herman. "Alfred Chandler's New Business History: A Review," *Politics and Society* 10, no. 1 (1980): 87–110.

Ehrenreich, Barbara. *Fear of Falling: The Inner Life of the Middle Class* (New York: Pantheon, 1989).

Ehrenreich, Barbara, and John Ehrenreich. "The Professional-Managerial Class," *Radical America* 2 (March–April 1977): 12–17.

Ehrenreich, John. *The Altruistic Imagination: A History of Social Work and Social Policy in the United States* (Ithaca: Cornell University Press, 1985).

Eichengreen, Barry G. *Golden Fetters: The Gold Standard and the Great Depression, 1919–1939* (New York: Oxford University Press, 1992).

Eichler, Ned. *The Merchant Builders* (Cambridge: MIT Press, 1982).

Ely, Richard T. *Ground under Our Feet: An Autobiography* (New York: Macmillan, 1938).

——. *Hard Times: The Way In and the Way Out* (New York: Macmillan, 1931).

——. "Landed Property as an Economic Concept and as a Field of Research," *American Economics Review* 7, no. 1 (March 1917).

——. *Property and Contract in Their Relations to the Distribution of Wealth* (Port Washington, N.Y.: Kennikat, 1971 [1914]).

——. "Research in Land and Public Utility Economics," *Journal of Land and Public Utility Economics* 1, no. 1 (January 1925).

Ely, Richard T., and Charles J. Galpin. "Tenancy in an Ideal System of Land Ownership," *American Economic Review* 9, no. 1 (March 1919): 180–212.

Ely, Richard T., and Edward W. Morehouse. *Elements of Land Economics* (New York: Macmillan, 1924).

Engels, Friedrich. *The Housing Question* (Moscow: Progress, 1975 [1872]).

Etzioni, Amitai. *The Semi-professions and Their Organization: Teachers, Nurses, Social Workers* (New York: Free Press, 1969).

Faludi, Susan. *Stiffed: The Betrayal of the American Male* (New York: William Morrow, 1999).

Filene, Peter G. *Him/Her/Self: Sex Roles in Modern America* (Baltimore: Johns Hopkins University Press, 1986).

Fishbein, Morris. *Fads and Quackery in Healing* (New York: Covici, Friede, 1932).

Fisher, Ernest M. *Principles of Real Estate Practice* (New York: Macmillan, 1923).

Fishman, Robert. "The American Planning Tradition: An Introduction and Interpretation," in Robert Fishman, ed., *The American Planning Tradition: Culture and Policy* (Washington: Woodrow Wilson Center, 2000), 1–29.

——. *Bourgeois Utopias: The Rise and Fall of Suburbia* (New York: Basic Books, 1987).

——. "Urbanity and Suburbanity: Rethinking the 'Burbs," *American Quarterly* 46, no. 1 (March 1994).

Flexner, Abraham. *Is Social Work a Profession?* (New York: New York School of Philanthropy, 1915).

Folsom, M. B. "The Organization of a Statistical Department," *Harvard Business Review* 2, no. 2 (January 1924): 178–93.

Freud, Sigmund. *Jokes and Their Relation to the Unconscious* (New York: W. W. Norton, 1989 [1909]).

Friedman, Milton. *A Monetary History of the United States, 1867–1960* (Princeton: Princeton University Press, 1963).

Friedman, Murray, ed. *Overcoming Middle Class Rage* (Philadelphia: Westminster, 1971).

Friedson, Eliot. *Professional Powers: A Study of the Institutionalization of Formal Knowledge* (Chicago: University of Chicago Press, 1986).

Funigiello, Philip. *The Challenge to Urban Liberalism: Federal-City Relations during World War II* (Knoxville: University of Tennessee Press, 1978).

Furner, Mary O. *Advocacy and Objectivity: A Crisis in the Professionalization of American Social Science, 1865–1905* (Lexington: University Press of Kentucky, 1975).

Galambos, Louis P. "The Emerging Organizational Synthesis in Modern American History," *Business History Review* 44, no. 3 (autumn 1970): 279–90.

Gallup Poll: Public Opinion, 1935–1971 (New York: Random House, 1972).

Gamber, Wendy. *The Female Economy: The Millinery and Dressmaking Trades, 1860–1930* (Urbana: University of Illinois Press, 1998).

Garreau, Joel. *Edge City: Life on the New Frontier* (New York: Doubleday, 1991).

Geison, Gerald, ed. *Professions and Professional Ideologies in America* (Chapel Hill: University of North Carolina Press, 1983).

Gilb, Corinne I. *Hidden Hierarchies: The Professions and Government* (New York: Harper and Row, 1966).

Gilbert, James B. *Designing the Industrial State: The Intellectual Pursuit of Collectivism in America, 1880–1940* (Chicago: Quadrangle, 1972).

——. *Work without Salvation: America's Intellectuals and Industrial Alienation, 1880–1910* (Baltimore: Johns Hopkins University Press, 1977).

Glazer, Penina Migdal, and Miriam Slater. *Unequal Colleagues: The Entrance of Women into the Professions, 1890–1940* (New Brunswick, N.J.: Rutgers University Press, 1986).

Gluck, Sherna Berger. *Rosie the Riveter Revisited: Women, the War, and Social Change* (Boston: Twayne, 1987).

Goldin, Claudia. *Understanding the Gender Gap: An Economic History of American Women* (New York: Oxford University Press, 1990).

Gordon, Colin. *New Deals: Business, Labor, and Politics in America, 1920–1935* (New York: Cambridge University Press, 1994).

Gordon, Linda. "Single Mothers and Child Neglect, 1880–1920," *American Quarterly* 37, no. 2 (summer 1985).

——. "Social Insurance and Public Assistance: The Influence of Gender in Welfare Thought in the United States, 1890–1935," *American Historical Review* 97, no. 1 (February 1992).

Grebler, Leo, David Blank, and Louis Winnick. *Capital Formation in Residential Real Estate: Trends and Prospects* (Princeton: Princeton University Press, 1956).

Grossberg, Michael. "Institutionalizing Masculinity: The Law as a Masculine Profession," in Mark C. Carnes and Clyde Griffen, eds., *Meanings for Manhood: Constructions of Masculinity in Victorian America* (Chicago: University of Chicago Press, 1990), 133–51.

Halttunen, Karen. *Confidence Men and Painted Women: A Study of Middle-Class Culture in America, 1830–1870* (New Haven: Yale University Press, 1982).

Harrison, Andrew. "Mr. Philadelphia: Albert M. Greenfield, 1887–1967" (PhD diss., Temple University, 1997).

Hartz, Louis I. *The Liberal Tradition in America; An Interpretation of American Political Thought since the Revolution* (New York: Harcourt, 1955).

Haskell, Thomas, ed. *The Authority of Experts: Studies in History and Theory* (Bloomington: Indiana University Press, 1984).

Hawley, Ellis P. "Herbert Hoover and Economic Stabilization, 1921–22," in Ellis P. Hawley, ed., *Herbert Hoover as Secretary of Commerce: Studies in New Era Thought and Practice* (Iowa City: University of Iowa Press, 1981).

———. "Herbert Hoover, the Commerce Secretariat, and the Vision of an 'Associative State,' 1921–1928," *Journal of American History* 62, no. 1 (June 1974).

Hayden, Dolores. *The Grand Domestic Revolution: A History of Feminist Designs for American Homes, Neighborhoods, and Cities* (Cambridge: MIT Press, 1981).

———. *Redesigning the American Dream: The Future of Housing, Work, and Family Life* (New York: W. W. Norton, 1984).

Hays, Samuel. *The Response to Industrialism, 1885–1914* (Chicago: University of Chicago Press, 1957).

Heermance, Edgar. *The Ethics of Business: A Study of Current Standards* (New York: Harper and Brothers, 1926).

Helper, Rose. *Racial Policies and Practices of Real Estate Brokers* (Minneapolis: University of Minnesota Press, 1969).

Henry, Nelson B., ed. *Education for the Professions: The Sixty-first Yearbook of the National Society for the Study of Education* (Chicago: University of Chicago Press, 1962).

Higham, John, and Paul K. Conkin, eds., *New Directions in American Intellectual History* (Baltimore: Johns Hopkins University Press, 1977).

———. *Strangers in the Land: Patterns of American Nativism, 1860–1925* (New Brunswick, N.J.: Rutgers University Press, 1955).

Hise, Greg. *Magnetic Los Angeles: Planning the Twentieth-Century Metropolis* (Baltimore: Johns Hopkins University Press, 1997).

Honey, Maureen. *Creating Rosie the Riveter: Class, Gender, and Propaganda during World War II* (Amherst: University of Massachusetts Press, 1984).

———, ed. *Breaking the Ties That Bind: Popular Stories of the New Woman, 1915–1930* (Norman: University of Oklahoma Press, 1992).

Hooks, Janet. *Women's Occupations through Seven Decades* (Washington: Zenger, 1978 [1947]).

Hoover, Herbert C. *The Memoirs of Herbert Hoover: The Cabinet and the Presidency, 1920–1933* (New York: Macmillan, 1952).

Hornstein, Jeffrey M. "A Nation of Realtors®: The Professionalization of Real Estate Brokerage and the Construction of a New American Middle Class" (PhD diss., University of Maryland, 2001).

Hounshell, David. *From the American System to Mass Production, 1800–1932: The Development of Manufacturing Technology in the United States* (Baltimore: Johns Hopkins University Press, 1984).

House, J. D. *Contemporary Entrepreneurs: The Sociology of Residential Real Estate Agents* (Westport, Conn.: Greenwood, 1977).

Hughes, Everett C. *The Growth of an Institution: The Chicago Real Estate Board* (New York: Arno, 1979 [1931]).

Hutchison, Janet A. "Building for Babbitt: The State and the Suburban Home Ideal," *Journal of Policy History* 9, no. 2 (1997).

——. "American Housing, Gender, and the Better Homes Movement, 1922–1935" (PhD diss., University of Delaware, 1989).

Isenstadt, Sandy M. "Little Visual Empire: The Visual Commodification of Landscape in the Real Estate Appraisal Industry, 1900–1992," *thresholds* 18 (1997).

Jackson, Kenneth T. *Crabgrass Frontier: The Suburbanization of the United States* (New York: Oxford University Press, 1985).

——. "Race, Ethnicity, and Real Estate Appraisal: The Home Owners Loan Corporation and the Federal Housing Administration," *Journal of Urban History* 6 (August 1980).

Johnson, Paul E. *A Shopkeeper's Millennium: Society and Revivals in Rochester, New York, 1815–1837* (New York: Hill and Wang, 1978).

Jorgensen, Emil O. *False Education in Our Colleges and Universities: An Exposé of Prof. Richard T. Ely and His "Institute for Research in Land Economics and Public Utilities"* (Chicago: Manufacturers and Merchants Federal Tax League, 1925).

Katz, Michael B. *Improving Poor People: The Welfare State, the "Underclass," and Urban Schools as History* (Princeton: Princeton University Press, 1995).

——, ed. *The "Underclass" Debate: Views from History* (Princeton: Princeton University Press, 1993).

Kaufman, Martin. *Homeopathy in America: The Rise and Fall of a Medical Heresy* (Baltimore: Johns Hopkins University Press, 1971).

Kazin, Alfred. *On Native Grounds: A Study of American Prose Literature from 1890 to the Present* (New York: Reynal and Hitchcock, 1942).

Kelly, Barbara M. *Expanding the American Dream: Building and Rebuilding Levittown* (Albany: State University of New York Press, 1993).

Kerber, Linda. "The Republican Mother: Women and the Enlightenment—An American Perspective," *American Quarterly* 28, no. 2 (summer 1976).

——. "Separate Spheres, Female Worlds, Women's Place: The Rhetoric of Women's History," *Journal of American History* 75, no. 1 (June 1988).

———. *Women of the Republic: Intellect and Ideology in Revolutionary America* (Chapel Hill: University of North Carolina Press, 1980).

Kimball, Bruce. *The "True Professional Ideal" in America: A History* (Cambridge, Mass.: Basil Blackwell, 1992).

Kimmel, Michael S. *Manhood in America: A Cultural History* (New York: Free Press, 1996).

———. "Masculinity as Homophobia: Fear, Shame, and Silence in the Construction of Gender Identity," in Joseph A. Kuypers, ed., *Men and Power* (Amherst, N.Y.: Prometheus, 1999).

Kirby, Andrew Martin. "The Great Desert of the American Mind: Concepts of Space and Time and Their Historiographic Implications," in JoAnne Brown and David Van Keuren, eds., *The Estate of Social Knowledge* (Baltimore: Johns Hopkins University Press, 1993).

Kloppenberg, James T. *Uncertain Victory: Social Democracy and Progressivism in European and American Thought, 1870–1920* (New York: Oxford University Press, 1986).

Knight, Peter E. "Real Estate Brokerage: A Must for Survival?," *Bottomline* 1, no. 6 (April 1984).

Kocka, Jürgen. *White Collar Workers in America, 1890–1940: A Social-Political History in International Perspective* (Beverly Hills: Sage, 1980).

Koven, Seth, and Sonya Michel. "Womanly Duties: Maternalist Politics and the Origins of Welfare States in France, Germany, Great Britain, and the United States, 1880–1920," *American Historical Review* 95, no. 4 (October 1990).

Kwolek-Folland, Angel. *Engendering Business: Men and Women in the Corporate Office, 1870–1930* (Baltimore: Johns Hopkins University Press, 1994).

———. *Incorporating Women: A History of Women and Business in the United States* (New York: Twayne, 1998).

Laclau, Ernesto, and Chantal Mouffe. *Hegemony and Socialist Strategy: Towards a Radical Democratic Politics* (New York: Verso, 1985).

Lamoreaux, Naomi R. *The Great Merger Movement in American Business, 1895–1904* (New York: Cambridge University Press, 1985).

Larson, Magali S. *The Rise of Professionalism: A Sociological Analysis* (Berkeley: University of California Press, 1977).

Layton, Edwin T., Jr. *The Revolt of the Engineers: Social Responsibility and the American Engineering Profession* (Baltimore: Johns Hopkins University Press, 1986).

Lears, T. J. Jackson. "The Concept of Cultural Hegemony: Problems and Possibilities," *American Historical Review* 90, no. 3. (June 1985), 567–93.

———. *Fables of Abundance: A Cultural History of Advertising in America* (New York: Basic Books, 1994).

———. "From Salvation to Self-Realization: Advertising and the Therapeutic Roots of Consumer Culture, 1880–1930," in T. J. Jackson Lears and Richard Wightman Fox, eds., *The Culture of Consumption: Critical Essays in American History, 1880–1980* (New York: Pantheon, 1983), 3–38.

——. *No Place of Grace: Antimodernism and the Transformation of American Culture, 1880–1920* (New York: Pantheon, 1981).

Lévi-Strauss, Claude. *The Savage Mind* (Chicago: University of Chicago Press, 1966).

Lewis, Sinclair. *Babbitt* (New York: Harcourt, Brace and World, 1950 [1922]).

——. *The Job: An American Novel* (Lincoln: University of Nebraska Press, 1994 [1917]).

Lloyd, Craig. *Aggressive Introvert: A Study of Herbert Hoover and Public Relations Management, 1912–1932* (Columbus: Ohio State University Press, 1972).

Lubove, Roy. *The Progressives and the Slums: Tenement House Reform in New York City, 1890–1917* (Westport, Conn.: Greenwood, 1974).

Lunbeck, Elizabeth. *The Psychiatric Persuasion: Knowledge, Gender, and Power in Modern America* (Princeton: Princeton University Press, 1994).

Lundberg, Ferdinand, and Marynia Farnham. *Modern Woman: The Lost Sex* (New York: Harper and Brothers, 1947).

Maisel, Sherman J., and Albert H. Schaaf. "Characteristics and Performance of Real Estate Brokers and Salesmen in California" (Berkeley: Real Estate Research Program, University of California, October 1956).

Manko, Katina L. "Ding-Dong! Avon Calling" (PhD diss., University of Delaware, 2001).

Marsh, Margaret S. "(Ms)Reading the Suburbs," *American Quarterly* 46, no. 1 (March 1994).

——. *Suburban Lives* (New Brunswick, N.J.: Rutgers University Press, 1990).

Maulitz, Russell. " 'Physician versus Bacteriologist': The Ideology of Science in Clinical Medicine," in Morris J. Vogel and Charles E. Rosenberg, eds., *The Therapeutic Revolution: Essays in the Social History of American Medicine* (Philadelphia: University of Pennsylvania Press, 1979).

May, Elaine Tyler. *Homeward Bound: American Families in the Cold War Era* (New York: Basic Books, 1988).

May, Ernest F. *The End of American Innocence: A Study of the First Years of Our Own Time, 1912–1917* (New York: Alfred A. Knopf, 1959).

McKenzie, Evan. *Privatopia: Homeowner Associations and the Rise of Residential Private Government* (New Haven: Yale University Press: 1994).

Melosh, Barbara. *"The Physician's Hand": Work Culture and Conflict in American Nursing* (Philadelphia: Temple University Press, 1982).

Mencken, Henry Louis. *The American Language: An Inquiry into the Development of English in the United States*, supplement 1 (New York: Alfred A. Knopf, 1975 [1945]).

Milkman, Ruth. "Gender, Consciousness, and Social Change: Rethinking Women's World War II Experience," *Contemporary Sociology* 16, no. 1 (January 1987).

Mills, C. Wright. *White Collar: The American Middle Classes* (New York: Oxford University Press, 1951).

Mills, John P. *Real Estate Salesmanship: A Few Hints to Salesmen on Attaining Success, Based upon Actual Experience* (Long Beach, Calif.: McArdle and West, 1923).

Mohun, Arwen P. "Laundrymen Construct Their World," *Technology and Culture* 38 (1997): 97–120.

Moore, J. Stuart. *Chiropractic in America: The History of a Medical Alternative* (Baltimore: Johns Hopkins University Press, 1993).

Muncy, Robyn. *Creating a Female Dominion in American Reform: 1890–1935* (New York: Oxford University Press, 1991).

———. "Trustbusting and White Manhood in America, 1898–1914," *American Studies* 38, no. 3 (fall 1997).

Nelson, Herbert U. *Administration of Real Estate Boards* (New York: Macmillan, 1925).

Noble, David F. *America by Design : Science, Technology, and the Rise of Corporate Capitalism* (New York: Alfred A. Knopf, 1977).

Orser, W. Edmund. *Blockbusting in Baltimore: The Edmondson Village Story* (Lexington: University Press of Kentucky, 1994).

Palm, Charles F. *The Middle Classes: Then and Now* (New York: Macmillan, 1936).

Parker, Richard T. *The Myth of the Middle Class: Notes on Affluence and Equality* (New York: Harper and Row, 1972).

Parsons, Talcott. "Professions," *International Encyclopedia of the Social Sciences*, vol. 12 (New York: Macmillan, 1968): 536–47.

Pegg, Betsy. *Dreams, Money, and Ambition: A History of Real Estate in Chicago* (Chicago: Chicago Real Estate Board, 1983).

Peiss, Kathy. " 'Vital Industry' and Women's Ventures: Conceptualizing Gender in Twentieth Century Business History," *Business History Review* 72 (summer 1998).

Perin, Constance. *Everything in Its Place: Social Order and Land Use in America* (Princeton: Princeton University Press, 1977).

Pocock, J. G. A. *The Machiavellian Moment* (Princeton: Princeton University Press, 1975).

Potter, David. *People of Plenty: Economic Abundance and the American Character* (Chicago: University of Chicago Press, 1954).

Pringle, Rosemary. *Secretaries Talk: Sexuality, Power, and Work* (New York: Verso, 1988).

Rader, Benjamin J. *The Academic Mind and Reform: The Influence of Richard T. Ely in American Life* (Lexington: University of Kentucky Press, 1966).

Radford, Gail. *Modern Housing for America: Policy Struggles in the New Deal Era* (Chicago: University of Chicago Press, 1996).

Riis, Jacob. *How the Other Half Lives: Studies among the Tenements of New York* (New York: Scribner's, 1890).

Rischin, Moses, ed. *The American Gospel of Success: Individualism and Beyond* (Chicago: Quadrangle, 1965).

Rodgers, Daniel T. "In Search of Progressivism," *Reviews in American History* 10, no. 4 (December 1982): 123.

Rosenberg, Charles. "The Therapeutic Revolution: Medicine, Meaning, and Social Change in Nineteenth-Century America," in Morris J. Vogel and Charles E. Rosenberg, eds., *The Therapeutic Revolution: Essays in the Social History of American Medicine* (Philadelphia: University of Pennsylvania Press, 1979).

Rosenberg, Rosalind. *Divided Lives: American Women in the Twentieth Century* (New York: Hill and Wang, 1992).

Ross, Andrew. *The Celebration Chronicles: Life, Liberty and the Pursuit of Property Values in Disney's New Town* (New York: Ballantine, 1999).

Ross, Dorothy. "Gendered Social Knowledge: Domestic Discourse, Jane Addams, and the Possibilities of Social Science," in Helene Silverberg, ed., *Gender and American Social Science: The Formative Years* (Princeton: Princeton University Press, 1998).

———. *Origins of American Social Science* (New York: Cambridge University Press, 1991).

Rotundo, Anthony F. *American Manhood: Transformations in Masculinity from the Revolution to the Modern Era* (New York: Basic Books, 1993).

Rubin, Joan Shelley. *The Making of Middle/Brow Culture* (Chapel Hill: University of North Carolina Press, 1992).

Rupp, Leila P. *Mobilizing Women for War: German and American Propaganda, 1939–1945* (Princeton: Princeton University Press, 1978).

Ryan, Mary. *Cradle of the Middle Class: The Family in Oneida County, New York, 1790–1865* (New York: Cambridge University Press, 1981).

Sakolski, Aaron M. *The Great American Land Bubble: The Amazing Story of Land-Grabbing, Speculations, and Booms from Colonial Days to the Present Time* (New York: Harper and Brothers, 1932).

Salter, Leonard T. *A Critical Review of Research in Land Economics* (Madison: University of Wisconsin Press, 1967).

Scott, Donald. "The Profession That Vanished: Public Lecturing in Mid-Nineteenth Century America," in Gerald L. Geison, ed., *Professions and Professional Ideologies* (Chapel Hill: University of North Carolina Press, 1983), chap. 2.

Scott, Joan W. "Gender: A Useful Category of Historical Analysis," in Joan W. Scott, *Gender and the Politics of History* (New York: Columbia University Press, 1988), 28–50.

Scranton, Philip. *Endless Novelty: Specialty Production and American Industrialization, 1865–1925* (Princeton: Princeton University Press, 1997).

Sharpe, William, and Leonard Wallock. "Bold New City or Built-Up 'Burb? Redefining Contemporary Suburbia," *American Quarterly* 46, no. 1 (March 1994): 1–30.

Shern, Mary. *Real Estate, A Woman's World: The Saga of Suzy Soldsine, Super Salesperson* (Chicago: Real Estate Education Company, 1977).

Shook, Robert L. *The Real Estate People: Top Salespersons, Brokers, and Realtors Share the Secrets of Their Success* (New York: Harper and Row, 1980).

Sies, Mary Corbin, and Christopher Silver. "The History of Planning History," in Mary Corbin Sies and Christopher Silver, eds., *Planning the Twentieth-Century American City* (Baltimore: Johns Hopkins University Press, 1996).

Silverberg, Helene, ed. *Gender and American Social Science: The Formative Years* (Princeton: Princeton University Press, 1998).

Siskin, Clifford. "Wordsworth's Prescriptions: Romanticism and Professional Power," in Gene W. Ruoff, ed., *The Romantics and Us: Essays on Literature and Culture* (New Brunswick, N.J.: Rutgers University Press, 1990).

Sklar, Kathryn Kish. *Catherine Beecher: A Study in American Domesticity* (New York: W. W. Norton, 1976).

Sklar, Martin J. *The Corporate Reconstruction of American Capitalism, 1890–1916: The Market, The Law, and Politics* (New York: Cambridge University Press, 1989).

Skowronek, Stephen T. *Building a New American State: The Expansion of National Administrative Capacities, 1877–1920* (New York: Cambridge University Press, 1982).

Smith-Cunnien, Susan. *A Profession of One's Own: Organized Medicine's Opposition to Chiropractic* (Lanham, Md.: University Press of America, 1998).

Sobel, Robert. *The Curbstone Brokers: The Origins of the American Stock Exchange* (New York: Macmillan, 1970).

Spilker, John, and Paul Gregory Cloud. *Real Estate Business as a Profession* (Cincinnati: Bachmeyer-Lutmer, 1921).

Stearns, Peter N. *Be a Man! Males in Modern Society* (New York: Holmes and Meier, 1979).

———. "The Middle Class: Toward a Precise Definition," *Journal of Comparative Studies in Society and History* 12 (1979).

Stilgoe, John. *Borderland: Origins of the American Suburb, 1820–1939* (New Haven: Yale University Press, 1988).

Stimson, Henry A. "The Small Business as a School of Manhood," *Scribners Magazine* 92, no. 557 (May 1904).

Strasser, Susan. "The Smile That Pays," in James B. Gilbert, ed., *The Mythmaking Frame of Mind: Social Imagination and American Culture* (Belmont, Calif.: Wadsworth, 1993).

Strom, Sharon Hartman. *Beyond the Typewriter: Gender, Class, and the Origins of Modern American Office Work, 1900–1930* (Urbana: University of Illinois Press, 1992).

Sugrue, Thomas P. *The Origins of the Urban Crisis: Race and Inequality in Postwar Detroit* (Princeton: Princeton University Press, 1996).

Swayze, Francis. "Ely's Property and Contract," *Quarterly Journal of Economics* 29, no. 4 (August 1915): 820–28.

Tanner, William R. "Herbert Hoover's War on Waste 1921–28," in Carl E. Krog and William R. Tanner, eds., *Herbert Hoover and the Republican Era: A Reconsideration* (Lanham, Md.: University Press of America, 1984).

Taylor, Henry C. *An Introduction to the Study of Agricultural Economics* (New York: Macmillan, 1909).

———. *The Story of Agricultural Economics in the United States, 1840–1932: Men, Services, Ideas* (Ames: Iowa State College Press, 1952).

Temin, Peter. *Did Monetary Forces Cause the Great Depression?* (New York: W. W. Norton, 1976).

Tobey, Ronald, Charles Wetherell, and Jay Brigham. "Moving Out and Settling In: Residential Mobility, Home Owning, and the Public Enframing of Citizenship, 1921–1950," *American Historical Review* 95 (December 1990).

Trachtenberg, Alan. *The Incorporation of America: Culture and Society in the Gilded Age* (New York: Hill and Wang, 1982).

U.S. Bureau of the Census. *1992 Census of Financial, Insurance, and Real Estate Industries: Establishment and Firm Size.*

———. *1997 Economic Census: Real Estate and Rental Leasing: Summary.*

U.S. Department of Housing and Urban Development. *U.S. Housing and Market Conditions: Fourth Quarter 1994* (February 1995).

Viña, Lynda de la. "An Assessment of World War II's Impact on Female Employment: A Study of the Decade 1940–1950" (PhD diss., Rice University, 1982).

Walkowitz, Daniel J. "The Making of a Feminine Professional Identity: Social Workers in the 1920s," *American Historical Review* 95, no. 4 (October 1990): 1051–75.

———. *Working with Class: Social Workers and the Politics of Middle-Class Identity* (Chapel Hill: University of North Carolina Press, 1999).

Walsh, Andrea S. *Women's Film and Female Experience, 1940–1950* (New York: Praeger, 1984).

Warner, W. Lloyd. *Social Class in America: A Manual of Procedure for the Measurement of Social Status* (New York: Harper and Row, 1960 [1949]).

Weiss, Marc A. "Real Estate History: An Overview and Research Agenda," *Business History Review* 63 (summer 1989): 241–82.

———. "Richard T. Ely and the Contribution of Economic Research to National Housing Policy, 1920–1940," *Urban Studies* 26 (1989).

———. *The Rise of the Community Builders: The American Real Estate Industry and Urban Land Planning* (New York: Columbia University Press, 1987).

Whitaker, John K. "Enemies or Allies? Henry George and Francis Amasa Walker One Century Later," *Journal of Economic Literature* 35, no. 4 (December 1997): 1891–1915.

Whyte, William H., Jr. *The Organization Man* (New York: Doubleday, 1957).

Wiebe, Robert. *Businessmen and Reform: A Study of the Progressive Movement* (Cambridge: Harvard University Press, 1962).

———. *Search for Order, 1877–1920* (New York: Hill and Wang, 1967).

Wilensky, Harold. "The Professionalization of Everyone?," *American Journal of Sociology* 70, no. 2 (September 1964): 137–58.

Witz, Anne. *Professions and Patriarchy* (New York: Verso, 1992).

Wood, Edith Elmer. *Recent Trends in American Housing* (New York: Macmillan, 1931).

Worley, William S. *J. C. Nichols and the Shaping of Kansas City* (Columbia: University of Missouri Press, 1991).

Wright, Gwendolyn. *Building the Dream: A Social History of Housing in America* (New York: Pantheon, 1981).

———. *Moralism and the Model Home* (Chicago: University of Chicago Press, 1980).

Wylie, Irving G. *The Self-Made Man in America: The Myth of Rags to Riches* (Toronto: Free Press, 1966).

Wylie, Philip. *Generation of Vipers* (New York: Rinehart, 1942).

Xueguang Zhou. "Occupational Power, State Capacities, and the Diffusion of Licensing in the American States, 1890–1950," *American Sociological Review* 58 (August 1993): 536–52.

Žižek, Slavoj. *The Sublime Object of Ideology* (New York: Verso, 1989).

Zunz, Olivier. *Making America Corporate* (New York: Oxford University Press, 1990).

INDEX

Women, as real estate brokers, 157, 173–74, 193–94

Women Realtors, 193–94

Women's Council of NAREB, 156, 157, 163, 167, 170, 171–72, 174–84, 186–87, 193–95, 198–99

Woodbury, Coleman, 143

Woolley, Edward Mott, 3

World's Columbian Exposition (1893), 19

Wright, Cora Ella, 163, 170, 172

Wylie, Philip, 181

YMCA, 30, 50, 79, 97, 100

Zoning, 10, 15, 18, 19, 21, 23, 27, 32, 62, 65, 104, 107, 110–14, 116, 139, 140–42, 149

Jeffrey Hornstein is an independent scholar and union organizer living in Philadelphia.

Library of Congress Cataloging-in-Publication Data

Hornstein, Jeffrey M., 1967–

A nation of realtors : a cultural history of the twentieth-century

American middle class / Jeffrey M. Hornstein.

p. cm. — (Radical perspectives)

Includes bibliographical references (p.) and index.

ISBN 0-8223-3528-x (cloth : alk. paper)

ISBN 0-8223-3540-9 (pbk. : alk. paper)

1. Real estate business—United States—History—20th century.

2. Middle class—United States—History—20th century.

3. Women real estate agents—United States—History—

20th century. I. Title. II. Series.

HD255.H63 2005

333.33'0973—dc22   2004023265